PEARSON LONGMAN

KEYSTONE

BUILDING BRIDGES

PEARSON English Learning System

Kaye Wiley

PEARSON

Upper Saddle River, New Jersey • Boston, Massachusetts • Chandler, Arizona • Glenview, Illinois

PEARSON English Learning System

Staff credits: The people who made up the *Longman Keystone Course 1A* team, representing editorial, production, design, manufacturing, and marketing, are John Ade, Rhea Banker, Liz Barker, Danielle Belfiore, Virginia Bernard, Kenna Bourke, Jeffrey Buckner, Diane Cipollone, Johnnie Farmer, Warren Fischbach, Patrice Fraccio, Charles Green, Aliza Greenblatt, Henry Hild, David L. Jones, Lucille M. Kennedy, Ed Lamprich, Linda Moser, Rebecca Ortman, Liza Pleva, Edie Pullman, Tania Saiz-Sousa, Chris Siley, Jane Townsend, Lauren Weidenman, and Adina Zoltan.

Text design: Kirchoff/Wohlberg, Inc.
Text composition: Kirchoff/Wohlberg, Inc., TSI Graphics
Text font: 12.5/16 Minion

Acknowledgments: See page 371.

Illustration and Photo credits appear on page 372, which constitute an extension of this copyright page.

Library of Congress Cataloging-in-Publication Data
Wiley, Kaye.
  Building Bridges / Kaye Wiley.
    p. cm.
  ISBN 1-42-843493-3
  1. English language — Textbooks for foreign speakers —
  Juvenile literature. 2. Readers (Secondary)
  [1. English Language — Textbooks for foreign speakers.
  2. Readers.]
  I. Title
  PE1128.M3326 2004
  428.6'4—dc22
                        2003023648

ISBN-13: 978-1-4284-349.
ISBN-10: 1-4284-349.

Printed in the United States of Amer
6 7 8 9 10 V057 16

Reviewers

Contents

INTRODUCTION

Getting Started

Contents

Journeys

Contents

UNIT 2

Hidden Forces

Contents

Play Ball!

Contents

Family Ties

Contents

The Power of Words

Contents

UNIT 6

Exploring the Senses

The World of Plants

Contents

Wings

Dear Student,

Welcome to **PEARSON LONGMAN**
KEYSTONE

This program will help you learn English for success in school. Some of the readings are about science and social studies. Other readings are about literature and culture. All of the readings have pictures to help you understand the text.

Before you begin each reading, look at the title and the pictures. Then read the list of Key Words. Ask yourself if you already know something about the topic. Then, as you read, stop and ask questions about what you are reading. Use the Reading Strategies. They will help you understand what you read. After you finish reading, discuss your ideas.

Each literature selection has a short play after it. The play retells the story that you read in the literature selection. You and your classmates can have fun speaking the different parts and rereading the story as a drama. You can also listen to recordings of all of the stories and plays.

The end of each unit has writing activities. Writing skills are a very important part of *Keystone*. The writing activities will help you practice your grammar skills and learn to organize your ideas. You will also practice taking tests.

As you read and write more English, the world of school will open up for you. May you soon become a shining star in all your classes!

Kaye Wiley

◀ **Kaye Wiley is an ESL teacher and writer from New Haven, Connecticut.**

1

INTRODUCTION

Getting Started

In this unit, you will learn and review numbers, letters of the alphabet, days of the week, and months of the year. You will talk about colors and shapes, and places and things in school. Later, you will read and write a folktale. You will also learn how to read and use maps, timelines, diagrams, and a graph. Finally, you will use math skills to solve equations and word problems. Are you ready? Let's get started.

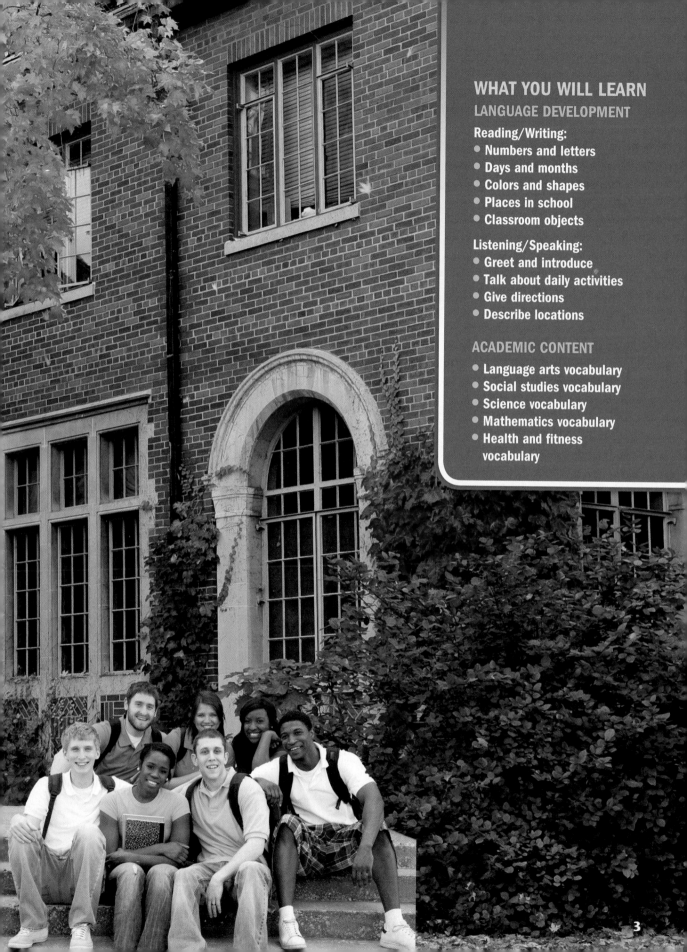

WHAT YOU WILL LEARN
LANGUAGE DEVELOPMENT
Reading/Writing:
- **Numbers and letters**
- **Days and months**
- **Colors and shapes**
- **Places in school**
- **Classroom objects**

Listening/Speaking:
- **Greet and introduce**
- **Talk about daily activities**
- **Give directions**
- **Describe locations**

ACADEMIC CONTENT
- **Language arts vocabulary**
- **Social studies vocabulary**
- **Science vocabulary**
- **Mathematics vocabulary**
- **Health and fitness vocabulary**

3

Numbers and Letters

A. Listen and read.

Nina:	Good morning. What's your name?
Mrs. Schmidt:	My name is Mrs. Schmidt.
Nina:	How do you spell your last name?
Mrs. Schmidt:	It's S-c-h-m-i-d-t.
Nina:	How long have you been a teacher?
Mrs. Schmidt:	Fifteen years.
Nina:	Thank you.

B. Learn capital and lowercase letters.

Aa Bb Cc Dd Ee Ff Gg Hh Ii Jj Kk Ll Mm Nn Oo Pp Qq Rr Ss Tt Uu Vv Ww Xx Yy Zz

C. Learn these numbers and words.

Cardinal Numbers

1	one	11	eleven	21	twenty-one	40	forty
2	two	12	twelve	22	twenty-two	50	fifty
3	three	13	thirteen	23	twenty-three	60	sixty
4	four	14	fourteen	24	twenty-four	70	seventy
5	five	15	fifteen	25	twenty-five	80	eighty
6	six	16	sixteen	26	twenty-six	90	ninety
7	seven	17	seventeen	27	twenty-seven	100	one hundred
8	eight	18	eighteen	28	twenty-eight	1,000	one thousand
9	nine	19	nineteen	29	twenty-nine	500,000	five hundred thousand
10	ten	20	twenty	30	thirty	1,000,000	one million

D. Write the words for each of these numbers in your notebook.

13: _thirteen_   60: _____

27: _____   19: _____

71: _____   1,000,000: _____

55: _____   1,000: _____

42: _____   86: _____

100: _____   99: _____

38: _____   11: _____

66: _____   500,000: _____

E. Play this game with a partner. Look at the alphabet chart. Partner 1 reads five letters to Partner 2, for example: *K, A, V, G, L.* Partner 2 then writes the five letters in alphabetical order on a sheet of paper. Take turns. Check your answers.

Reading Skill
Remember that we read English text from left to right.

Workbook
Pages 1–2

Days and Months

A. Listen and read.

Luis: Hi, Sara. What day is it today?
Sara: It's Monday, July 7th. My basketball game is tonight. Do you want to come, Luis?
Luis: Sure. See you later!

B. Learn these numbers and words.

Reading Skill
Read the chart from top to bottom and from left to right.

Ordinal Numbers

1st first	11th eleventh	21st twenty-first	40th fortieth
2nd second	12th twelfth	22nd twenty-second	50th fiftieth
3rd third	13th thirteenth	23rd twenty-third	60th sixtieth
4th fourth	14th fourteenth	24th twenty-fourth	70th seventieth
5th fifth	15th fifteenth	25th twenty-fifth	80th eightieth
6th sixth	16th sixteenth	26th twenty-sixth	90th ninetieth
7th seventh	17th seventeenth	27th twenty-seventh	100th one hundredth
8th eighth	18th eighteenth	28th twenty-eighth	1,000th one thousandth
9th ninth	19th nineteenth	29th twenty-ninth	500,000th five hundred thousandth
10th tenth	20th twentieth	30th thirtieth	1,000,000th one millionth

C. Look at the calendar. Answer the questions about Sara's activities in your notebook.

Monday	Tuesday	Wednesday	Thursday
plays basketball	*reads a book*	*watches TV*	*cooks dinner*

Friday	Saturday	Sunday
washes the dishes	*goes to the movies*	*plays the guitar*

1. When does Sara watch TV?
   She watches TV on Wednesday.
2. When does she wash the dishes?
3. When does she cook dinner?

4. When does she go to the movies?
5. When does she play the guitar?
6. When does she read a book?
7. When does she play basketball?

D. Learn these words.

Months of the Year

January	February	March	April	May	June
July	August	September	October	November	December

Complete the sentences about months in your notebook.

1. August is the __*eighth*__ month of the year.
2. The new year begins in _____.
3. _____ usually has twenty-eight days.
4. November is the _____ month of the year.
5. I like the month of _____ best.
6. May is the _____ month of the year.

Workbook
Pages 3–4

Colors and Shapes

A. Listen and read.

Martin: What color is Japan's flag?

Laura: Japan's flag is red and white.

Martin: What shapes are in it?

Nadia: It has a red circle inside a white rectangle.

B. Learn the colors.

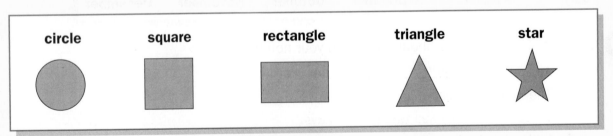

| red | pink | blue | purple | green | yellow |
| orange | brown | black | gray | white | tan |

C. Learn the shapes.

| circle | square | rectangle | triangle | star |

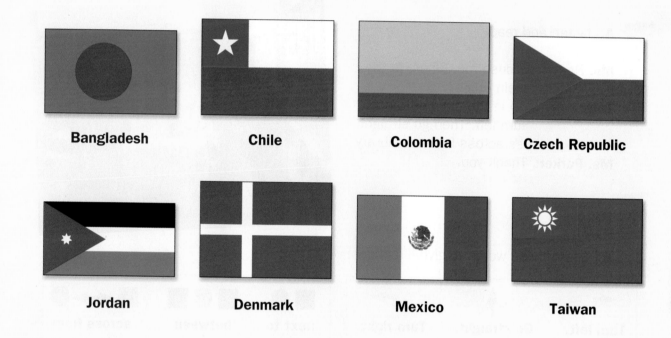

Bangladesh **Chile** **Colombia** **Czech Republic**

Jordan **Denmark** **Mexico** **Taiwan**

D. Look at the flags. Answer these questions in your notebook.

1. What color is Colombia's flag?
   Colombia's flag is yellow, blue, and red.
2. What color is Jordan's flag?
3. What shapes are in Denmark's flag?
4. Which flags have circles?
5. Which flags have squares?
6. Which flags have triangles?
7. Which flags have stars?
8. Which flags have rectangles?

E. Draw with a partner. Make a new flag.
Use many shapes and colors.
Describe your flag to your partner.

Workbook
Pages 5–6

Directions

A. Listen and read.

Ms. Parker: Excuse me. Where is the main office?

Tara: Go in the main entrance. Turn left. Then go straight. It's across from the library.

Ms. Parker: Thank you.

B. Learn these words to give directions.

| Turn left. | Go straight. | Turn right. |

| next to | between | across from |

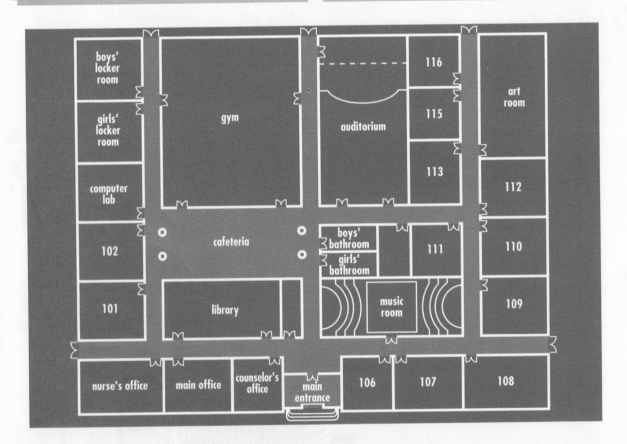

C. Write in your notebook. Give directions. Use the school map. Begin from the main entrance. Take turns reading your directions aloud with a partner.

1. Where is the library?

   Turn left. Then go straight. It's across from the main office and the counselor's office.

2. Where is the cafeteria?

3. Where is the music room?

4. Where is the gym?

5. Where is the auditorium?

D. Play this game with a partner. Ask each other questions.

1. What is across from the gym? *The cafeteria*

2. What is between the art room and the auditorium?

3. What is next to the library?

4. What is across from the counselor's office?

5. What is between the nurse's office and the counselor's office?

Workbook
Pages 7–8

Classroom Objects

A. Listen and read.

Steve: What is that?
Carla: It's a globe.
Steve: What are those?
Carla: They're books.

B. Learn classroom words.

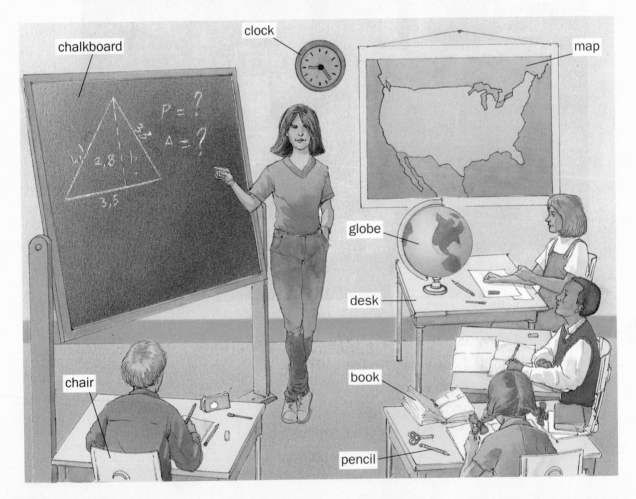

C. Write five sentences about objects in your classroom. Use numbers in your sentences.

> *There is one clock in my classroom.*
>
> *There are 32 chairs in my classroom.*

D. Work with a partner. Look at the drawing on page 12. Ask and answer the questions.

1. What is across from the chalkboard?
2. What is between the chalkboard and map?
3. What color is the clock?
4. What color is the chalkboard?
5. What shape is the clock?
6. What shape is the map?
7. What shape is the globe?

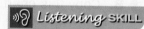 **Listening** SKILL

Listen to your partner. Rephrase his or her responses as complete sentences.

Workbook
Pages 9–10

Language Arts

▶ **READING**

 Nonfiction is about real people, places, and events. Science and social studies texts are types of nonfiction.

READING STRATEGY	FIND MAIN IDEA AND DETAILS

When you read nonfiction, find the **main idea** and **details**.

- The main idea is the biggest or most important idea.
- Details are ideas or facts about the main idea.

 A. Read this social studies text. Look for the main idea.

Antarctica

The continent of Antarctica is very cold. An ice sheet covers most of the land. The average winter temperature is -60°C (-76°F). Few animals can live there all year. In the summer, animals such as penguins, whales, and seals come to Antarctica to eat food and to breed, or have babies.

B. Copy this chart. Write the details about the main idea.

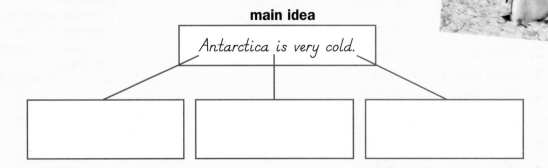

main idea

Antarctica is very cold.

Fiction is about characters and events that writers make up. Myths, folktales, and short stories are types of fiction.

READING STRATEGY	IDENTIFY CHARACTERS, PLOT, AND SETTING

As you read fiction, think about the **characters**, **plot**, and **setting**.

- The characters are the people or animals in the story.
- The plot is what happens in the story.
- The setting is the time and place of the story.

 C. Read this Native American folktale.

How Bear Lost His Tail

Many years ago in North America, Bear had a long tail.

One cold winter day, Bear saw Fox at the lake. Fox was sitting on the ice next to many fish. "How did you catch those fish?" Bear asked.

"With my tail," Fox lied. He wanted to fool Bear. Bear put his tail into the icy water. Soon Bear was asleep. Fox went home to eat his fish.

When Fox returned, Bear was still sleeping. "Bear!" Fox shouted. "Can you feel a fish on your tail?"

Bear jumped up, and his frozen tail broke off.

And that's why bears have short tails today.

 D. Read the folktale again with a partner. Answer these questions.

1. Who are the characters?
2. What is the plot?
3. What is the setting of the story?

Workbook
Pages 11–12

➤ WRITING

A process is a way of doing something. Usually
a process has a number of steps, or actions, that
help you learn to do it.

 A. Read about the writing process.

The Writing Process
The writing process is a series of steps that help you
write. Many writers use the writing process to think of
ideas and then to organize, write, and revise their
writing. Here are the steps.

Prewrite Before you can write, you need ideas.
Brainstorming is a way of getting ideas. When you
brainstorm, write down all the ideas you can think of
about a topic. Make a list.
    Look at your list. Choose the best ideas. Then make
notes to organize your ideas.

Draft Use your notes to write your report or story. Write
your ideas about your topic in sentences.

Revise Read your draft. What changes can you make to
improve it? Are your ideas clear? Did you include details
to support your ideas? Do your sentences flow smoothly?
If not, you need to revise, or make changes to your draft.
Ask a partner to read your writing and give you feedback.

Edit Write a new draft that includes your revisions. Then
check your work for errors in spelling and punctuation.

Publish Share your writing with the class.

B. Read the notes the writer made before writing "How Bear Lost His Tail."

> *Notes for "How Bear Lost His Tail"*
>
> *Beginning:* Bear had a long tail.
>
> *Middle:* Fox wanted to fool Bear. Fox said he had caught fish with his tail. Bear put his tail into the icy water. Bear fell asleep.
>
> *End:* Bear's frozen tail broke off.

C. Compare the writer's notes with the folktale on page 15. Answer the questions in your notebook.

   1. How are the notes different from the folktale?

   2. How did the writer use the notes to write the folktale?

   3. Are the writer's notes mostly about character, plot, or setting? Explain.

D. Write a folktale about something in nature, for example, "Why the Moon Is White." First, make a list of ideas in your notebook. Next, make notes to organize your ideas. Then write the folktale.

E. Trade folktales with a partner. Read your partner's story. Give your partner ideas for how to make his or her story better. Listen to your partner's ideas about your story. Then revise your story.

Workbook
Pages 13–14

Social Studies

► **MAPS**

Social studies textbooks often have maps. Maps help you understand where people live and where events take place.

 A. Work in groups. Study the map below. Then answer the questions.

1. What countries are on the map?
2. What oceans are on the map?
3. Name three cities on the map.
4. Name two bays on the map.

B. Read about a compass rose.

Many maps use a compass rose to show direction. This compass rose shows the directions north (N), south (S), east (E), and west (W).

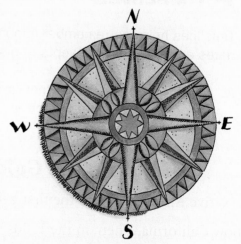

C. Work with a partner. Study the map. Answer the questions.

THE UNITED STATES OF AMERICA

1. What state is north of New Mexico?
2. What state is west of North Dakota?
3. What state is east of Georgia?
4. What state is south of Utah?

Reading Skill

Direction words appear routinely in textbooks that include maps. These words allow you to discuss the information presented in the maps.

Workbook
Pages 15–16

Timelines help you remember important dates and the order of events in history.

A. Read this text with a partner. It tells about part of the history of California.

California, the Golden State

Native Americans were the first people to live in what is now California. Then, in the 1500s, Spanish explorers came to the land. At that time, Spain also controlled the territory where the country of Mexico is today.

In 1821, Mexico won its independence from Spain. As a result, California became a part of Mexico. Soon more people came to California. Some people sailed in ships around the tip of South America. Others traveled in wagons across the United States.

In 1846, Mexico and the United States fought a war. When the peace treaty was signed on February 2, 1848, California became a territory of the United States. Two weeks before, a man named James Marshall discovered something amazing near Sacramento, California. John Sutter, a Swiss settler, hired Marshall to help him build a sawmill. On January 24, 1848, Marshall saw shiny pieces of yellow metal in a stream by Sutter's Mill. They were pieces of gold!

Many people came to California to find gold. They were called "forty-niners" because they came in 1849. Soon people came from all over the world, including China and Australia. On September 9, 1850, California became the thirty-first state in the United States.

B. Look at the timeline. Answer the questions with a partner.

1500s — Spanish explorers come.

1821 — Mexico wins independence from Spain.

1848 — Marshall discovers gold.

1850 — California becomes a state.

1. When did Spanish explorers come to California?
2. When did Mexico win its independence from Spain?
3. When did James Marshall discover gold?
4. When did California become a state?

Reading Skill

Remember that we read English text from left to right and top to bottom.

 C. Make a timeline of other important dates in California's history or in the history of another state. Use the library or the Internet to find information.

Workbook
Pages 17–19

James Marshall discovered gold at Sutter's Mill, near Sacramento, in 1848. ▶

 Gold-mining area

Science

 MATTER

 Everything you can touch or see is matter. Matter has three states, or forms: solid, liquid, and gas.

A. Read about the three states of water.

solid   liquid   gas

Three States of Water

Water is an important liquid. Water covers about 70 percent of the earth's surface. Your body is about two-thirds water. When water is in its liquid state, you can pour it. As a liquid, water takes the shape of its container. The water in the picture above takes the shape of the glass.

When water gets very cold, it freezes. It changes from a liquid to a solid. The freezing point of water is 0°C (32°F). Ice and snow are solid forms of water.

When water gets very hot, it boils. Then it changes from a liquid to a gas. This gas is called water vapor or steam. The boiling point of water is 100°C (212°F).

> **)) Listening SKILL**
>
> Play the Audio CD. Listen for patterns of intonation. Listen to the way the voice rises and falls. Intonation provides information about what's important in the text.

B. Work with a partner. Complete the sentences.

1. _____ and _____ are solid forms of water.
2. When water gets very hot, it _____.
3. The _____ point of water is 0°C.
4. Very hot water changes from a liquid to a _____.

C. Read about the water cycle.

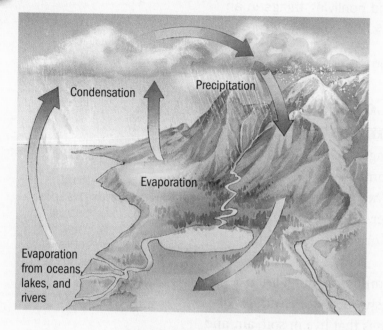

Condensation

Precipitation

Evaporation

Evaporation
from oceans,
lakes, and
rivers

Reading SKILL

Trace the movement of
water by following the
arrows with your finger.

The Water Cycle

The movement of water from the ground to the air and
back is called the water cycle. In the water cycle, water
changes its state as it moves. The sun heats water on the
ground and changes it to water vapor. This change is called
evaporation. Then water vapor moves up in the air and
forms clouds. Water vapor cools in the clouds and changes
into water drops. This change is called condensation.
When the water drops become large enough, they fall from
the clouds down to the ground as precipitation, such as
rain or snow.

D. Work in groups. Study the diagram again. Then answer
the questions.

1. What is water called after it evaporates?
2. What happens to water vapor in clouds?
3. Name two kinds of precipitation.
4. Explain how water changes its state in the water
cycle.

»🎧 *Listening* SKILL

Listen to your
classmates. Rephrase
their responses in
complete sentences.

Workbook
Pages 20–21

► ECOSYSTEMS

 An ecosystem is all the living and nonliving things in an area. Living things include plants and animals.

 A. Read about the living things in an ecosystem.

Producers, Consumers, and Decomposers

There are three kinds of living things in an ecosystem: producers, consumers, and decomposers.

Most plants are producers. They produce, or make, their own food. Animals are consumers. Animals cannot make their own food. They consume, or eat, plants or other animals.

Fungi and bacteria are decomposers. Fungi are like plants, but they live in dark places. Mushrooms are examples of fungi. Bacteria are very tiny things that live in soil, air, and water. Fungi and bacteria decompose, or break down, dead plants and animals. They help the dead plants and animals become part of the soil.

Word Skill

The word *animal* comes from the Latin root *anim,* meaning "life, spirit." What other forms of life are discussed in this passage?

Plants are producers.

Animals are consumers.

Fungi are decomposers.

B. Work with a partner. Match the words and their meanings.

_____ **1.** A consumer   **a.** makes its own food.

_____ **2.** A decomposer   **b.** eats plants and animals for food.

_____ **3.** An ecosystem   **c.** breaks down dead plants and animals.

_____ **4.** A producer   **d.** is all the living and nonliving things in an area.

C. Read about a food chain. Look at the drawing.

A Food Chain

The way food moves through an ecosystem is called a food chain. A food chain begins with a producer—a plant, such as grass. A small consumer, such as a mouse, eats the grass. Then a larger consumer, such as a hawk, eats the mouse. Decomposers, such as bacteria, break down the hawk when it dies. Its body becomes part of the soil.

D. Work with a partner. Look at the pictures. In your notebook, number the pictures to make a food chain.

snake	grass	owl	grasshopper	toad
—	—	—	—	—

Workbook
Pages 22–23

Mathematics

▶ OPERATIONS AND WORD PROBLEMS

Use symbols and words to show addition, subtraction, multiplication, and division.

Operations:	addition	subtraction	multiplication	division
Symbols:	+	−	×	÷
Words:	plus	minus	times	divided by

 A. Read the examples of these four operations.

Addition

$$\begin{array}{r} 4 \\ +\,2 \\ \hline 6 \end{array}$$ or $4 + 2 = 6$ or   Four plus two equals six.

Subtraction

$$\begin{array}{r} 8 \\ -\,3 \\ \hline 5 \end{array}$$ or $8 - 3 = 5$ or   Eight minus three equals five.

Multiplication

$$\begin{array}{r} 6 \\ \times\,3 \\ \hline 18 \end{array}$$ or $6 \times 3 = 18$ or   Six times three equals eighteen.

Division

$$6\overline{)12}\ \ ^2$$ or $12 \div 6 = 2$ or   Twelve divided by six equals two.

 B. Write the problems in your notebook. First write them in words. Then use numbers. Solve the problems.

1. Twenty-five plus eleven equals _____.
2. Thirty-seven minus twenty-two equals _____.
3. Twelve times ten equals _____.
4. Sixty divided by fifteen equals _____.

C. Read about word problems.

A word problem is a math problem with words and numbers. You can use addition, subtraction, multiplication, and division to solve word problems. Follow these steps:

1. Read the word problem carefully.

2. Ask yourself, "What operation do I use to solve the problem?"

3. Look for words in the problem that help you decide which operation to use.

4. Sometimes a picture can help you solve a word problem.

D. Work with a partner. Read the word problems. Follow the steps above and solve each problem.

1. José is fourteen years old. José's sister is five years older than José. José's brother is three years younger than José. How old are José's sister and brother?

2. A redwood tree in California is about 111 meters tall. It is 18 meters taller than the Statue of Liberty in New York. How tall is the Statue of Liberty? (*Hint:* Look at the picture. Do you need to add or subtract to solve the problem?)

3. Kim has a box of oranges. The box has twenty-one oranges. Kim eats one orange each day. In how many weeks will Kim eat all the oranges? (*Hint:* How many days are in one week?)

4. Tom reads three books every week. How many books does he read in one year? (*Hint:* How many weeks are in one year?)

Workbook
Pages 24–25

FRACTIONS, DECIMALS, AND PERCENTS

 A. A fraction is a number smaller than one. Read the examples.

 This is 1/2 (one-half).

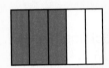 This is 3/4 (three-fourths or three-quarters).

 This is 4/5 (four-fifths).

A fraction has two numbers divided by a line. Look at the examples.

2/3 (two-thirds)

3/5 (three-fifths)

5/8 (five-eighths)

 B. In your notebook, write the fraction—numbers and words—for each picture.

 1. _____ or _____

 2. _____ or _____

 3. _____ or _____

 4. _____ or _____

Word Skill

The word *fraction* comes from the Latin root *fract*, meaning "break." How do the illustrations of fractions on this page show this meaning?

C. A decimal is a number smaller than one. A decimal has a decimal point (.) and a number. For example, .3 and .25 are decimals. Read about the U.S. dollar.

The U.S. dollar is based on decimals. Ten pennies equals one dime. One penny is 1/10 of a dime. You can write the fraction 1/10 as the decimal .1. You say the fraction and the decimal the same way: *one-tenth*.

          =

Ten dimes equals one U.S. dollar. One dime is 10/100 of a dollar, or .10 as a decimal.

          =

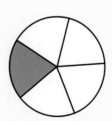 **D.** A percent is a part of 100. A percent has a number and a percent symbol (%). For example, 10% means ten percent (of 100).

Fractions, decimals, and percents can show the same amount or part of something.

Fraction: 1/5 of the circle is blue. [1/5 = 1 divided by 5]

Decimal: .20 of the circle is blue. [1/5 = 20/100 = .20]

Percent: 20% of the circle is blue. [.20 × 100 = 20%]

E. In your notebook, write the answer as a fraction, a decimal, and a percent.

Fraction: _____ of the circle is blue.

Decimal: _____ of the circle is blue.

Percent: _____ of the circle is blue.

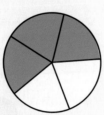

Workbook Pages 26–28

Health and Fitness

➤ YOUR BODY

 Diagrams help you understand and remember important information. Many diagrams use pictures with labels, or words.

 A. Work in groups. Study the diagram. Then answer the questions.

1. What parts of the body help you see?
2. What parts help you write?
3. What part helps you smile?
4. What parts help you hear?
5. What parts help you run?
6. What part connects your foot to your leg?
7. What part helps you bend your arm?
8. What part helps you smell?

head
hair
eye
nose
chin
ear
mouth
neck
arm
shoulder
wrist
thumb
finger
hand
elbow
leg
knee
ankle
toe
foot

B. Read about physical exercise.

Physical exercise is good for your body. It helps your bones and muscles stay strong. Some people like aerobic exercise. Others enjoy sports such as golf or tennis.

A calorie is a unit for measuring how much energy your body gets from food. Exercise burns, or uses, calories to keep your body healthy and strong.

C. Bar graphs compare information. Read the bar graph. It compares different activities. It shows how many calories each activity burns in one hour. Then answer the questions with a partner.

▲ Exercise helps keep you healthy.

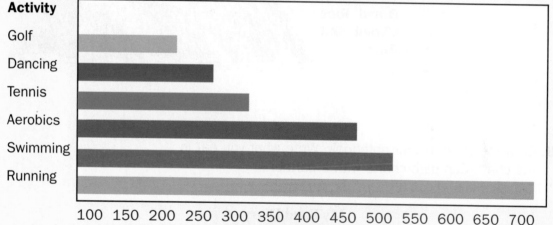

Exercise and Calories

Activity

Golf
Dancing
Tennis
Aerobics
Swimming
Running

100 150 200 250 300 350 400 450 500 550 600 650 700

Calories Burned in One Hour

1. Which activity uses the most calories?
2. Which activity uses the least calories?
3. Which uses more calories, swimming or dancing?
4. Which is your favorite activity? Explain.

Workbook
Pages 29–30

➤ KEEPING HEALTHY

You are what you eat. It is important to eat a variety of healthy foods every day. Do you have good eating habits?

 A. Read the Food Pyramid diagram.

To keep healthy, eat more foods from the bottom of the pyramid. Foods from the top, such as candy and cake, have a lot of fat and sugar. Eat less of these foods.

Fats and Sweets

Dairy Products

Meat, Poultry, Fish, Beans, and Eggs

Vegetables

Fruit

Bread, Rice, Cereal, and Pasta

 B. Copy the chart in your notebook. Write what you eat in the chart. Compare charts with a partner.

My Food Diary

Food Group	Example
Fats and sweets	cookies
Meat, poultry, fish, beans, eggs	
Dairy products	
Fruit and vegetables	
Bread, rice, cereal, pasta	

C. Read about healthy habits.

A habit is something you do often or every day. Exercise and eating healthy food are two examples of good, or healthy, habits. Smoking and eating a lot of sweet and fatty foods are examples of bad, or unhealthy, habits.

D. Copy the chart in your notebook. Work with a partner. Take turns asking questions about healthy habits.

Healthy Habits	Your Partner	You
Exercise every day.		
Eat a healthy diet.		
Wear a helmet when biking or skating.		
Go to your doctor for check-ups.		
Brush your teeth and visit your dentist.		
Get plenty of sleep.		
Keep yourself clean and neat.		
Drink plenty of water.		
Wear a seatbelt in the car.		

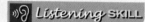
»))) Listening SKILL

Listen to your partner. In your chart, take notes about his or her habits.

 E. Play this game in small groups. One person acts out a healthy habit. The first player to guess the habit gets to act out another habit. Play until everyone has had a turn.

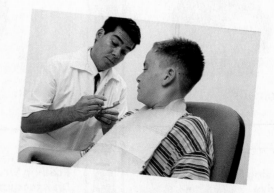

Workbook
Pages 31–32

Journeys

Some people do not live in one place. Instead, they move from place to place. These people are called nomads. The selection "Nomads" tells about how these people live. Some nomads live in the desert. The folktale "Jewel in the Sand" is about desert nomads. "The U.S. Camel Corps" tells how camels helped the U.S. Army.

Reading

1 Social Studies	2 Folktale	3 Social Studies

"Nomads"	"Jewel in the Sand"	"The U.S. Camel Corps"
Reading Strategy: Preview	**Reading Strategy:** Draw conclusions	**Connect to Reading:** Draw conclusions; Text structure

Listening and Speaking

In this unit, you will retell a story.

Writing

In the unit, you will practice freewriting, write a journal entry, and learn about different writing genres.

Quick Write

Have you been on a journey? Write two or three sentences about a place you traveled to.

DVD **VIEW AND RESPOND**
Watch the Unit 1 DVD. As you watch, answer the questions on page 55.
www.LongmanKeystone.com.

What You Will Learn

Reading

- Vocabulary building: *Context; dictionary skills*

- Reading strategy: *Preview*

- Text type: *Informational text (social studies); nonfiction*

Academic Content

- Social studies vocabulary

- Nomads

- Different kinds of shelters

➤ **BUILD BACKGROUND**

"Nomads" tells about real people. It is nonfiction. Nonfiction is factual information. You read it in textbooks. The nonfiction you will read is a social article about nomads who live and travel in the desert.

▲ These nomads live in a tent.

Workbook Page 33

USE PRIOR KNOWLEDGE

1. Why do some people live in tents?

2. What do you think the woman in the picture is doing?

➤ VOCABULARY

Listening and Speaking: Key Words

Look at the pictures and the captions, or words underneath the pictures. They will help you learn the words in the box. Write the meaning of each highlighted word, then read them aloud with a partner. Then check your work in a dictionary.

Key Words

buffalo
camels
desert
herds
nomads
tents

Audio

▲ Some nomads live in the desert. They often travel with camels.

▲ Nomads move from place to place. These nomads from Mongolia (mon-GO-lee-uh) live in round tents. Mongolia is in Asia.

▲ The Sioux (SOO) people were nomads of North America. They hunted buffalo. The buffalo moved in groups called herds.

Workbook
Page 34

READING STRATEGY | PREVIEW

To **preview** means to look at the pages before you read.

- Look at the headings in dark type.
- Look at all the pictures and maps.
- Try to predict what the text is about.

Workbook
Page 35

Set a purpose for reading Nonfiction gives true information. "Nomads" tells about people who travel from place to place. Preview the pages. What do the pictures and headings tell you about nomads?

NOMADS

What Are Nomads?

Nomads are people who do not live in one place. They move from place to place to find food and water. They carry their homes with them on their **journeys**. In **prehistoric** times most people were nomads. They hunted animals and looked for seeds and plants to eat.

Are All Nomads Hunters?

Some nomads today are hunters, but most are herders. They travel with herds of sheep, goats, or camels. They look for places that have grass and water for their animals. These nomads often live in tents. They travel in large family groups called tribes.

---

journeys, long trips
prehistoric, before people started writing down history

▲ This cave painting shows prehistoric nomads hunting elk.

Woman herder with long-haired lamb ▶

MAKE CONNECTIONS

1 How large is your family group? Count your family members.
2 Are there nomads in your home country? Explain.

Where Do Nomads Live?

Most nomads live on open land. Some live in the desert. Others live on **grassy plains**. In the past, nomads also lived in the ice and snow of the Arctic.

Who Are the Bedouins?

The Bedouins (BED-oo-inz) are desert nomads. They travel across the deserts of the Middle East and northern Africa. They have herds of camels. Camels are good desert animals because they can go many days without food or water.

Some Bedouins camp near water. Then they can keep horses, sheep, and goats. The women make tents and rugs from camel hair and goat hair. Bedouin families camp in groups called clans. The clan leader is called a sheik. Many clans together make a tribe.

---

grassy plains, large areas of land where grass grows

Reading Skill

To understand the highlighted words, read the definition at the bottom of the page.

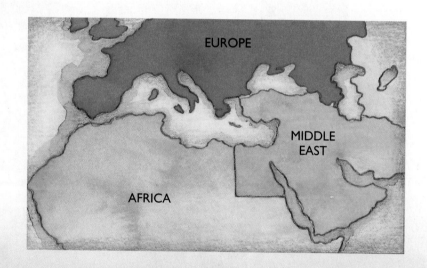

Bedouins traveling across the desert with camels and other animals ▼

BEFORE YOU GO ON

1. Why are camels good desert animals?

2. What do Bedouin women make from camel and goat hair?

3. What is a clan?

Reading 1 **39**

Who Are Mongolian Nomads?

Mongolian nomads live in Asia. They travel with herds of horses, sheep, cows, and goats. They live in round tents called yurts. Yurts are made of wool from sheep. Yurts protect the nomads from bad weather.

Mongolian nomads are famous horseback riders. Men and women ride horses and shoot arrows for fun. Young children even learn to race horses.

◀ Mongolian yurts

◀ Mongolian children get ready for a horse race.

Make Connections

1. What do you think it's like to live in a yurt?
2. What kinds of sports and races are there in your home country? Describe them.

▲ Sioux hunters on the Great Plains

▲ Sioux

Are There Nomads in North America?

There are very few nomads left in North America. Before 1850, there were many nomads. The Sioux, for example, hunted buffalo on the plains. They used buffalo meat for food. They made tents and blankets from buffalo skins. The tents were called tepees.

The Inuit, who live in the most northern part of North America, were also nomads. In summer they lived in tents by the sea and fished. In winter they hunted seals and polar bears. They used small boats called kayaks. Today most Inuit live in towns or villages. They are no longer nomads.

▲ This tepee is made of buffalo skins.

▲ Inuit

▼ Inuit hunting in a kayak

BEFORE YOU GO ON

1 What animals did the Sioux hunt?

2 What animals did the Inuit hunt in the winter?

Reading 1 **41**

Review and Practice

► RETELL AND REVIEW

1. Tell a partner what you learned about nomads. Use the headings and the pictures on pages 38–41 to help you. Use the Key Words. If you can't think of a word, describe it, use a synonym, or ask your teacher.

2. How did previewing the headings and pictures in "Nomads" help you get ready to read? Did you guess what the text was about? Explain.

 **Listening** SKILL

Look at pages 38–41 as you listen to your partner. If you don't understand something, ask a question.

► COMPREHENSION

Workbook
Page 36

Write the sentences below in your notebook. Use the words in the box to complete the sentences.

buffalo	herds	~~nomads~~	tribes
camels	kayak	desert	yurt

1. People who travel from place to place are called _nomads_.
2. Nomads often keep _____ of animals.
3. Some nomads live in the _____.
4. A _____ is a round Mongolian tent.
5. Nomads travel in large family groups called _____.
6. A _____ is a large animal that the Sioux hunted.
7. The Inuit fish in a boat called a _____.
8. Many Bedouins travel with herds of _____.

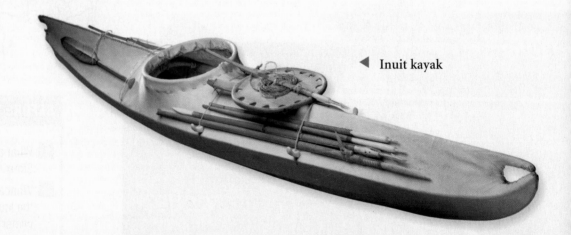

◄ Inuit kayak

Extension

Different Kinds of Shelters

A shelter is a place where people live. It is a home. It protects the people inside from bad weather. Look at the shelters below. How are they alike? How are they different?

A. Talk about your home with a partner.

1. What kind of shelter is it?
2. How does it protect you from bad weather?
3. Draw a picture of your home.
4. Compare your home with the shelters shown on this page. Take notes.

> 🔊》 *Speaking* SKILL
>
> You may use informal language when speaking with your partner.

B. Find out more about shelters. Follow these steps:

1. Look at a map or globe.
2. Choose a country.
3. Find information about that country. Use the Internet or library books.
4. Read about the shelters or homes in that country.
5. Draw a picture of a home from that country.
6. Share your picture and the information you learned with the class.

Workbook
Page 37

Reading 1 **43**

What You Will Learn

Reading

■ Vocabulary building:
  Context; dictionary skills

■ Reading strategy:
  Draw conclusions

■ Text type: *Literature (folktale and play)*

Grammar
Articles

Writing
Write a journal entry

➤ **BUILD BACKGROUND**

"Jewel in the Sand" is a folktale. Folktales are stories that people, or folk, tell one another. Folktales began as oral stories, told by word of mouth. In time people wrote down the stories. Sometimes folktales teach a lesson. Sometimes people tell them just for fun.

> **TRY TO PREDICT**
>
> **1** Where do you think the story takes place?
> **2** What do you think the story is about?

➤ VOCABULARY

Listening and Speaking: Key Words

Look at the pictures and the captions. They will help you learn the words in the box. Write the meaning of each highlighted word, then read them aloud with a partner. Check your work in a dictionary.

Key Words

daughter
earrings
jewels
nephew
princess
uncle
welcomed

Audio

▲ This princess is wearing earrings. The earrings have jewels in them. A princess is the daughter of a prince or a king.

▲ The young woman welcomed the old woman into her tent.

◀ The man is the boy's uncle. The boy is the man's nephew. The man is the brother of the boy's mother or father.

Workbook
Page 38

READING STRATEGY | DRAW CONCLUSIONS

To **draw** a **conclusion** means to decide something is true based on information. For example, you see someone wearing expensive clothes. You might draw the conclusion that the person is wealthy.

- As you read the story, think about how the three main characters act.

- Based on the characters' actions, what conclusions can you draw about them?

Workbook
Page 39

Set a purpose for reading "Jewel in the Sand" is a folktale that teaches a lesson about giving. As you read, think about how the characters act. What conclusions can you draw about them?

Jewel in the Sand

Adapted from *Arab Folktales*, edited by Inea Bushnaq

Sheik Hamid and his nephew Ali were riding their horses across the desert. The sheik was telling a long story. Suddenly, Ali saw something bright in the sand. Was it a jewel? He was **curious**, but he did not stop. It was not polite to **interrupt**. his uncle's story.

Instead, Ali had an idea. On his back he carried a long sword. Ali put the point of the sword into the sand. It made a long line behind him as he rode home. Ali wanted to follow the line back to the jewel later.

Soon the two riders arrived at their camp. Friends welcomed them. The sheik went to his tent, but Ali turned his horse around. Quickly, he followed the line back through the sand. Was the jewel still there? Yes, it was. He picked it up. It was a beautiful green stone with gold around it. "This jewel must belong to a princess," Ali said.

---

curious, wanting to know about something
interrupt, stop a person who is talking

| **MAKE CONNECTIONS** |
Did you ever find something special? Explain.

Ali returned and showed the jewel to his uncle. "The work on this jewel is very fine," said the sheik. "The owner of such a beautiful jewel must be a princess. We must find her." The sheik called an old woman to help him. He gave her the jewel. "Take this," he said. "Visit all the tribes around us. Find the person who lost this jewel."

The old woman went from camp to camp. No one knew who owned the jewel. Finally, she came to a big camp full of black tents. She entered a long tent. A beautiful young woman welcomed her. "Come in, Grandmother," she said.

The old woman sat for a while and rested. Then she opened the cloth that held the jewel. "Do you know who lost this jewel?" she asked. The girl's eyes opened wide. She ran to a wooden box. She took out a matching jewel.

"Here is my earring," said the young girl. "I lost the other one in the desert." She showed the old woman the two jewels in her hand. "Do you see how they match?"

The old woman saw that the jewels matched. "My child, take your jewel. But tell me your name and the name of your tribe."

The girl answered, "Grandmother, my name is not important. I want you to keep both jewels. You worked hard to find me. I give you the earrings as a gift."

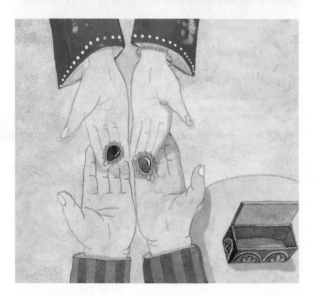

BEFORE YOU GO ON

1. Why do you think the princess called the old woman "Grandmother"?

2. How do you show respect for older people in your home country?

The old woman returned to her camp to tell the news to Sheik Hamid. He wanted to meet this princess. She was as **generous** as a king! He decided to ride to the camp of the black tents. He wanted to ask permission to marry the princess. The people there welcomed the sheik. The men brought food for his horses. The women cooked a big feast.

After three days, the sheik spoke to the prince, the father of the princess, "I rode here for a reason," said the sheik. "I came to ask to marry your daughter."

The prince looked sad. Then he said, "How can I refuse such a guest? My daughter and I bow our heads to you." The prince prepared marriage gifts to send with his daughter. "I give you seventy camels, many rugs, and many servants," he said. "My daughter will now be your bride. She is the jewel of the desert."

Soon the wedding day came. Sheik Hamid was walking to the wedding tent when a young man appeared. "Grant me the right to speak, Sheik Hamid!" he cried.

"You may speak without fear," said the sheik.

"The princess and I love each other. Her father knew this. But he could not refuse you because you were his guest. Please let me marry her!"

The sheik looked at the man. Then he said, "You ask only for what is fair. May you and your bride find joy."

So it is when people do what is right.

---

generous, giving

BEFORE YOU GO ON

1 Why did the princess give the earrings to the old woman?

2 What kind of person is the princess?

3 Why does her father call her "the jewel of the desert"?

Jewel in the Sand ❀ A Play

Now read the same folktale as a play. There are eight parts.

CHARACTERS

Narrator	Princess
Ali	Prince
Sheik Hamid	Young Man
Old Woman	Chorus

Narrator: Sheik Hamid and his nephew Ali were riding their horses in the desert. The sheik was telling a story. Suddenly, Ali saw something bright in the sand.

Ali *(to himself):* Is that a jewel?

Narrator: Ali did not stop to look. It was not polite to interrupt his uncle's story. But he lowered his sword into the sand to make a line behind him as he rode.

Chorus: Later that day, Ali followed the line back to the jewel.

Ali *(to himself):* There it is! What a fine jewel.

Chorus: Ali returned and showed the jewel to his uncle.

Sheik Hamid: The owner of such a beautiful jewel must be a princess. We must find her. *(to the old woman)* Grandmother! We need your help! *(He gives the old woman the jewel.)* Find the person who lost this jewel.

Old Woman: Yes, Sheik Hamid.

Narrator: The old woman went from camp to camp. No one knew who owned the jewel. Finally, she came to a camp with big black tents. A beautiful princess welcomed her.

Princess: Come in, Grandmother. How can I help you?

Old Woman *(holding out the jewel):* Do you know who lost this?

Princess *(taking something out of a box):* Look, here is my earring. I lost its mate in the desert. See how they match!

Old Woman *(nodding):* Yes. Take back your jewel. But please tell me your name.

Princess: My name is not important. Here, I give you the two jewels as a gift.

Chorus: The old woman returned to her camp. She showed the sheik the jewels.

Sheik Hamid: I must meet this princess. She is as generous as a king.

Chorus: He rode to the camp with the black tents. There, he met the prince, the father of the princess.

Sheik Hamid: Good Prince, I came here to ask to marry your daughter.

Prince *(sadly):* How can I refuse such a guest? My daughter will be your bride. She is the jewel of the desert.

Narrator: Soon the wedding day came. The sheik was near the wedding tent when a young man spoke to him.

Young Man: The princess and I love each other. Her father knew this. But he could not refuse you because you were his guest. Please let me marry her!

Sheik Hamid: You ask only for what is fair. May you and your bride find joy.

Chorus: So it is when people do what is right.

Review and Practice

➤ RETELL AND REVIEW

1. Look back at the pictures in "Jewel in the Sand" on pages 46–48. Cover the words on each page. Retell the events of the story to a partner, using only the pictures. Use the Key Words. If you can't think of a word, describe it, use a synonym, or ask your teacher.

2. What conclusions did you draw about Ali, Sheik Hamid, and the princess? What kind of person was Ali? The sheik? The princess? How do you know?

➤ COMPREHENSION  Workbook Page 41

Write the sentences below in your notebook. Write **Yes** if statement is true. Write **No** if it is not true. Then rewrite the statement correctly. Reread the selection silently to increase your comprehension.

1. Sheik Hamid and Ali were riding camels across the desert. *No.*
   Sheik Hamid and Ali were riding horses across the desert.
2. Ali saw something bright in the sand.
3. He put the point of a stick into the sand.
4. The sheik went to his yurt.
5. Ali returned and showed the jewel to his grandfather.
6. The sheik called an old woman to help him.
7. The princess gave the jewels to the sheik.
8. The prince prepared birthday gifts to send back with the sheik.

Extension

Birthstones

Birthstones are special jewels. There is a birthstone for each month. For example, the birthstone for January is a garnet. Look at the birthstones chart.

A. Talk about birthstones in small groups.

1. What is your birthstone?
2. What color is it?
3. Does anyone in your group have the same birthstone as you?
4. Which birthstone do you like the most? Why?

B. Make a poster about your birthstone. Follow the steps below:

1. Use the Interent or library books to find more information about your birthstone. Take notes.
2. Paste or draw a picture of it in the middle of your poster. Write its name below the picture.
3. Write some facts about your birthstone around the picture. For example, tell what month your birthstone goes with. Tell what color it is, where it comes from, and what people make with it. You might also tell other interesting facts about it.
4. Draw lines from each fact to the picture of your birthstone.
5. Work with a partner. Tell each other about your birthstones.

BIRTHSTONES

JANUARY	FEBRUARY	MARCH
Garnet	Amethyst	Aquamarine
APRIL	MAY	JUNE
Diamond	Emerald	Pearl
JULY	AUGUST	SEPTEMBER
Ruby	Peridot	Sapphire
OCTOBER	NOVEMBER	DECEMBER
Opal	Topaz	Turquoise

Listening SKILL

Listen closely to your partner. What are his or her main points? Write them down as you listen.

Garnet is the birthstone for January.

Garnet

Some travelers carry garnets to protect themselves from accidents.

Grammar

Articles

Articles are words that identify nouns. Nouns are the names of persons, places, or things. Use **a** or **an** to talk about one general person, place, or thing. Use **a** or **an** before singular nouns you can count.

> **A** princess lost **an** earring. (One princess lost one earring.)

- Use **a** before a consonant sound.

> He saw **a** jewel. They sleep in **a** tent.

- Use **an** before a vowel sound.

> Ali has **an** uncle. He had **an** idea.

🔊 *Speaking* **SKILL**

Remember to use articles correctly when you speak as well as when you write.

- Do not use **a** or **an** before nouns you cannot count.

> I eat **rice** for dinner. We drink **coffee** in the morning.

- Use **the** to talk about one or more specific persons, places, or things.

> **The** Inuit were nomads. (The Inuit are specific people.)
> Ali found **the** earring. (Ali found the specific earring that the princess lost.)

- Do not use **a, an,** or **the** before names of places, months, days, or languages.

> My friends in **Canada** can speak **English** and **French.**
> I visited them in **July.**

Practice  Workbook Page 42

Write these sentences in your notebook. Underline the article(s).

1. The Sioux hunted buffalo on the plains.
2. A sheik is a Bedouin leader.
3. The Mongolian nomads are an Asian people.
4. The sheik asked an old woman to find the owner of the earring.
5. The Inuit used boats called kayaks.
6. Many clans together make a tribe.

▲ Bedouin bags for coffee beans

Writing

Ongoing Writing Skills Practice

Write a Journal Entry

People write in journals to record their thoughts and feelings about things that happen in their lives. Each separate writing in a journal is called an entry. A journal entry is personal and informal. **You** choose what to write about. You don't always need to write in complete sentences because you are writing for yourself. Writing journal entries can help you remember important events. It can also help you express your ideas and feelings more easily.

Imagine that the princess in "Jewel in the Sand" had a journal. Read the following entry. Then answer the questions in your notebook.

Monday

What a terrible day! My father and I went to visit another camp. We were riding our horses in the desert, and it was windy. I reached up to get my hair out of my face. When my hand brushed past my ear, I didn't feel my earring. It was gone! I couldn't believe it. I felt my ear again. No earring. It must have fallen in the sand. How will I ever find it? What am I going to tell my father? Those earrings were his grandmother's! He will be so angry with me.

1. How was the princess feeling when she wrote this entry? How do you know?
2. How is her entry personal?
3. How is her entry informal?

Workbook
Pages 43–44

Practice

Workbook Page 45

Write a journal entry about something special you lost, a fun trip you took, or a gift someone gave you.

1. **Read** Reread the journal entry on page 53. What was special about the earring that the princess lost?

Writing Strategy: Freewriting

Journal entries are a kind of freewriting. When you freewrite, you write down thoughts and feelings quickly. A good way to freewrite is to time yourself. Set a timer for five minutes and start writing. Don't stop until the time is up. Use informal language. Don't think about grammar or punctuation. Write as many ideas as you can.

In the entry below, the writer is freewriting about a trip she took last summer.

> I took a trip with my family to San Francisco last summer. It was so much fun! We rode the cable cars up and down the many big hills. We ate lunch by San Francisco Bay and saw some seagulls. In the evening we ate dinner in Chinatown. The next day we visited Golden Gate Park and went to the Golden Gate Bridge. I bought a really cool model of the Golden Gate Bridge. My sister and brother got one too. What a great city—I want to go back there!

---

2. **Freewrite your journal entry** Think about something special you lost, a fun trip you took, or a gift that means a lot to you. Once you have an idea, take out a sheet of paper. Set a timer for five minutes and write without stopping. Using informal language, write everything you remember about the idea or experience. Make sure you include your feelings.

Prepare to Read

► BUILD BACKGROUND

You will now read a social studies article called **The U.S. Camel Corps**. In the nineteenth century, the U.S. Army needed animals to carry things in the deserts of the Southwest. It was not easy to find food and water in the desert. The solution was to use camels. Camels can survive very well in the desert. They can live for weeks without water and for months without food, and they are very strong.

Have you ever been in a desert? Share with the class.

What You Will Learn

Reading
- Vocabulary building: *Synonyms and antonyms*
- Connect to reading: *Draw conclusions; Text structure*
- Text type: *Informational text (social studies)*

Writing
Writing genres

"Camels" ►

BOOST YOUR LISTENING COMPREHENSION

Unit 1: Journeys
Your teacher will play the DVD for this unit. After you listen, answer these questions.

1. Why is rain so rare in the desert?

2. What is the largest desert in the world?

3. What are two ways that people can survive in dry regions?

4. Who are the Bedouins? How have they survived?

5. What technique makes farming possible in dry areas of Israel?

6. What are three important sources of water in the Middle East? Why is the demand for water growing in this area?

► CONNECT TO VOCABULARY

Synonyms and Antonyms

A **synonym** is a word that means the same as, or almost the same as, another word. For example, the word *quick* is a synonym for the word *fast*. An **antonym** is a word that means the opposite of another word. The word *slow* is an antonym for the word *fast*.

Look at the word map below. It shows you a way to learn new words.

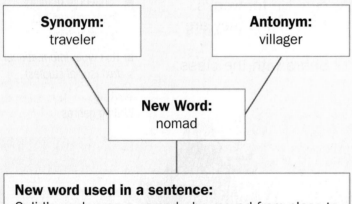

| Synonym: traveler | Antonym: villager |

New Word: nomad

New word used in a sentence:
Salid's uncle was a <u>nomad</u> who moved from place to place all his life.

Practice

Workbook Pages 46–47

Make a word map for each word below. Write a synonym and an antonym for each word. Then write a sentence using the word.

1. journey

2. herds

3. curious

4. welcomed

5. generous

➤ CONNECT TO READING

Draw Conclusions

To **draw conclusions** means to decide that something is true based on information. When you read, you draw conclusions based on facts from the text. For example, you read that a character is eating a large meal. You might draw the conclusion that the character is hungry.

Look at the chart below. It shows facts from the story "Jewel in the Sand." These facts were stated in the story. The chart also shows conclusions. These conclusions were not stated in the story. You can use the facts to decide that the conclusions are true.

Facts and Details	Draw a Conclusion
Ali finds a jewel in the desert. He traces a line to it with his sword.	Ali is clever.
An old woman returns the jewel to the princess.	The old woman is honest.
The princess gives the jewel to the old woman.	The princess is generous.

Practice

Workbook
Page 48

Read each fact or detail from "Jewel in the Sand." Then answer each question to draw a conclusion.

1. Ali does not interrupt his uncle's story because he does not want to be impolite. What conclusion can you draw about Ali?

2. Friends welcome Ali and his uncle when they return to camp. How do the friends feel about Ali and his uncle?

3. The princess shows the old woman an earring that matches the earring the old woman brings. Why does the princess do this?

Text Structure

The way a text is put together, or organized, is called its **structure**. A text may be organized in different ways. Clue words can help you figure out a text's structure. Three common kinds of structures are compare, contrast, and time order.

Read the examples on the chart.

Structure	Description	Clue Words	Example
Compare	A text **compares** when it tells how things are alike.	*same* *both* *alike* *similar*	Texas and Alaska are <u>both</u> large states.
Contrast	A text **contrasts** when it tells how things are different.	*but* *different* *unlike* *instead of*	Texas is a large state, <u>but</u> Alaska is larger.
Time order	A text is in **time order** when it gives actions in the order in which they happened.	*first, next, then, finally*	<u>First</u>, we will do homework. <u>Then</u>, we will watch TV.

Practice

Workbook Page 49

Write the sentences below in your notebook. Underline the text structure clue word in each sentence. Then write *Compare*, *Contrast* or *Time Order* next to the sentence.

1. Spanish and Italian are similar languages. *Compare*

2. Deserts are hot during the day, but they are cold at night.

3. Snow is the same as frozen water.

4. Read the story. Next, answer the question.

Set a purpose for reading "The U.S. Camel Corps" is a nonfiction article. Nonfiction articles give facts about a subject. As you read, look for clue words that help you understand the text structure.

The U.S. Camel Corps

Audio

In the 1850s, the United States was growing. The country's new land in the Southwest contained large, dry deserts. The U.S. Army traveled through the deserts of the Southwest. The soldiers used horses and mules to carry the things they needed. It was hard to find food and water in the desert for the animals.

In 1855, Jefferson Davis was the United States Secretary of War. He had a solution to the Army's problem. Davis knew that camels live in dry places. Davis decided that the Army should use camels to carry **supplies** through the Southwestern deserts.

---

supplies, things people need, such as food and water

BEFORE YOU GO ON

1 What did the soldiers use to carry their things?

2 Why did the U.S. Army decide to buy camels?

First, Davis sent men from the U.S. Army to North Africa. Camels live there. When the men arrived, they liked what they saw. Horses could carry heavy **loads**, but camels could carry heavier loads. Camels ate different things from horses, too. Horses ate oats and grain, but camels ate desert plants. Unlike horses, camels could go days without drinking water. The camels would solve the problem of finding food and water for animals in the desert.

The U.S. Army decided to buy thirty camels. They also hired people to handle, or work with, the camels. The camel handlers traveled back to the United States with the camels. Finally, in 1856, the U.S. Camel Corps began at Camp Verde, Texas.

The camels were very useful to the Army. They ate wild plants that horses and mules would not eat. The camels carried heavy loads across all types of land. They even kept going in heavy rain. Wagon wheels could get trapped in the mud, but the camels kept going.

The camels worked in the U.S. Army for five years. Then, in 1861, the southern states **broke away** from the United States. The southern states formed the Confederacy. Texas was part of the Confederacy. The camels became part of the Confederate Army.

---

loads, large amounts
broke away, separated

"The camels were very useful to the Army."

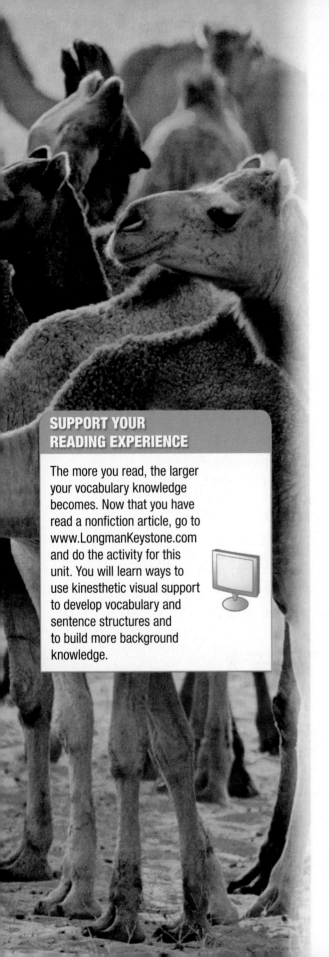

The Civil War began in 1861. The Confederacy fought the U.S., or Union, Army for four years. The Confederacy did not use the camels during the war.

Then, in 1865, the war ended. The Confederacy lost the war. As a result, the camels belonged to the U.S. Army again. However, the U.S. Army no longer wanted them. Some camels were sold. Others were released into the desert to live on their own. Time passed, and all the camels **disappeared**.

---

disappeared, died

SUPPORT YOUR READING EXPERIENCE

The more you read, the larger your vocabulary knowledge becomes. Now that you have read a nonfiction article, go to www.LongmanKeystone.com and do the activity for this unit. You will learn ways to use kinesthetic visual support to develop vocabulary and sentence structures and to build more background knowledge.

Workbook
Pages 50–51

BEFORE YOU GO ON

1. Who started the U.S. Camel Corps in 1856?

2. How were the camels different from horses?

3. What are some clue words in the article that tell you a comparison or contrast is made?

4. What are some clue words in the article that tell you time order is being used?

Writing

Writing Genres

Genre is the kind of writing you are reading or writing. Here are three genres you may have used.

Genre	Explanation
Letter	A letter is a written message sent through the mail. A letter begins with a greeting, such as "Dear Maria." A letter ends with a closing, such as "Sincerely." After "Sincerely," the letter writer signs his or her name. Letters can be formal or informal, but they are usually more formal and private than e-mail. Letters should always be polite.
E-mail	E-mails are electronic messages. You read, write, and send e-mails over the Internet on a computer. After the heading "To," type the e-mail address of the person who will receive your e-mail. After the heading "Subject," type what your e-mail is about.
Editorial	An editorial is an opinion expressed in a newspaper or magazine. The purpose of an editorial is to state a position on an issue. You state your opinion near the beginning of the editorial. Then you give reasons that people should agree with your opinion.

1. You want to give your opinion about a new law in your town. You want a lot of people to read your opinion. Which genre would you use and why?

2. You want to thank someone for a gift. The person does not have a computer. Which genre would you use and why?

3. You want to ask a friend about homework. The homework is due tomorrow. Which genre would you use and why?

Workbook
Pages 52–53

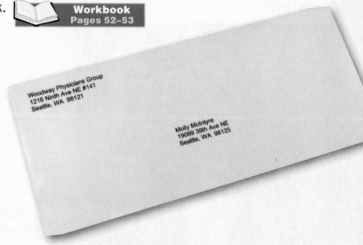

Woodway Physicians Group
1216 Ninth Ave NE #141
Seattle, WA 98121

Molly McIntyre
19089 39th Ave NE
Seattle, WA 98125

Link the Readings

Make a chart like the one below to compare the readings in this unit. Look at each word in the column. Put an **X** under "Nomads" if the word reminds you of that selection. Put an **X** under "Jewel in the Sand" if the word reminds you of the folktale. Put an **X** under "The U.S. Camel Corps" if the word reminds you of that selection. Put an **X** in all places if the word reminds you of all selections.

	"Nomads"	"Jewel in the Sand"	"The U.S. Camel Corps"
fiction	_____	___X___	_____
nonfiction	_____	_____	_____
desert	_____	_____	_____
tribe	_____	_____	_____
sheik	_____	_____	_____
buffalo	_____	_____	_____
tents	_____	_____	_____
camels	_____	_____	_____

Check Your Knowledge

Language Development
1. Do you think the people in "Jewel in the Sand" are Bedouins? Explain.
2. Name the three articles you learned about in this unit. Use each one in a sentence.
3. Give an example of drawing a conclusion. Use "Jewel in the Sand," another text, or your own experience.

Academic Content
1. Why do nomads travel from place to place?
2. Who are the Bedouins? Describe their way of life.
3. Why are animals important to nomads? Give examples.
4. How did the Sioux of North America use the buffalo that they hunted?
5. Why were camels important to the U.S. Army?

Hidden Forces

Sometimes there are surprises hidden inside things. "The Trojan Horse" is a story from the past. The horse has a secret hidden inside it. There are also surprises inside the earth. "Earthquakes" tells of forces hidden in the earth. These forces can make the earth move suddenly. Finally, you will read two different viewpoints about oil drilling and earthquakes.

Reading

1 Legend

"The Trojan Horse"

Reading Strategy:
Look for problems and solutions

2 Science

"Earthquakes"

Reading Strategy:
Look for causes and effects

3 Science

"Oil Drilling and Earthquakes"

Connect to Reading:
Visuals in informational articles; Main ideas and details

Listening and Speaking

In this unit, you will retell a legend.

Writing

In this unit, you will create a sequence-of-events chart, write a personal narrative, and learn to structure ideas to write an informational article.

Quick Write

Have you ever felt an earthquake? Write two or three sentences about your experience. If you have never felt an earthquake, what do you think it would feel like?

VIEW AND RESPOND
Watch the Unit 2 DVD. As you watch, answer the questions on page 85.
www.LongmanKeystone.com.

Prepare to Read

What You Will Learn

Reading

- Vocabulary building: *Context; dictionary skills*
- Reading strategy: *Look for problems and solutions*
- Text type: *Literature (legend and play)*

➤ **BUILD BACKGROUND**

"The Trojan Horse" is a Greek legend. A legend is a story that people tell and retell over many, many years. Legends often change over time.

▲ The Trojans lived in the ancient, or very old, city of Troy. Troy is marked with a star.

USE PRIOR KNOWLEDGE

1 How do you think the Greeks traveled to Troy? Look at the map.

2 How do you think a big wooden horse could help an army?

▲ Model of the Trojan Horse at the site of ancient Troy in Turkey.

Workbook
Page 54

➤ VOCABULARY

Listening and Speaking: Key Words

Look at the pictures and the captions. They will help you learn the words in the box. Write the meaning of each highlighted word, then read them aloud with a partner. Then check your work in a dictionary.

▲ Queen Helen was a prisoner inside the palace at Troy.

▲ The strong walls around Troy made the city safe.

◀ These Greek soldiers were ready to attack their enemies, the Trojans.

Workbook
Pages 55–56

READING STRATEGY | LOOK FOR PROBLEMS AND SOLUTIONS

In this legend, the Greeks had a **problem**. They needed to solve it, or find a **solution**. Read the story to find out what the problem was and how the Greeks solved it. Ask yourself these questions:

- What did the Greeks want to do?
- Why couldn't they do it?
- How did they solve their problem?

Workbook
Page 57

Set a purpose for reading As you read, think about how the Greeks solved their problem with the Trojans. As you read, fill in a problem-and-solution graphic organizer.

THE TROJAN HORSE

Helen was queen of the Greeks. She was very beautiful. A Trojan prince made her a prisoner and took her to his home in Troy. Helen's husband wanted Helen back in Greece. He sailed to Troy with many ships and many soldiers. For ten years he and the other Greeks **camped** outside the walls around the city. They attacked Troy many times, but the walls were too strong.

Finally, the Greeks asked two of their gods, Athena (uh-THEE-nuh) and Poseidon (po-SI-dun), for help. Athena wanted the Greeks to beat their enemies. She gave an idea to Odysseus (oh-DISS-ee-yus), one of the Greeks. Odysseus said, "We can trick the Trojans! We can build a huge wooden horse and hide inside it. Then, as soon as the Trojans bring the horse through the city walls, we will surprise them."

---

camped, lived in tents

And that is what the Greek soldiers did. When the wooden horse was ready, they carved words on the side. The words said: *For Athena. The Greeks ask you for a safe return home.* The Greeks knew that the people of Troy also **honored** Athena. They knew there was a **temple** to Athena inside the city walls. This was their plan: "The Trojans will take the horse into the city to the temple. We will be hiding inside the horse."

That night, Odysseus and twenty other soldiers climbed inside the horse. They closed the small door and waited quietly. All the other Greeks sailed away in their ships, but they did not go far.

The next morning, the Trojans looked outside the walls. The Greeks were gone. Their camp was empty. Nothing was left outside the walls of Troy but the big wooden horse.

The Trojans saw the huge horse and were curious about it. One Trojan warned that the horse was a trick. But the others did not listen. They decided to bring it through the city walls. It was very heavy. With great effort, they pulled it into the city. When the horse was inside, the people of Troy covered it with flowers.

---

honored, treated as special; respected
temple, place where people worship in some religions

BEFORE YOU GO ON

1 Who gave Odysseus the idea to build a horse?

2 Why did the Greeks think the Trojans would take the horse into the city?

At night the king of Troy had a party at the palace. At last the war was over. Queen Helen came outside to look at the horse. "I wonder what is inside this horse," she said quietly to herself. The men inside the horse wanted to call out to Helen, but Odysseus stopped them.

"Shhh," he said to his men. "Do not say a word or the Trojans will **discover** us." Helen guessed that Greek soldiers were inside the horse, but she kept the secret.

Late that night, all the Trojans were asleep. The Greek soldiers opened the small door in the horse. They climbed out. A few of them ran to the top of the city walls. They waved at their ships to return. The Greek soldiers on the ships saw them and sailed back to the city.

Then Odysseus and his men opened the city gates. All the other Greek soldiers rushed inside. They killed the Trojans and burned the city. Queen Helen was saved. The long war was over.

---

discover, find

BEFORE YOU GO ON

1 Why did Odysseus tell his men not to call out to Queen Helen?

2 How did the horse help the Greeks win the war?

THE TROJAN HORSE * A Play

Now read the same legend as a play. There are twelve parts.

CHARACTERS

Narrator	First Trojan Soldier
Helen's Husband	Second Trojan Soldier
Athena	Trojan Man
Odysseus	Trojan King
First Greek Soldier	Queen Helen
Second Greek Soldier	Chorus

Narrator: Helen, queen of the Greeks, was a prisoner in Troy. Her husband wanted her back in Greece.

Helen's Husband (to soldiers): We must get Helen out of Troy!

Narrator: The Greeks sailed to Troy. They attacked the city for ten years. But the walls around Troy were very strong.

Chorus: The Greeks called to the gods for help. Athena! Poseidon!

Athena: I will help my people win. I will give an idea to Odysseus.

Odysseus: I have an idea! We can trick the Trojans. We can build a huge horse and hide inside it.

First Greek Soldier: We'll carve these words on it: *For Athena. The Greeks ask you for a safe return home.*

Odysseus: The Trojans will think the horse is for Athena. They honor her just as we do.

Second Greek Soldier: The Trojans will bring the horse inside their city. Then we will surprise them.

Narrator: The Greek soldiers built the huge horse. When it was ready, Odysseus and twenty other soldiers climbed inside.

Odysseus: Close the door! Be quiet!

Chorus: The Greeks' ships left Troy, but they did not go far.

First Trojan Soldier: Look! What did the Greeks leave behind?

Second Trojan Soldier: It is a gift for Athena. Call the others. We can take it into the city.

Trojan Man: No! Wait. It must be a trick.

Chorus: Don't listen to him!

First Trojan Soldier: Open the gates! We have a gift for Athena.

Narrator: The Trojans pulled the horse into the city.

Trojan King: The war is over. Now we will have a feast at the palace.

Queen Helen (to herself, looking at the horse): What is inside this horse?

Odysseus (quietly, to the other men inside the horse): Shhh! Don't say a word!

Narrator: The Greek soldiers came out of the horse. The people of Troy were asleep.

First Greek Soldier: I will climb the walls and wave at the ships.

Second Greek Soldier: I will open the gates.

All the Greek Soldiers: Now, soldiers! Attack! Burn the city!

Chorus: So the Greeks won the war, and Helen was saved.

Review and Practice

► RETELL AND REVIEW

1. Took back at the pictures in "The Trojan Horse" on pages 68–70. Cover the words on each page. Retell the events of the story to a partner, using only the pictures. Use the Key Words. If you can't think of a word, describe it, use a synonym, or ask your teacher.

2. What problem did the Greeks have to solve?

3. How did the Greeks solve their problem?

► COMPREHENSION  Workbook Page 58

Complete the sentences. Choose the correct word from the column on the right. Write the completed sentences in your notebook.

1. The walls around Troy were very _strong_.	Odysseus
2. Helen was a _____ in Troy.	~~strong~~
3. Athena gave an idea to _____.	Athena
4. The Trojans thought the horse was a gift for _____.	returned
5. All the other Greeks sailed away in their _____.	prisoner
6. The Trojans pulled the horse through the city _____.	saved
7. The Trojan king had a feast at the _____.	asleep
8. Late at night, all the Trojans were _____.	palace
9. The Greek soldiers on the ships _____.	ships
10. The Greeks _____ Helen and won the war.	gates

Extension

Greek Gods

A. With a partner, take turns reading the following text aloud.

Poseidon was a Greek god. He was the god of the sea. The Greeks asked Poseidon for help in fighting against the Trojans. The Greeks believed Poseidon could make storms in the sea. They also believed he could shake the earth, making walls and buildings fall. Poseidon was also the god of horses. Some people think that the Trojan horse really stood for Poseidon. They think that the walls around Troy fell because Poseidon made the earth shake.

B. Find out more about Poseidon or another Greek god. Follow these steps:

1. Read library books or use the Internet.
2. Choose a Greek god to write about.
3. Write a paragraph. Answer these questions:
   - What does the god look like?
   - What does the god do?
   - What powers does the god have?
4. Read your paragraph to the class.

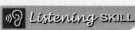

Listening SKILL

Listen to your classmates' paragraphs. What are the main points? What details support these points?

Workbook
Page 59

Prepare to Read

What You Will Learn

Reading

- Vocabulary building: *Context; dictionary skills*

- Reading strategy: *Look for causes and effects*

- Text type: *Informational text (science)*

Academic Content

- Science vocabulary

- Earthquakes

Grammar

Simple past tense: regular and irregular verbs

Writing

Write a personal narrative

➤ BUILD BACKGROUND

"Earthquakes" is nonfiction. It is like the text you find in science books. It tells how and why earthquakes happen.

Earthquakes can cause great damage, or harm. Some people think that an earthquake caused the walls of Troy to fall. Troy was in a part of the world where many earthquakes have happened. Why do earthquakes happen more often in some places than in others? Read "Earthquakes" to find out.

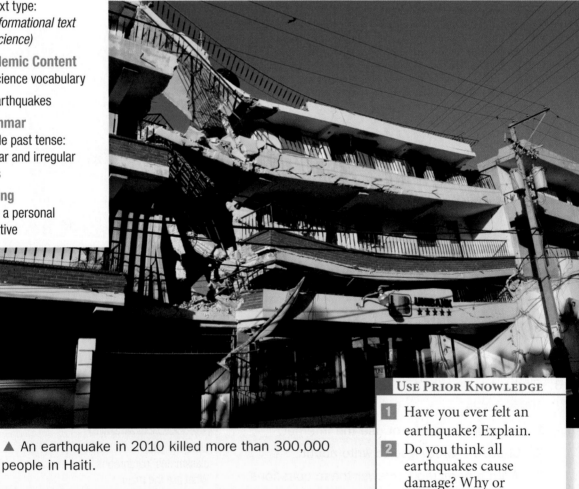

▲ An earthquake in 2010 killed more than 300,000 people in Haiti.

USE PRIOR KNOWLEDGE

1. Have you ever felt an earthquake? Explain.
2. Do you think all earthquakes cause damage? Why or why not?

► VOCABULARY

Listening and Speaking: Key Words

Look at the pictures and the captions. They will help you learn the words in the box. Write the meaning of each highlighted word, then read them aloud with a partner. Then check your work in a dictionary.

▲ A powerful earthquake can destroy buildings.

◄ These are plates, pieces of the earth's crust. They are moving in different directions.

▲ Living in places where earthquakes happen can be dangerous.

Workbook
Page 60

READING STRATEGY | **LOOK FOR CAUSES AND EFFECTS**

"Earthquakes" tells why earthquakes happen. Why something happens is a **cause**. What happens is an **effect**. Writers often use the words cause and causes to show cause and effect.

- Read to find out why earthquakes happen.
- Look for the words *cause* and *causes*.
- Read to find out some effects of earthquakes.

Workbook
Page 61

Set a purpose for reading "Earthquakes" is nonfiction text that tells where and how earthquakes happen. As you read, think about the causes and effects of earthquakes.

EARTHQUAKES

What Is an Earthquake?

An earthquake is a sudden moving or shaking of the ground. *Quake* is another word for *shake*. Earthquakes can be mild or very powerful. Powerful earthquakes can destroy buildings and bridges. They can also cause rivers to change direction. Earthquakes under the ocean can cause

▲ A powerful earthquake in 1985 destroyed many buildings in Mexico City.

huge waves, called tsunamis (soo-NAH-meez), to crash onto the land. Few earthquakes last more than thirty seconds.

What Is the Earth's Crust?

The earth's crust is a layer of rock that covers the earth. It is underneath all the land and water on the earth. The crust is made of huge pieces of rock called plates. The plates move very slowly. Where the plates touch, they can push against each other. These areas are called faults.

What Happens along the Faults?

Along the faults, the rocks press together. The **pressure** builds up between the plates until one of the plates snaps past the other. This causes the rock along the faults to shake. The shaking is an earthquake. During an earthquake, the earth's crust can crack. These huge cracks usually happen along the faults.

---

pressure, force created by pressing

▲ An underwater earthquake in 2004 caused a tsunami that crashed onto the island of Phuket in Thailand. It destroyed everything in its path.

▲ The earth's crust is made up of plates.

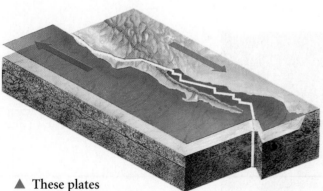

▲ These plates are moving in opposite directions. This causes pressure to build up where the plates touch. In time, the plates will snap past each other, causing an earthquake.

BEFORE YOU GO ON

1 What kinds of damage can earthquakes cause?

2 What are plates?

3 What happens when pressure builds up between plates?

Workbook
Page 62

Where Do Earthquakes Happen?

Most earthquakes happen along the faults, where the plates meet. Look at the map. It shows the plates in the earth's crust. One of the places where earthquakes happen is Turkey, where the city of Troy once was. Other places where earthquakes happen include Mexico, Japan, and California. As you can see, earthquakes can happen all over the world!

Reading Skill

Read the caption with each map, diagram, or photo. This will help you understand the information it presents.

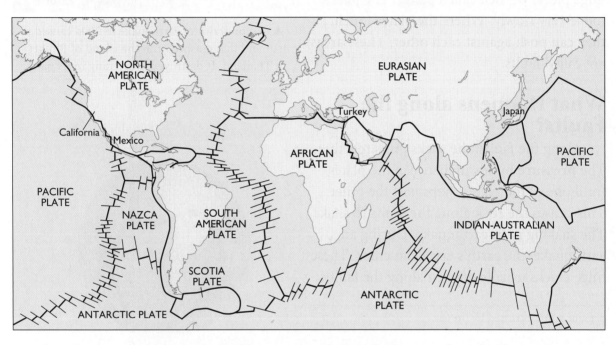

▲ This map shows the plates in the earth's crust. Most earthquakes happen where the plates meet.

◀ An earthquake with a magnitude of 8.8 hit the city of Concepción, Chile, in 2010.

What Is the San Andreas Fault?

The San Andreas Fault in California is famous. It is where the Pacific plate slides against the North American plate. Earthquakes along this fault usually happen closer to the earth's surface than at other places. They cause more shaking. These types of earthquakes are more dangerous than ones deep under the ground.

How Do We Measure Earthquakes?

We measure earthquakes by using a special machine called a seismograph (SIZE-moh-graf). The word *seismograph* comes from the Greek word *seismos,* which means "earthquake." Earthquakes cause waves to pass through the earth's crust. Stronger earthquakes make bigger waves, and weaker earthquakes make smaller waves. A seismograph records the size of the waves and how far away the earthquake is.

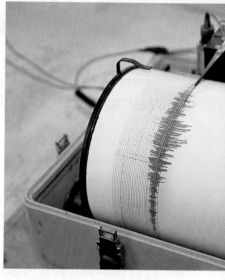

▲ A seismograph measures earthquakes by recording the force of the waves.

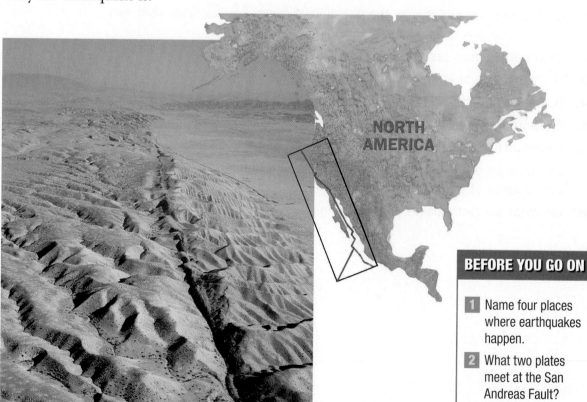

NORTH AMERICA

▲ San Andreas Fault in California

BEFORE YOU GO ON

1 Name four places where earthquakes happen.

2 What two plates meet at the San Andreas Fault?

3 Why are earthquakes along the San Andreas Fault often dangerous?

Review and Practice

➤ RETELL AND REVIEW

1. Tell a partner what you learned about earthquakes. Use the headings and the pictures on pages 76–79 to help you. Use the Key Words. If you can't think of a word, describe it, use a synonym, or ask your teacher.

2. What causes and effects did you find when you read "Earthquakes"? List each cause and effect that you found.

🔊 Listening SKILL

Look at pages 76–79 as you listen to your partner. If you don't understand something, ask a question.

➤ COMPREHENSION  Workbook Page 63

Write the sentences below in your notebook. Write Yes if the statement is true. Write No if it is not true. Then rewrite the statement correctly. Reread the selection silently to increase your comprehension.

1. Earthquakes cannot change the direction of rivers. *No. Earthquakes can change the direction of rivers.*

2. Most earthquakes last for hours.

3. The earth's crust is made up of solid rock.

4. During an earthquake the earth's crust can crack.

5. Pressure in the earth's crust causes earthquakes.

6. Earthquakes can cause tsunamis.

7. Earthquakes deep under the ground cause more damage than earthquakes at the surface.

8. We measure earthquakes with thermometers.

Models

People use models to show what something is like. For example, a globe is a model of the earth. A globe has the same shape as the earth. It shows the earth's land and oceans.

You can make a model showing what happens when plates that make up the earth's crust push against each other. Follow the steps below.

You will need:

- modeling clay in three colors
- a rolling pin
- a strong plastic knife
- a small empty box (size of paper-clip box)

1. Put the three pieces of modeling clay on a table.
2. Rolleach piece of clay into a slab 1 centimeter (½ in.) thick.
3. Cuteach clay slab into a square measuring 16 x 16 centimeters (6 x 6 in.).
4. Place one square on top of the other, like a sandwich.
5. Cutthe clay "sandwich" in half, making two rectangles, 8 x 16 centimeters (3 x 6 in.) each.
6. Turnthe pieces so that the long, smooth sides are touching, side by side.
7. Balancea small empty box on one rectangle.
8. Pushthe rectangles in opposite directions. Keep them pressed against each other as they slowly move past each other.

What happened to the box? How is that like an earthquake? Tell a partner.

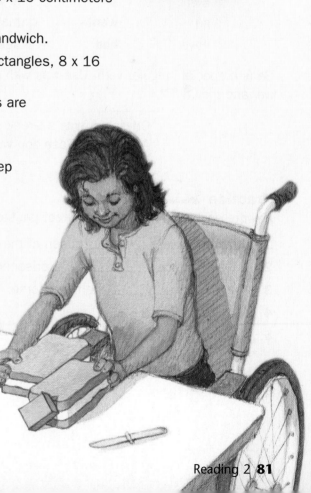

Grammar

The Simple Past Tense: Regular and Irregular Verbs

Use the **simple past tense** to talk about completed actions in the past.
For most **regular** verbs, add -ed to the base form.

Speaking SKILL

It is important to use the simple past correctly when you speak as well as when you write.

> The Greeks sail**ed** to Troy.
> The soldiers camp**ed** outside the walls.
> The earthquake happen**ed** in Mexico City.

When a regular verb ends in -e, add -d.

> The Greek soldiers close**d** the door.
> He use**d** a seismograph to measure the earthquake.

Many verbs have **irregular** past-tense forms. The chart gives some examples.

base form	simple past	base form	simple past
do	**did**	keep	**kept**
give	**gave**	know	**knew**
go	**went**	make	**made**
have	**had**	see	**saw**

Be is a special irregular verb. Use *was* with *I, he, she,* or *it*. Use *were* with *you, we,* and *they*.

> Odysseus **was** a Greek soldier.
> Athena and Poseidon **were** Greek gods.

Practice

Workbook Page 64

Rewrite each sentence with a correct past-tense verb. Use the charts above.

1. Beautiful Helen ___was___ queen of the Greeks. (be)

2. A Trojan prince _____ her a prisoner. (make)

3. The Trojans _____ the huge horse. (see)

4. At last the war _____ over. (be)

5. Queen Helen _____ that soldiers were inside the horse. (know)

Writing

Ongoing Writing Skills Practice

Write a Personal Narrative

A narrative tells a story. A **personal narrative** tells a story about an experience you had. You usually tell a personal narrative in the order that the events happened.

You can use sequence words to show the order of events. Sequence words usually come at the beginning of a sentence. Some sequence words are *first, next, then, after that,* and *finally.*

Read about Zin's unusual experience. Then answer the questions in your notebook.

Zin Dong

Our Shaky Day

Last Tuesday, my mother and I had breakfast as usual. But it wasn't usual for long. First, our glasses of orange juice shook. Then the table shook. After that, we watched our glasses slide. Crash! They fell off the table and broke on the floor. We knew it was an earthquake!

My mother felt really scared, but I remembered what to do. First, I helped her stand up. Then we stood in the doorway between the kitchen and the hall. A doorway is the safest place in an earthquake. Next, we breathed slowly to stay calm. Finally, the earthquake was over! It only lasted for about thirty seconds, but it seemed like thirty minutes.

---

1. What happened to Zin and her mother?
2. How do you know that this is a personal narrative?
3. What words show the order of events?

Workbook Page 65

Practice

Workbook
Page 66

You will write a personal narrative about an unusual experience you had.

1. Read Reread the personal narrative on page 83.

Writing Strategy: Sequence-of-Events Chart

A sequence-of-events chart helps you tell events in the order that they happened. Zin created this chart to write her personal narrative.

Our glasses of orange juice shook.

↓

The table shook.

↓

The glasses slid and fell off the table.

↓

I helped my mom stand up.

↓

We stood in the doorway between the kitchen and the hall.

↓

We breathed slowly to stay calm.

↓

The earthquake was over!

---

2. Make a sequence-of-events chart Make a chart about your experience in your notebook. Write the events in the order that they happened.

3. Write Write a personal narrative. Use the events from your chart. Remember to use sequence words to show the order of events. Edit your work. Make sure you form the simple past correctly. Check for spelling errors.

Prepare to Read

➤ BUILD BACKGROUND

You will now read a science article that presents two different viewpoints on the topic of oil drilling and earthquakes. When people have an opinion about an issue, they often try to convince others to agree with them. Opinions should be based on facts and research, not on emotion or what other people think. You should arrive at your own opinion after you have considered all the facts.

Do you have a strong opinion about an issue? Share with the class.

▼ Students discussing an issue

BOOST YOUR LISTENING COMPREHENSION

Unit 2: Hidden Forces

Your teacher will play the DVD for this unit. After you listen, answer these questions.

1. What causes an earthquake?

2. What is the San Andreas Fault? Where is it located?

3. How do scientists record and measure the force of seismic waves?

4. How many kinds of seismic waves does an earthquake produce? What are they called?

5. What have scientists learned by studying P waves and S waves?

6. How are the two layers of the earth's core different from each other? How are they the same?

➤ CONNECT TO VOCABULARY

Roots and Cognates

A **root** is a basic part of a word. It tells part of the meaning of the word. Many English words come from Greek and Latin roots. Can you guess the meaning of the word *biology* by thinking about the meanings of the parts of the word? (*bio* means "life"; *logy* means "the study of")

Study the following roots. They can help you figure out the meanings of words in your classes.

Root	Origin of the Word	Meaning
geo	Greek	Earth
sect	Latin	to cut
tele	Greek	far away

A **cognate** is a word with a root that is the same in different languages. Spanish and English share many roots. Spanish and English cognates usually look and sound similar. In many cases, that means the words have the same definition, too.

Spanish Word	English Cognate
terrible	terrible
importante	important
directo	direct
naturalmente	naturally

Practice 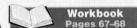 **Workbook**
Pages 67–68

Read the sentences. Use the charts to figure out the meanings of the underlined words. Write the meanings in your notebook.

1. We <u>dissected</u> a frog in science class today.

2. In <u>geology</u> class, we learn about rocks.

3. It is <u>important</u> to understand the story.

4. I asked him to <u>direct</u> me to the nearest grocery store.

▶ CONNECT TO READING

Visuals in Informational Articles

Visuals such as diagrams, photographs, and pictures often appear in books that give information. They help the reader better understand the ideas in a story or article.

Look at "The Trojan Horse." The words tell how the Greeks made a huge wooden horse. The pictures show men making a giant wooden horse. They help readers understand how big the horse was. It is clearer to show the size than to describe it in words.

Some informational articles have diagrams. They can help make ideas clearer. For example, look at the earth diagram on page 77. You cannot see the earth's crust in real life. The diagram helps you understand it.

Sometimes, it is faster to find facts in a chart than in a paragraph. Look at the chart below.

Number of Earthquakes Worldwide, 2006–2007			
How Powerful (10 is most powerful)	**2006**	**2007**	**2008**
8.0–9.9	1	4	0
7.0–7.9	10	14	12
6.0–6.9	142	172	166

Source: National Earthquake Information Center, U.S. Geological Survey

Could you quickly find all the facts in the chart if they were in a paragraph instead? You can get the same information much faster from a chart.

Practice  Workbook Pages 69–70

Work in a small group. Answer the questions.

1. Look at the chart. How many earthquakes happened in 2007?

2. Look at the map on page 78. Where do the plates meet in North America?

3. You are writing about teenagers and credit cards. You want to tell how many teenagers in each state have credit cards. Would you use a chart or words? Why?

Main Ideas and Details

All authors have a viewpoint. A viewpoint is the author's beliefs about a topic. The author presents his or her viewpoint through **main ideas** and **details**. The main idea is the most important idea. Details are facts, definitions, examples, or other ideas. They explain the main idea.

The headings, or subtitles, in a text are often clues to the main idea for each section. In the nonfiction article "Earthquakes," a paragraph follows each heading. The heading asks a question. The paragraph then gives information to answer that question.

For example, "Earthquakes" begins with the heading "What Is an Earthquake?" This question is the main idea of the section. The paragraph then answers the question with details. The details include facts about earthquakes.

Main Idea: What is an earthquake?

↓

Detail: An earthquake is a sudden moving or shaking of the ground.

↓

Detail: Earthquakes can be mild or powerful.

↓

Detail: Earthquakes under the ocean can cause tsunamis.

Practice  **Workbook** Pages 71–72

Work with a partner. Choose a section from "Earthquakes." In your notebook, make a chart like the one above. Fill in the main idea and details from the section you chose.

Set a purpose for reading As you read each different viewpoint, synthesize, or put together, the information. Then you can form your own ideas about the topic.

Oil Drilling and Earthquakes

Audio

DRILLING CAUSES EARTHQUAKES

Scientists have shown that drilling for oil can cause earthquakes. Since drilling for oil can cause earthquakes, it may be dangerous to allow more drilling in the United States.

Earthquakes happen a lot in the United States. Almost every year, there are earthquakes large enough for people to feel. In some places, there are very small earthquakes every few days.

Earthquakes can kill people and damage buildings. In 1989, an earthquake in San Fransisco killed 63 people and left thousands more homeless, yet offshore oil drilling continues in California. It's just too dangerous.

MINOR EARTHQUAKES:
NO REASON TO STOP DRILLING FOR OIL

Scientists have shown that drilling for oil may cause some earthquakes. This has happened in a few oil fields around the United States. However, these earthquakes are very small. There is almost no danger to people or buildings. Therefore, there is no reason to stop oil drilling in the United States.

In some parts of the United States, there are earthquakes every few days. Most earthquakes are very small. Sometimes, though, there is an earthquake that people can feel. Studies have shown that these earthquakes are not caused by oil drilling.

Even if people feel the earthquake, earthquakes almost never cause damage. In 2011, an earthquake damaged some buildings in the Northeast. Since then, however, there has been no serious earthquake damage anywhere. Oil drilling is safe.

SUPPORT YOUR READING EXPERIENCE

The more you read, the larger your vocabulary knowledge becomes. Now that you have read two nonfiction articles, go to www.LongmanKeystone.com and do the activity for this unit. You will learn ways to use kinesthetic visual support to develop vocabulary and structures and to build more background knowledge.

BEFORE YOU GO ON

1 Which facts in the articles are the same?

2 How are the two authors' viewpoints different?

3 How would you synthesize the ideas to form your own viewpoint?

Writing

Ongoing Writing Skills Practice

Write an Informational Article

A good informational, or nonfiction, article has a clear main idea and supporting details. It often starts with an interesting idea or question. This **rhetorical device**, or writer's tool, can make people want to read the article.

As you write, remember your main idea. You should also connect ideas. Use transition words to show how ideas fit together. A **transition** is a word that signals a change from one thought to another. A transition shows the relationship between sentences and paragraphs.

Transition Words and Phrases	
therefore	Shows that one thing caused another. • It was raining. <u>Therefore</u>, we left early.
however	Shows a contrast with what came before it. • The CD cost a lot. <u>However</u>, I got it anyway.
for example	Shows that an example will follow. • I like sweets. <u>For example</u>, I enjoy cake.

Here is a student's paragraph about earthquakes. After you read it, answer the questions in your notebook.

> Some people think that all earthquakes cause damage. It is true that some earthquakes are extremely dangerous. However, some earthquakes are very small. For example, many earthquakes in California are small. People do not usually even notice them.

1. What is the main idea of the paragraph?

2. What two transition words are used in the paragraph?

3. How do the transitions help you connect the ideas?

Workbook
Pages 73–74

Practice

Write a short informational article about oil drilling and earthquakes. Make sure your article has a clear main idea, supporting details, and transitions.

1. **Read** Reread the student's paragraph on the previous page. Think about what you want to say in your article.

2. **Plan with a chart** Make notes for your article. Use the chart on this page as a model.

Writing Strategy: Writing an Informational Article

Think about your article. What is your main idea? What details will support that main idea? Make a chart like the one below. Use it to structure your writing.

What is my main idea?
What is my first supporting detail?
What is my second supporting detail?
What headings can I use to organize information?
How can I make my first paragraph interesting to the reader?

---

3. **Write** Use your notes to write an informational article. Include some visuals, if possible.

IMPROVE YOUR WRITING SKILLS

When you write, you write for a particular reader, or "audience." Good writers are careful about selecting the correct genre and determining an appropriate topic to write about. Go to www LongmanKeystone. com and do the activity for this unit. You will learn strategies to help you convey meaning appropriately to differen types of audiences.

Link the Readings

Make a chart like the one below to compare the readings in this unit. Look at each word in the column. Put an **X** under "The Trojan Horse" if the word reminds you of the legend. Put an **X** under "Earthquakes" if the word reminds you of that selection. Put an **X** under "Oil Drilling and Earthquakes" if the word reminds you of that selection. Put an **X** in all places if the word reminds you of all selections.

	"The Trojan Horse"	"Earthquakes"	"Oil Drilling and Earthquakes"
legend	_____	_____	_____
science text	_____	_____	_____
Athena	_____	_____	_____
Poseidon	_____	_____	_____
plates	_____	_____	_____
faults	_____	_____	_____
hidden forces	_____	_____	_____
social studies text	_____	_____	_____

Check Your Knowledge

Language Development

1. What is a legend? How is it different from a folktale? Explain and give an example.
2. How does thinking about problems and solutions help you as you read?
3. Give examples of verbs with regular and irregular past-tense forms.
4. What is a sequence-of-events chart? What does it show?

Academic Content

1. What was the Trojan Horse?
2. Name three places in the world where earthquakes have happened.
3. What do scientists think causes an earthquake?
4. How are earthquakes measured?

Play Ball!

Ball games are part of our history. "The Bouncing Ball" tells how the rubber ball came to us a long time ago. "Roberto Clemente" is the story of a great player of one of America's favorite ball games—baseball. Clemente was a hero in other ways, too. Finally, "My Life in the Desert" is about growing up in Arizona.

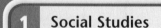

Reading

1 Social Studies	2 Biography	3 Personal Essay

"The Bouncing Ball"	"Roberto Clemente"	"My Life in the Desert"
Reading Strategy: Ask questions	**Reading Strategy:** Understand chronological order	**Connect to Reading:** Literary nonfiction

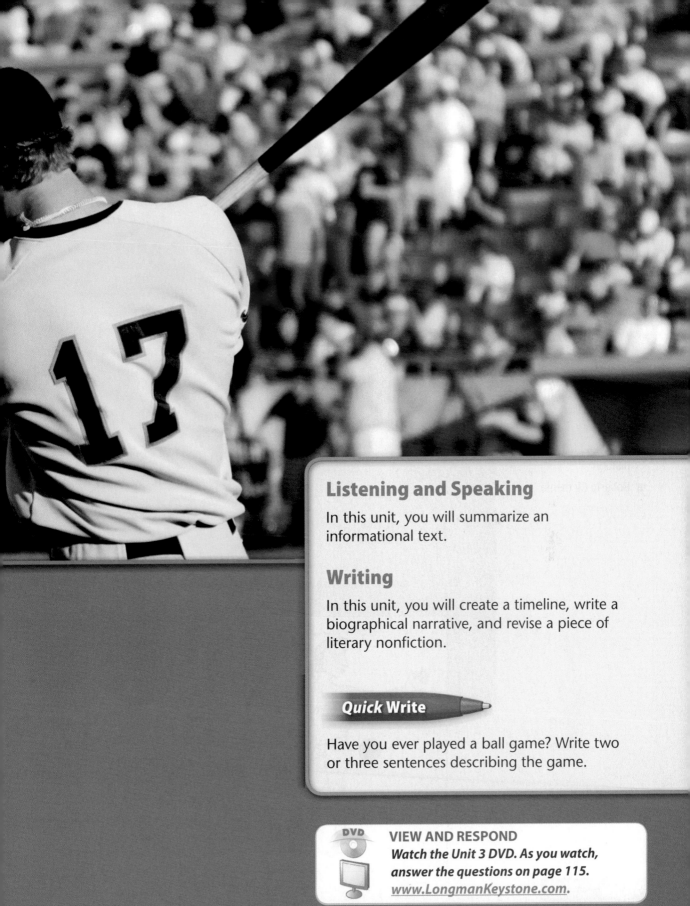

Listening and Speaking

In this unit, you will summarize an informational text.

Writing

In this unit, you will create a timeline, write a biographical narrative, and revise a piece of literary nonfiction.

Quick **Write**

Have you ever played a ball game? Write two or three sentences describing the game.

DVD

VIEW AND RESPOND
Watch the Unit 3 DVD. As you watch, answer the questions on page 115.
www.LongmanKeystone.com.

What You Will Learn

Reading

- Vocabulary building: *Context; dictionary skills*
- Reading strategy: *Ask questions*
- Text type: *Informational text (social studies); nonfiction*

Academic Content

- Social studies vocabulary
- Aztec and Maya history
- Roberto Clemente

➤ **BUILD BACKGROUND**

"The Bouncing Ball" is nonfiction. It gives you facts about the history of the rubber ball.

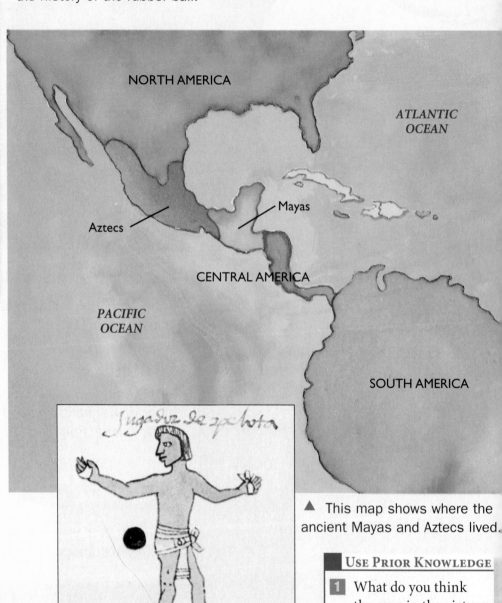

▲ This map shows where the ancient Mayas and Aztecs lived.

USE PRIOR KNOWLEDGE

1. What do you think the man in the picture is doing?
2. Look at the map showing where the Mayas and Aztecs lived. What countries are in this area today?

Workbook Page 75

▶ VOCABULARY

Listening and Speaking: Key Words

Look at the pictures and the captions. They will help you learn the words in the box. Write the meaning of each highlighted word and say them aloud with a partner. Then check your work in a dictionary.

Key Words

artifact
bounce
explorers
rubber
statue

◀ This statue of a Maya ballplayer is an artifact. An artifact is an object made by people. We learn about ancient peoples from the artifacts they leave behind.

▲ Rubber comes from the liquid inside rubber trees. Most balls made of rubber can bounce up and down.

▲ Spanish explorers traveled to the Americas in the 1500s. There they met the Aztec (AZ-tek) and Maya (MY-uh) peoples.

Workbook
Pages 76–77

READING STRATEGY | ASK QUESTIONS

Ask questions as you read to check what you know and don't know. For example, ask yourself, "What ideas or words don't I understand?"

- Write down words or ideas you don't understand.
- Reread the text and look for the meanings of these words or ideas.
- Use a dictionary or ask your teacher for help when necessary.

Workbook
Page 78

Set a purpose for reading Nonfiction gives you facts about a subject. "The Bouncing Ball" tells about the ball games people played a long time ago. As you read, ask yourself questions about the text.

The Bouncing Ball

Where Did This New Ball Come From?

Most people in Europe did not know about rubber balls until the 1500s. Before that time, Europeans played games with balls made of wood or leather. They did not have balls that bounced. They did not play ball games like basketball, soccer, or tennis.

In the early 1500s, explorers from Spain went to what is now Mexico and Central America to look for gold. There the Spanish explorers met the Aztec and Maya peoples. The Aztecs and the Mayas played games with a new kind of ball. This ball bounced up and down. At first, the Spanish were afraid of this strange ball. What made it bounce? Was there something inside it? Did the Aztecs and Mayas have a secret?

▲ Maya ballplayer

▲ Players tried to bounce a rubber ball through a stone ring.

USE PRIOR KNOWLEDGE

Why do you think the Spanish were afraid of the bouncing ball?

▲ Rubber tree

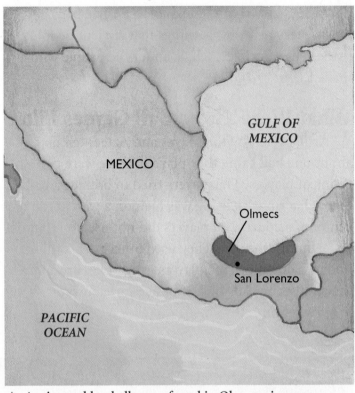

▲ Ancient rubber balls were found in Olmec ruins near San Lorenzo, Mexico.

▲ An ancient rubber ball

This strange ball was heavy. It was not made of wood or leather. It was made of rubber. The Aztecs and Mayas made rubber from the **sap** of rubber trees. The Spanish did not know about rubber trees. Rubber trees did not grow in Spain.

Who Were the Olmecs?

No one knows exactly when people first used rubber balls. Scientists think the Olmec people had rubber balls as early as 1000 B.C.E. The Olmecs lived in parts of what is now Mexico and Central America before the Aztecs and Mayas. Their name, *Olmec*, means "rubber people."

In 1989, scientists found three ancient rubber balls in Olmec **ruins** near San Lorenzo, Mexico. They also

sap, liquid inside trees
ruins, remains of buildings where people lived long ago

BEFORE YOU GO ON

1 What were European balls made of?

2 How did the Aztecs and Mayas make rubber?

3 Look at the map. Do you think rubber trees grew near San Lorenzo? Why or why not?

discovered clay statues of ballplayers. The balls and the statues are artifacts, things that ancient people made. These artifacts tell us about the people who made them.

What Were These Ball Games Like?

Artifacts left by the Mayas and Aztecs tell us about one ball game they played. There were two teams of players. The players tried to bounce a ball through a ring. The ring was high on a wall in the center of a court. The players did not use their hands or feet to hit the ball. They used other parts of their bodies. Sometimes the players wore yokes around their waists or pads on their knees or elbows for protection.

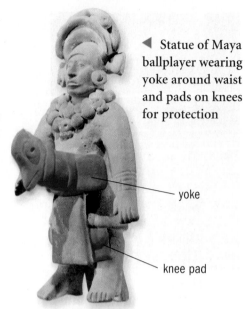

◀ Statue of Maya ballplayer wearing yoke around waist and pads on knees for protection

yoke

knee pad

▲ This ancient ball court in Mexico has stone rings placed high on its walls. Why do you think the rings are so high up?

MAKE CONNECTIONS

1. Is the ball game that the Mayas and Aztecs played like any game you know? Explain.
2. What is your favorite sport? Why do you like it?

How Are Our Ball Games Like Theirs?

The Spanish explorers took Aztec and Maya ballplayers back to Europe in 1521. Europeans loved the new ball games. They began to use rubber balls themselves and made up new games. Later, when Europeans came to North America, they invented other ball games. Many of the sports we play today come from the early Aztec and Maya games in some way. Here are some examples:

- In most of our sports today, we use balls that bounce.
- We play ball games on ball courts or fields.
- Two teams play against each other.
- Sometimes the players wear pads to protect themselves.

When you play games with a bouncing ball, you are part of history. You are continuing games that began on ancient ball courts 3,000 years ago.

▲ Soccer players pass the ball without using their hands or arms. They wear pads to protect their legs.

▲ Volleyball is played on a court.

▲ Basketball players throw the ball through a hoop at the end of a court.

BEFORE YOU GO ON

1 Why did the ballplayers wear yokes and pads?

2 When did ancient ball games begin?

3 What sports today use a bouncing ball? Explain.

Review and Practice

▶ RETELL AND REVIEW

1. Tell a partner what you learned about Aztec and Maya ball games. Use the headings and the pictures on pages 98–101 to help you. Use the Key Words. If you can't think of a word, describe it, use a synonym, or ask your teacher.

2. What questions did you ask yourself as you read "The Bouncing Ball"? How did you answer these questions?

»⁀ Listening SKIL

If you don't understand something, ask your partner to clarify it.

▶ COMPREHENSION

Workbook
Page 79

Write the questions below in your notebook. Then write an answer after each question. Use complete sentences. Reread the selection to find supporting evidence for your answers.

1. Why did Spanish explorers go to the Americas in the early 1500s?
   Spanish explorers went to the Americas to look for gold.
2. What did the Spanish think of the rubber ball when they first saw it?
3. What is an artifact? What do artifacts tell us?
4. What kinds of balls did Europeans use in their games before the 1500s?
5. What is rubber made from?
6. How did the Aztecs and Mayas play their ball games?
7. How did the rubber ball get to Europe?
8. List three ways in which Aztec and Maya ball games are like our sports.

Extension

Artifacts

Why Are Artifacts Important?

Artifacts tell us how people from a different time lived. They answer questions like these:

- Where did the people live?
- What did these people wear?
- What did they eat?
- What games did they play?

A. Work in a small group. Look at the pictures. Discuss what each object tells about how people live today.

B. Pretend that it is the year 4010. A scientist finds the ruins of your house. There are many artifacts there. Which artifacts tell the scientist the most about how you lived?

1. Make a list of artifacts that the scientist might find. Choose artifacts that would give answers to the questions at the top of the page.

2. Make a chart. In the left column, copy your list of artifacts. In the right column, explain what each artifact tells about how you lived.

Artifact	What It Tells
Cell phone	People had to talk to each other a lot.

3. Paste the chart onto a sheet of paper. Then add photos or drawings of the artifacts.

4. Share your work with the class.

Workbook
Page 80

Prepare to Read

What You Will Learn

Reading

- Vocabulary building: *Context; dictionary skills*

- Reading strategy: *Understand chronological order*

- Text type: *Literature (biography and play)*

Grammar
Information questions

Writing
Write a biographical narrative

➤ BUILD BACKGROUND

"Roberto Clemente" is a biography. A biography is the true story of a person's life. It is written by someone else. A biography is nonfiction because the people and events in it are real.

▲ Roberto Clemente was born in Puerto Rico. He became a great baseball player.

USE PRIOR KNOWLEDG

1. What do you know about baseball? Tell a partner some things you like and dislike about it.

2. Find Puerto Rico on the map below. Share some things you know about Puerto Rico with your classmates.

Florida

CUBA

JAMAICA

HAITI

DOMINICAN REPUBLIC

PUERTO RICO

▶ VOCABULARY

Listening and Speaking: Key Words

Look at the pictures and the captions. They will help you learn the words in the box. Write the meaning of each highlighted word and say them aloud with a partner. Then check your work in a dictionary.

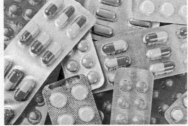

◀ The Pittsburgh Pirates gave Roberto Clemente the opportunity to play baseball.

▲ One of Roberto Clemente's greatest achievements was being voted Most Valuable Player of the National League in 1966.

▲ Rescue workers bring medicine and other supplies to people in need.

Workbook
Page 81

READING STRATEGY | UNDERSTAND CHRONOLOGICAL ORDER

A biography tells events in **chronological**, or time, **order**. Writers use time phrases such as *in 1934, on May 30,* and *the next year* to tell you when events happen.

- As you read, look for time phrases and important events.
- Make a T-chart to help you remember the dates and events. On the left side, write the dates. On the right side, write the events.

Workbook
Page 82

Set a purpose for reading "Roberto Clemente" is a biography. It is the true story of Roberto Clemente's life. The people and events in it are real. As you read, look for time phrases that tell when events happened.

ROBERTO CLEMENTE

Reading Skill

Read the text aloud with a partner. Listen for pauses and stressed words as your partner reads. This will help you understand the text.

Roberto Clemente was born in Carolina, Puerto Rico, in 1934. His father worked on a sugar cane **plantation**, and his mother worked in a grocery store. As a boy, Roberto loved baseball. His family didn't have much money, so Roberto had to make his own baseballs. He took old golf balls and wrapped string and tape around them to make them the right size.

Roberto played baseball in high school. After high school, he played for a team in Puerto Rico. In 1953, the Brooklyn Dodgers asked Roberto to join one of their **minor league** teams in Montreal, Canada. The next year, the Pittsburgh Pirates chose him to play for them in the **major leagues**. Roberto moved to Pittsburgh, Pennsylvania, and played **right field** for the Pirates for the next eighteen years. He became one of the best players in the major leagues.

---

plantation, large farm
minor league, less important group of teams of baseball players
major leagues, most important groups of teams of baseball players
right field, position in a baseball field

USE PRIOR KNOWLEDGE
What do you think Roberto Clemente's childhood was like? Explain.

His fans called him "The Great One." Roberto didn't speak English well, so reporters and sports writers sometimes **made fun of** him. Roberto didn't listen to them. He played great baseball and helped other Spanish-speaking players.

In 1971, the Pirates played against the Baltimore Orioles in the World Series, the games that decide the best baseball team in North America. Roberto was amazing! In seven games, he had 12 hits, including 2 **home runs**, 2 **doubles**, and 1 **triple**. The Pirates won the Series, and Roberto was voted Most Valuable Player of the Series.

Another of Roberto's great achievements happened on September 30, 1972. He got his three-thousandth hit as a major league player. At that time, he was only the eleventh player ever to get that many hits. But the hit was to be his last.

▲ Roberto with his wife and son and the trophy for Most Valuable Player of the National League in 1966

---

made fun of, laughed at, said unkind things about
home runs, hits that let the batter run around all the bases and score a run
doubles, hits that get the batter to second base
triple, hit that gets the batter to third base

▲ Clemente batting in the World Series, 1971

BEFORE YOU GO ON

1 What did Roberto use for "baseballs" when he was a boy?

2 What were some of Roberto's major achievements?

3 Have you ever been on a winning team? Tell about it.

Workbook
Page 83

▲ "The Great One"

ROBERTO CLEMENTE WALKER
PITTSBURGH N. L. 1955–1972

MEMBER OF EXCLUSIVE 3,000-HIT CLUB. LED
NATIONAL LEAGUE IN BATTING FOUR TIMES. HAD
FOUR SEASONS WITH 200 OR MORE HITS WHILE
POSTING LIFETIME .317 AVERAGE AND 240 HOME
RUNS. WON MOST VALUABLE PLAYER AWARD 1966.
RIFLE-ARMED DEFENSIVE STAR SET N. L. MARK BY
PACING OUTFIELDERS IN ASSISTS FIVE YEARS.
BATTED .362 IN TWO WORLD SERIES, HITTING IN
ALL 14 GAMES.

▲ Roberto Clemente was elected to the Baseball Hall of Fame.

On December 23, 1972, three earthquakes hit the city of Managua, Nicaragua. More than 10,000 people died, and more than 250,000 people lost their homes. Most of the buildings in the city were destroyed. The city had no water, electricity, or gas. Rescue workers there needed help.

Roberto had once said, "Anytime you have an opportunity to make things better and you don't, you are wasting your time on this earth." Roberto now had a chance to help the people of Nicaragua. On New Year's Eve, he and four friends loaded a plane with medicine and other supplies and took off from Puerto Rico to Nicaragua. But they never got there. The plane crashed into the ocean, and Roberto and his friends died.

After he died, people honored Roberto in many ways. Sports writers **elected** him to the **Baseball Hall of Fame** in 1973. He was the first player from Latin America ever to receive this honor. People all over the world named schools and hospitals after him. And his wife and sons collected money to build a sports center for children in Puerto Rico. It was something Roberto had always planned to do.

---

elected, chose
Baseball Hall of Fame, museum in New York State that honors people important to baseball

BEFORE YOU GO ON

1 What did Roberto do when he heard about the earthquakes in Nicaragua?

2 What happened to Roberto and his friends?

3 Why do you think so many people loved Roberto Clemente?

Roberto Clemente ⚾ A Play

Now read the same story as a play.
There are eight parts.

CHARACTERS

Narrator   Sports Writer 2
Roberto's Mother   Fans
Roberto   Reporter
Sports Writer 1   Chorus

Narrator: Roberto Clemente was born in Carolina, Puerto Rico, in 1934. His father worked on a sugar cane plantation, and his mother worked in a grocery store.

Roberto's Mother: Roberto loved baseball. As a boy, he played baseball whenever he could. We didn't have much money, so we couldn't buy baseballs for him. He used to make baseballs out of old golf balls.

Narrator: In 1953, Roberto got great news.

Roberto's Mother *(proudly):* The Brooklyn Dodgers asked Roberto to play for one of their minor league teams in Canada!

Narrator: The next year, Roberto received better news.

Roberto: The Pittsburgh Pirates have chosen me to play in the major leagues!

Sports Writer 1: Roberto Clemente can do it all. He can run, hit, catch, and throw.

Sports Writer 2: He doesn't talk to reporters much. His English isn't very good.

Roberto: It is hard for Spanish-speaking players to play baseball in the United States. I must do all I can to help them.

Fans: Roberto, you are a great ballplayer *and* a great person. You are "The Great One"! We love you!

Narrator: In 1971, the Pirates beat the Baltimore Orioles in the World Series.

Sports Writer 1: Roberto Clemente was voted Most Valuable Player of the Series.

Narrator: A year later, Roberto got his three-thousandth hit as a major league player.

Roberto's Mother *(sadly):* That was Roberto's very last hit.

Reporter: On December 23, 1972, three earthquakes hit Managua, Nicaragua.

Chorus: Thousands of people died. Thousands of others lost their homes.

Roberto: Anytime you have an opportunity to make things better and you don't, you are wasting your time on this earth. I must help the people of Nicaragua.

Narrator: Roberto and four friends tried to fly to Nicaragua from Puerto Rico.

Chorus: Their plane crashed on New Year's Eve and Roberto and his friends died.

Sports Writer 1: Today, we honor Roberto Clemente by electing him to the Baseball Hall of Fame.

Chorus: People all over the world named schools and hospitals after him.

Roberto's Mother: Roberto's family built a sports center for the children of Puerto Rico.

Chorus: It's what The Great One always wanted to do.

Review and Practice

► **RETELL AND REVIEW**

1. Tell a partner what you learned about Roberto Clemente. Use the pictures and the captions on pages 106–108 to help you. Use the Key Words. If you can't think of a word, describe it, use a synonym, or ask your teacher.

2. How did your T-chart of events help you to understand the biography better? Work with a partner to compare the events you listed.

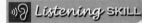
► **COMPREHENSION**  **Workbook Page 84**

Complete the sentences. Choose the correct answer from the column on the right. Write the completed sentences in your notebook.

1. Roberto Clemente was born in *Puerto Rico*.   Nicaragua
2. Roberto made his own baseballs from old _____.   English
3. Roberto did not speak _____ very well.   home runs
4. Roberto hit two _____ during the 1971 World Series.   plane crash
5. People called Roberto _____.   golf balls
6. People all over the world named _____ after him.   ~~Puerto Rico~~
7. In 1972 there were three earthquakes in _____.   "The Great One"
8. Roberto died in a _____.   hospitals

Extension

Games

People play many different games. What are the most popular games in your home country?

Find out more about your favorite games. Share what you learn with the class. Follow these steps:

1. Choose a game that you want to learn more about.
2. Talk to your family and friends. Ask them about the game.
3. Find information about the game in books or on the Internet. Take notes.
4. Make a poster about the game.
5. Write the rules of the game on a sheet of paper. Tape the rules to your poster.
6. Write the names of important players on the poster. Add pictures if you can.
7. Give an oral report about your game to the class. Show your poster. Use formal language.

Grammar

Information Questions

Information questions begin with a question word. Many information questions in the simple past use *did* before the subject. For the main verb in the question, use the base form. Do not use *-ed* or an irregular past-tense ending.

Information Questions			Answers
question word	subject	main verb	
What **did**	the ball	**do?**	It **bounced** up and down.
Where **did**	the Aztecs	**live?**	They **lived** in what is now Mexico.
When **did**	explorers	**go** to the Americas?	They **went** in the early 1500s.
Who **did**	explorers	**meet** there?	They **met** Aztecs and Mayas.
How **did**	the Olmecs	**make** rubber?	They **made** it from sap.
Why **did**	ballplayers	**wear** pads?	They **wore** pads for protection.

Practice  Workbook Page 85

Read the statements below. In your notebook, write the correct question word in the blank to complete each question. Use the underlined words to help you.

1. The Aztecs and Mayas played <u>games with a rubber ball</u>.

    ___*What*___ did the Aztecs and Mayas play?

2. Explorers went to the Americas <u>to look for gold</u>.

    _____ did explorers go to the Americas?

3. <u>In 1989</u>, scientists found three ancient rubber balls.

    _____ did scientists find three ancient rubber balls?

4. The Mayas and Aztecs played ball <u>on a court</u>.

    _____ did the Mayas and Aztecs play ball?

5. Scientists know <u>from their artifacts</u> that the Olmecs had rubber.

    _____ do scientists know the Olmecs had rubber?

6. The Olmecs came before <u>the Aztecs and the Mayas</u>.

    _____ did the Olmecs come before?

Reading Skill

Questions beginning with question words appear routinely in textbooks. Note that each question word asks about a particular kind of information. For example, who asks about people.

Writing

Ongoing Writing Skills Practice

Write a Biographical Narrative

A biographical narrative tells the true story of a real person's life. It usually includes a problem that the person had to solve. Writers usually tell events in a biographical narrative in chronological order—in the order that they happened.

Read the example below about Olympic athlete Wilma Rudolph. Then answer the questions in your notebook.

> Alejandro Landin
>
> Wilma Rudolph: Olympic Champion
>
> Wilma Rudolph was born in Tennessee in 1940. As a child, she became sick with polio. Her doctor said she would never walk again. But Wilma was strong and worked hard. By age 11, she could walk without help. Wilma became a star runner and basketball player in high school. In 1956, she won a bronze medal in the women's 400-meter relay in the Olympic Games in Melbourne. Four years later, in the Olympic Games in Rome, Wilma won gold medals in the 100-meter and 200-meter dash, and the women's 400-meter relay. She was the first American woman to win three gold medals! Wilma wrote her autobiography, _Wilma_, in 1977. She was elected to the U.S. Olympic Hall of Fame in 1983.

1. How old was Wilma when she ran in the Melbourne Olympics?
2. How old was she when she won three gold medals in the Rome Olympics?
3. What problem did Wilma have? How did she solve it?

Workbook
Pages 86–87

Practice

You will write a biographical narrative of someone you think is a hero.

1. **Read** Reread the biographical narrative on page 113. Then think of a hero to write about. It can be someone you know or someone you have read about.

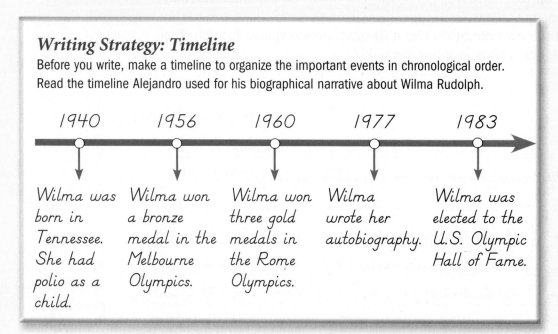

Writing Strategy: Timeline

Before you write, make a timeline to organize the important events in chronological order. Read the timeline Alejandro used for his biographical narrative about Wilma Rudolph.

1940 — Wilma was born in Tennessee. She had polio as a child.

1956 — Wilma won a bronze medal in the Melbourne Olympics.

1960 — Wilma won three gold medals in the Rome Olympics.

1977 — Wilma wrote her autobiography.

1983 — Wilma was elected to the U.S. Olympic Hall of Fame.

2. **Make a timeline** Think about the person you will write about. Make a timeline of important events. Include a problem the person had.

3. **Write** Use your timeline to write a biographical narrative. Tell the important events in chronological order. Talk about a problem and how the person solved it. Edit your work. Make sure you use regular and irregular verb tenses correctly. Check the spelling of words with the CVCe pattern.

Prepare to Read

➤ **BUILD BACKGROUND**

You will now read a personal essay about growing up in the Sonoran Desert in Arizona. Personal essays are a type of literary nonfiction. That means the places are real and the events really happened. A personal essay is told from the author's point of view about memories and experiences that are important to the author.

Do you have strong memories about a place from your childhood? Share with the class.

What You Will Learn

Reading
- Vocabulary building: *Word meanings and histories*
- Connect to reading: *Literary nonfiction*
- Text type: *Literature (personal essay)*

Writing
Revising your writing: Revising literary nonfiction

BOOST YOUR LISTENING COMPREHENSION

Unit 3: Play Ball!
Your teacher will play the DVD for this unit. After you listen, answer these questions.

1. When and where was Roberto Clemente born?

2. What were two of Clemente's achievements as a baseball player?

3. What other honor did Clemente receive?

4. Why did Clemente decide to go to Nicaragua?

5. When and how did Roberto Clemente die?

6. What is the Roberto Clemente sports complex? Who works there?

➤ CONNECT TO VOCABULARY

Word Meanings and Histories

Where can you find definitions besides in a dictionary? Look in a **thesaurus**. It is a book of synonyms and antonyms for words. If you look up the word *fast* in a thesaurus, you will find synonyms like these: *quick, speedy, rapid.* You will also find antonyms like these: *slow, pokey, sluggish.* Dictionaries and thesauruses come in book form and electronic form (on the Internet).

You can also find definitions in word lists, or **glossaries**, in some books. For example, in the back of this book is a glossary that defines words relating to grammar and literature.

Dictionaries can give you more than definitions. They can also have word histories, or **etymologies**. The etymology of a word tells what language it came from. It also tells when the word was first used in English and what the word first meant. Look at the histories below.

> **artifact** – (1821) from the Italian *artefatto*, meaning "anything made by human art."
> **bounce** – (1586) from the Middle French *bondir*, meaning "to leap."
> **explore** – (c. 1450) from the Latin *explorare*, meaning "search out."

Some dictionaries and thesauruses also explain the different feelings, or **connotations**, that go along with words. For example, *confident, proud,* and *stuck-up* have the same **denotation**, or definition, but very different connotations. Negative, or bad, feelings go along with the word *stuck-up*. Positive, or good, feelings go along with the word *confident*. The word *proud* is neutral.

Practice
Workbook
Pages 89–90

For 1–3, use a dictionary to find the etymology of each word. In your notebook, tell what language the word comes from, when it was first used in English, and what the word first meant. For 4, tell each word's connotation—positive, negative, or neutral.

1. rubber

3. knee

2. statue

4. small, petite, puny

► CONNECT TO READING

Literary Nonfiction

Literary nonfiction is a mix of facts and personal examples and descriptions. Like all nonfiction, literary nonfiction has ideas that can be proven to be true. Unlike many other kinds of nonfiction, literary nonfiction also has opinions, or personal beliefs that cannot be proven to be true. Literary nonfiction may explain a subject. It may describe a person or situation. It may give a writer's viewpoint, or beliefs, about a subject.

Often, literary nonfiction contains sensory details. These details tell how something looks, sounds, tastes, smells, or feels.

Literary nonfiction may be structured, or organized, in different ways. Study the chart below.

Structure	Example
Spatial: Describing something in a logical order, such as from left to right, top to bottom, front to rear, outside to inside	It was a pretty box of candy. The top was gold. The bottom was red. Inside the box were chocolates wrapped in white paper.
Comparison/Contrast: Telling similarities and differences between people, places, or things	During the day, the city is beautiful but noisy. At night, the city is still beautiful, but it is much quieter.
Time Order: Telling what happened in the order that it happened	First, we went to English class. Next, we went to gym class. Then, we ate lunch.

Practice  **Workbook** Pages 91–92

Read the paragraph. Then answer the questions in your notebook.

When I was young, Mother's hands were tender. Her palms were like cotton. By the time I was twelve, Mother's hands were as rough as concrete. We lived near a new car factory. Mother had a job there. "I want to take good care of you," she said. Soon, she was able to buy us many things. I was able to take dance lessons. She gave up soft hands to give us soft lives.

1. Which details are facts? Which details are opinions?

2. What are some sensory details in the paragraph?

3. What is the structure of the paragraph?

Set a purpose for reading "My Life in the Desert" is literary nonfiction. As you read, look for facts, personal examples, and sensory details.

My Life in the Desert

I have lived in Arizona all my life, and all my life I have wondered at the Sonoran Desert. I can feel its warmth from my porch. I can taste its dryness and hear its many sounds. A desert is not like an island. You cannot see where it starts and where it ends. You know you are in it when it feels like the sun has wrapped its arms around you.

Weather is harsh in the desert. It will beat on you like a drum. In the daytime the sun stretches across the sky. The heat swallows you like a cup of water. The night is so cold you forget the sun ever visited. It is as if the sun has been tossed in the ocean. All that is left is black sky, moon, and cold. The stars are there, too. I watch them blink. They are crystal eyes in the sky. I wish the sun could meet them, but they always leave before she arrives. When the sun rises again, she throws heat over the land like a heavy blanket. Then night falls. Before you know it, the cold rushes in again.

My father wants to move away from the desert. He is from the North, where it is cold. He says it is time for us to go. He is tired of the desert and the heat. "I've had enough of this desert," he says. "Let's go somewhere cool."

I do not see things as he does. To me, the Sonoran desert is beautiful. It is the most beautiful land my toes have touched. It is the most beautiful air my nose has breathed. It is the most beautiful song my mouth has sung. There are so many colors. I lose track counting. There are bright, blue skies. There are red mountains. There are dry green cactuses. There is a strong orange sun. There is a quiet white moon.

The animals must think the Sonoran desert is special, too. They live all around me. I have seen mountain lions, bobcats, golden eagles, coyotes, and great horned owls. They all dance in the desert sand. They drink its tiny bits of water. They must love the land as much as I do.

A desert is not home to many plants. Not many trees are as brave as the cactus. A cactus is a strange plant. It grows roots in the dry land. It holds on with very little water. It has a tight grip on the land. Somehow, it finds the strength to grow. The cactus proves that the desert is alive. It reminds me of a soldier. It fights for its life. The cactus inspires me, and it talks to me.

BEFORE YOU GO ON

1. What is the weather like in the desert?

2. What are some of the author's strongest memories about the desert?

3. Why does the author's father want to leave the desert?

The cactus says something special to me. It helps me know that I can live here, too.

However, the desert cannot be home for long. Rain never visits enough. My father is right. Sometimes, it does not rain for months. Rain is not a good friend of the desert. It does not visit as often as it should. When it does visit, it does not stay long. For that reason, people and animals cannot stay in one spot for long. They must travel the desert. They must follow its clues. I tell my father, "This is why we do not live in the desert. We live along its rim."

This evening, I will ask my father to close his eyes. I will ask him to think about the desert's beauty. When he closes his eyes, I hope he sees colors: red, yellow, green, gold. "Can you see your life without these colors?" I will ask. I hope he will open his eyes with a smile. I hope he will say we can stay.

"To me, the Sonoran desert is beautiful."

SUPPORT YOUR READING EXPERIENCE

The more you read, the larger your vocabulary knowledge becomes. Now that you have read a personal essay, go to www.LongmanKeystone.com and do the activity for this unit. You will learn ways to use kinesthetic visual support to develop vocabulary and structures and to build more background knowledge.

Workbook
Pages 93–94

BEFORE YOU GO ON

1 Does the author want to keep living in the Sonoran desert? Why?

2 Which ideas in the essay are facts? Which are personal opinions?

3 Would you like to live in the desert? Why or why not?

Writing

Revise Your Writing

When you **revise** your writing, you change it in order to make it better. Sometimes, you might revise to meet your **purpose**, or reason for writing. If your purpose is to entertain your **audience**, you might make a sentence funnier.

Other times, you might revise to make something clearer in order to inform your audience. Suppose your audience does not know anything about your subject. You might write an easy word in place of a hard word your readers do not know. Or, you might add **figurative language**, or language that you do not take literally, such as poetic comparisons.

You may also revise to follow the rules of a **genre**, or kind of writing. For instance, you might forget to sign, or write your name, at the end of a letter. Letters are supposed to end with the writer's name, so you add your name.

Here are some revisions the author made to the first draft of "My Life in the Desert."

The ~~desert~~ animals must think the ^Sonoran^ desert is special, too.
They live all around me. I have seen ^mountain lions, bobcats, golden eagles,
coyotes, and great horned owls. They all ~~walk~~ ^dance^ on the desert sand.
They drink its tiny bits of water. They must love the land as
much as I do.

---

1. Which edit changes the essay's word choice?

2. Which edit makes a sentence longer?

3. How does adding the word "Sonoran" make the author's purpose clearer?

Workbook
Pages 95–96

◄ A mountain lion

Practice

You will revise a piece of literary nonfiction. You will think about the purpose of the writing, the audience who will read it, and the genre of the writing.

1. **Read** Look at the paragraph below. It is from a student's writing. The purpose of the writing is to inform and entertain. The audience is teenagers who do not know the subject of the writing. The genre is literary nonfiction.

Writing Strategy: Revising Literary Nonfiction

Think about the paragraph. What do you think needs improving?

> I like to bake. I especially like to bake sugar cookies. When I bake sugar cookies, I make sure I have all the ingredients I need in front of me. I put my recipe on the kitchen table. I can read it while I work. I like the way the cookie batter looks and tastes while I am making it. After I put the cookies in the oven, I like the way the kitchen smells. When the cookies are cool, I decorate them. They look pretty.

IMPROVE YOUR WRITING SKILLS

Now that you have practiced writing a piece of literary nonfiction, go to www.LongmanKeystone com and do the activity for this unit. You will find suggestions for planning future written works, including how to determine appropriate topics through a range of strategies.

2. **Discuss** Work with a partner. Decide what revisions you would make. Think about the purpose, audience, and genre. Answer these questions.

   - Are there any words the audience will not know? What would you put in their place?

   - Where could you add sensory details or figurative language? What would you add?

   - The sentences all sound the same. How would you revise them to add variety?

3. **Revise** Work with a partner. Use the question list to edit each other's work.

4. **Write** Write a final draft of your paragraph.

Link the Readings

Make a chart like the one below to compare the readings in this unit. Look at each word in the column. Put an **X** under "The Bouncing Ball" if the word reminds you of that selection. Put an **X** under "Roberto Clemente" if the word reminds you of the biography. Put an **X** under "My Life in the Desert" if the word reminds you of the essay. Put an **X** in all places if the word reminds you of all selections.

	"The Bouncing Ball"	"Roberto Clemente"	"My Life in the Desert"
explorers	_____	_____	_____
major league	_____	_____	_____
statue	_____	_____	_____
artifact	_____	_____	_____
achievement	_____	_____	_____
opportunity	_____	_____	_____
ruins	_____	_____	_____
personal essay	_____	_____	_____

Check Your Knowledge

Language Development
1. How did asking questions help you to understand the reading?
2. What is a biography?
3. How do you form an information question in the simple past? Give an example.
4. What is a timeline? What does it help you to do?
5. What are sensory details? Give an example.

Academic Content
1. Describe a ball game that the Mayas and Aztecs played.
2. What did the Spanish think of the rubber ball when they first saw it?
3. What can we learn from artifacts?
4. What modern games are like the Aztec and Maya ball game? Explain.

Family Ties

In "The Clever Daughter-in-Law," a father wants his three sons to marry. The story has a riddle, or puzzle, in it. One girl answers the riddle and surprises everyone. Grandparents, parents, and children often have many things in common. Their eye color or hair color may be the same. "Family Traits" tells about how people in families are alike. Finally, you will read two speeches on the same subject.

Reading

1 **Folktale**

"The Clever Daughter-in-Law"

Reading Strategy:
Predict

2 **Science**

"Family Traits"

Reading Strategy:
Reread

3 **Social Studies**

"Daytime Curfew?"

Connect to Reading:
Opinions and evidence

Listening and Speaking

In this unit, you will retell a folktale and summarize a science text.

Writing

In this unit, you will create a *Wh-* question chart, write a personal letter, learn to use feedback to revise your writing, and write a critique.

Quick Write

Do you have a small family or a large family? Write two or three sentences describing your family.

DVD **VIEW AND RESPOND**
Watch the Unit 4 DVD. As you watch, answer the questions on page 145.
www.LongmanKeystone.com.

What You Will Learn

Reading

- Vocabulary building: *Context; dictionary skills*

- Reading strategy: *Predict*

- Text type: *Literature (folktale and play)*

▶ BUILD BACKGROUND

"The Clever Daughter-in-Law" is a folktale from China. China is a large country in Asia.

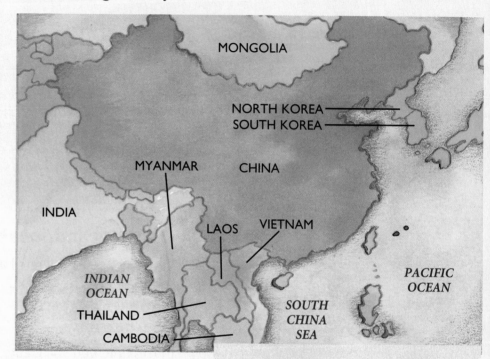

MONGOLIA

NORTH KOREA

SOUTH KOREA

MYANMAR

CHINA

INDIA

LAOS

VIETNAM

INDIAN OCEAN

THAILAND

CAMBODIA

SOUTH CHINA SEA

PACIFIC OCEAN

> ### USE PRIOR KNOWLEDGE
>
> **1** What do you know about China?
>
> **2** Look at the picture of the girl. What is she doing?

▲ A Chinese farm girl from long ago

Workbook
Page 97

► **VOCABULARY**

Learn Key Words

Look at the pictures and the captions. They will help you learn the words in the box. Write the meaning of each highlighted word. Then check your work in a dictionary.

▲ Chinese lantern

▲ A wife calls her husband's father father-in-law. She is his daughter-in-law. One daughter-in-law in this story is clever, or smart.

◄ The sisters missed their mother, so they asked their father-in-law if they could go to see her.

Workbook
Pages 98–99

READING STRATEGY | **PREDICT**

To **predict** means to guess what will happen.

- Look for clues in the story and in the pictures.
- Think about what will happen next.
- At the end of the story, see if what you predicted was correct.

Workbook
Page 100

Set a purpose for reading "The Clever Daughter-in-Law" has a riddle, or puzzle, in it. This makes the folktale fun to tell. As you read, see if you can predict the ending of the story.

The Clever Daughter-in-Law

Adapted from *Celebrate the World: Twenty Tellable Folktales for Multicultural Festivals*, by Margaret Read MacDonald

Long, long ago in China, there was a rich old man. He lived in a big house. He had three sons. One day he said to his sons, "It is time for you to marry. I am getting old. I need a big family around me to help me in my old age."

Two of the sons found lovely wives. The two wives were sisters from a family in the next town. Soon the sisters came to live in the big house with their new husbands and their father-in-law. The old man was very happy. But he still needed to find a wife for his third son.

The two sisters liked the big new house, but they missed their mother terribly. Every month they wanted to visit her. "Kind Father-in-law," they said, "may we go home again for a few days?" The old man agreed, but he did not like them to go away so often.

One day the old man had an idea. The two sisters came as usual and said, "Kind Father-in-law, may we go to visit our mother for a few days?"

"Of course," said the old man. "But please bring me two gifts when you return."

"Certainly," said the young wives. They wanted to please their father-in-law. "What gifts may we bring you?" they asked.

To the first wife the old man said, "You must bring me the wind wrapped in paper." And to the second wife he said, "You must bring me fire wrapped in paper." The two sisters were shocked. They left quickly. Then they walked along the road **silently** for some time.

"How can I find wind wrapped in paper?" the first sister asked.

"How can I find fire wrapped in paper?" asked the second sister. Neither sister had an answer. They sat down under a tree and began to cry loudly.

Soon a young farm girl saw them. She was walking with her **water buffalo**. "Why are you crying?" she asked. The sisters told her of the gifts they needed for their father-in-law. "Is that all?" the girl asked. "I can help you. Go to visit your mother and enjoy yourselves. I will have the gifts ready for you when you return."

---

silently, very quietly
water buffalo, large buffalo of Asia, often used as a
    farm animal

BEFORE YOU GO ON

1 Why does the old man want his sons to marry?

2 What gifts does the old man ask for?

3 What gifts do you think the farm girl will have ready for the sisters?

The two sisters returned the next day. The farm girl was waiting. "Here is the wind wrapped in paper," she said. In her hand was a paper fan. It made a gentle **breeze** when she waved it. Then she said, "And here is fire wrapped in paper." This time she held up a paper lantern with a bright candle inside.

"What a clever girl you are!" said the sisters. "Thank you so much!" They took the gifts and walked quickly back to the big house.

"Did you bring me the gifts?" asked the old man.

"Yes, good Father-in-law," said the two wives.

"Here is the wind wrapped in paper," said the first wife, and she showed him the fan.

"And here is fire wrapped in paper," said the second wife, and she showed him the lantern.

"How clever you are!" said the old man. "How did you think of these things?"

"Oh, we are not the clever ones," they said. "The young girl with the water buffalo was the clever one."

The old man invited the clever girl to meet his third son. They liked each other right away. Soon they married.

"How lucky I am," said the old father. "Now I have a happy house and a clever new daughter-in-law."

---

breeze, mild wind

BEFORE YOU GO ON

1 Does the clever farm girl remind you of anyone you know? Describe the person.

2 The farm girl solved the riddle. Do you know any riddles? Share them with a partner.

The Clever Daughter-in-Law
A Play

Now read the same folktale as a play. There are six parts.

CHARACTERS

Narrator	Young Wife 2
Old Man	Farm Girl
Young Wife 1	Chorus

Narrator: Long, long ago in China, there was a rich old man with three sons. Two of the sons married sisters from the next town. The sisters came to live in the big house.

Old Man: I am very happy. But I still must find a wife for my third son.

Narrator: The wives missed their mother.

Young Wife 1: Kind Father-in-law, may we go to visit our mother for a few days?

Chorus: The old man did not like his daughters-in-law to go away so often. He had an idea.

Old Man: You may go, but please bring me two gifts when you return.

Young Wife 2: Certainly. What may we bring to you?

Old Man: First wife, you bring me the wind wrapped in paper. Second wife, you bring me fire wrapped in paper.

Chorus: The two sisters were shocked. They left quickly.

Young Wife 1 (crying): How can I find wind wrapped in paper?

Young Wife 2 (crying): How can I find fire wrapped in paper?

Narrator: A young farm girl saw them. She was walking with her water buffalo.

Farm Girl: Why are you crying?

Chorus: The sisters told her their problem.

Farm Girl: Is that all? Go visit your mother. I will have the gifts ready when you return.

Narrator: The next day the two sisters returned. The farm girl was waiting.

Farm Girl (holding out a fan): Here is the wind wrapped in paper.

Young Wife 1: Oh, thank you. You are so clever!

Farm Girl (holding up a lantern with a candle): And here is fire wrapped in paper.

Young Wife 2: What a clever girl you are! Thank you so much!

Narrator: They took the gifts and walked quickly back to the big house.

Old Man: Did you bring me the gifts?

Chorus: They showed him the fan and the lantern.

Old Man: How clever you are! How did you think of these things?

Young Wife 1: Oh, we are not the clever ones. It was a farm girl.

Narrator: The old man invited the clever girl to meet his third son. They liked each other right away. Soon they married.

Old Man: How lucky I am! Now I have a happy house and a clever new daughter-in-law.

Review and Practice

➤ RETELL AND REVIEW

1. Look back at the pictures in "The Clever Daughter-in-Law" on pages 128–130. Cover the words on each page. Retell the story to a partner, using only the pictures. Use the Key Words. If you can't think of a word, describe it, use a synonym, or ask your teacher.

2. What did the farm girl do that was clever? Explain.

3. What gifts did you predict the farm girl would have ready for the sisters?

➤ COMPREHENSION  Workbook Page 101

Write the sentences below in your notebook. Write *Yes* if the statement is true. Write *No* if it is not true. Then rewrite the statement correctly. Reread the selection silently to increase your comprehension.

1. The rich old man lived in ancient Greece. *No. The rich old man lived in ancient China.*

2. Two of his sons married two sisters.

3. The young wives never left the big house.

4. The sisters wanted to visit their brother.

5. The old man asked for three gifts.

6. The old man wanted the wind wrapped in fire.

7. A farm girl was walking with her horse.

8. The paper lantern had a candle in it.

9. The farm girl was very clever.

10. The farm girl married the first son.

Extension

Chinese Lantern Festival

A. Read about a special Chinese festival.

The Chinese have a special lantern festival called *Yuanxiao Jie*. The Lantern Festival takes place on the fifteenth day of the first month of the Chinese New Year. People hang colorful lanterns in houses and buildings to celebrate the full moon and new year. Other people make lanterns and carry them on streets and in parks. Everyone comes out at night to see the colorful lanterns. People also watch dragon dances, play games, and light firecrackers. The Lantern Festival is a fun time for young and old.

▲ Paper lanterns in a temple during the Lantern Festival

People eat a special food called *yuanxiao*—named for the Lantern Festival. Yuanxiao is a kind of round dumpling made of sticky rice. One kind of yuanxiao is sweet and has nuts or fruit inside. Another kind is salty and has meat or vegetables inside.

B. Work in small groups. Take turns. Talk about a special festival in your home country. Ask and answer these questions about the festival.

1. Where and when do people celebrate the festival?
2. What special activities do people do?
3. What special food do they eat?
4. Are there special customs for the festival?
5. What do you like most about the festival? Why?

> **🔊 *Speaking* SKILL**
>
> You may use informal language when speaking with your classmates. But be sure to use formal language when speaking to your teacher.

Workbook
Page 102

Prepare to Read

What You Will Learn

Reading

- Vocabulary building: *Context; dictionary skills*
- Reading strategy: *Reread*
- Text type: *Informational text (science)*

Academic Content

- Science vocabulary
- Family traits
- Gregor Mendel

Grammar
Adverbs

Writing
Write a personal letter

➤ BUILD BACKGROUND

"Family Traits" is nonfiction. It explains why children look so much like their parents. It is the kind of text you find in a science book.

▲ Do you think these young men are brothers? Why or why not?

▲ Do you think these baby ducks have the same parents? Why or why not?

USE PRIOR KNOWLEDGE

What do you think makes people or animals in the same family look alike?

▲ Why do you think this flower is the color it is?

➤ VOCABULARY

Listening and Speaking: Key Words

Look at the pictures and the captions. They will help you learn the words in the box. Write the meaning of each highlighted word and say them aloud with a partner. Then check your work in a dictionary.

Key Words

experiments
generations
inherit
members
traits

▲ Family members make up a family. There are three generations in this family. The grandparents are one generation. Their son and his wife are a second generation. Their daughters are a third generation.

▲ These twins look alike. They have the same traits. Children inherit, or get, traits from their parents.

◄ Scientists test their ideas by doing experiments. Experiments help scientists learn about the world.

Workbook
Page 103

READING STRATEGY | REREAD

To **reread** means to read again. Each time you read the text, you figure out a little more.

- Stop if you don't understand what you are reading.
- Reread sentences and paragraphs slowly.
- Reread key words and headings.

Workbook
Page 104

Set a purpose for reading "Family Traits" tells why people in a family look alike. Read the text slowly. Reread any parts that you don't understand.

FAMILY TRAITS

What Are Family Traits?

Family traits are ways in which family members are alike. You may have the same color hair as your mother. You may have the same color eyes as your father. Eye color and hair color are family traits. Another family trait is how tall you are. Traits like these are passed on through families. You inherit, or get, these traits from your parents and your grandparents. You will pass on these traits to your own children.

> **MAKE CONNECTIONS**
> What family traits did you inherit from your parents or grandparents? Explain.

◀ These twins inherited the same traits from their parents and their grandparents. That is why they look alike.

▲ How can green birds have a blue chick?
Read the rest of this text to find out.

Do Children Always Look Like Their Parents?

Sometimes children do not look like their parents. For example, parents with brown eyes can have a child with blue eyes. This happens with other animals and even plants, too.

Look at the chart above. It shows that two green birds had four chicks. Three of the chicks are green, and one chick is blue. How can a chick inherit blue feathers when its parents' feathers are green? Many people wondered about this question. One of these people was a man named Gregor Mendel.

Workbook
Page 105

Reading Skill

Pause the Audio CD at the end of each section. Then answer the question that the subheading asks.

BEFORE YOU GO ON

1. Give two examples of family traits.

2. Who do you inherit your traits from?

3. Two orange cats can have a gray kitten. How is this idea like the idea of green birds having a blue chick?

Who Was Gregor Mendel?

Gregor Mendel (1822–1884) was a scientist and a monk who worked with plants. Mendel wanted to learn more about inherited traits. How can a trait that you cannot see in parents be passed on to their young? He did many experiments with pea plants. Mendel worked hard to find out the answer.

What Did Mendel Learn about Traits?

Mendel grew many generations of pea plants. Most of the pea-plant flowers were red, but some were white. This made him think that the trait for red flowers was stronger than the trait for white flowers. His experiments showed that this was true. In pea-plant flowers, redness is a strong, or dominant, trait. Whiteness is a weak, or recessive, trait.

Mendel believed that each trait was **determined** by a pair of **factors**. Each parent passes on one factor for every trait to its young. The way the factors combine determines what its young will look like. Today we call these factors genes.

▲ Gregor Mendel in his garden

---

determined, decided
factors, things that produce a result

Reading Skill

Study the subheadings in the selection. This will help you identify the most important ideas.

When Do Recessive Traits Appear?

Look at the chart of Mendel's flowers. In the top row are a red and a white flower. This is the first generation. The red flower has two dominant genes (RR). The white flower has two recessive genes (rr). In the next row is the second generation. All the flowers are red because they have one dominant gene and one recessive gene (Rr). The dominant gene determines the color of the flower in these cases.

In the third generation one white flower appears. That flower is white because it has two recessive genes (rr). Mendel learned that the recessive color white appears only when there is no dominant gene (R) present in the pair.

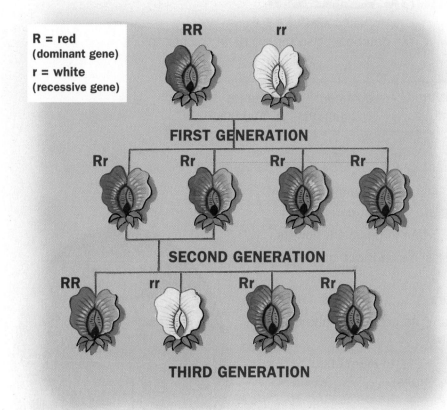

R = red
(dominant gene)
r = white
(recessive gene)

RR   rr

FIRST GENERATION

Rr   Rr   Rr   Rr

SECOND GENERATION

RR   rr   Rr   Rr

THIRD GENERATION

◄ This chart shows how pea-plant flowers pass on traits for the colors red and white.

BEFORE YOU GO ON

1 What did Gregor Mendel want to find out?

2 Why are there so many more red pea-plant flowers than white?

Review and Practice

➤ RETELL AND REVIEW

1. Tell a partner what you know about family traits. Use the headings and the pictures on pages 136–139 to help you summarize the selection. Use the Key Words. If you can't think of a word, describe it, use a synonym, or ask your teacher.

2. Which parts of "Family Traits" did you reread? How did rereading help you understand the text?

➤ COMPREHENSION  Workbook Page 106

Write the sentences below in your notebook. Use the words in the box to complete the sentences.

recessive	family trait	dominant	genes
~~generation~~	inherit	experiments	members

1. Children are in a different *generation* than their parents.
2. One _____ is the color of your eyes.
3. We _____ family traits from our parents.
4. Redness is a _____ trait in pea-plant flowers.
5. _____ traits do not show up if one of the genes in a pair is dominant.
6. Brothers and sisters are _____ of the same family.
7. The pea-plant flower is white because it has two recessive _____ (rr).
8. Gregor Mendel did _____ to learn about dominant and recessive traits.

▲ Gregor Mendel

Extension

Family Tree

A family tree is a chart of family information. It usually has names and birth dates. The top row on the chart shows grandparents. The next row shows parents. The bottom row shows children.

1. Copy the chart below on a large sheet of paper. It is an outline for a family tree.

FAMILY TREE

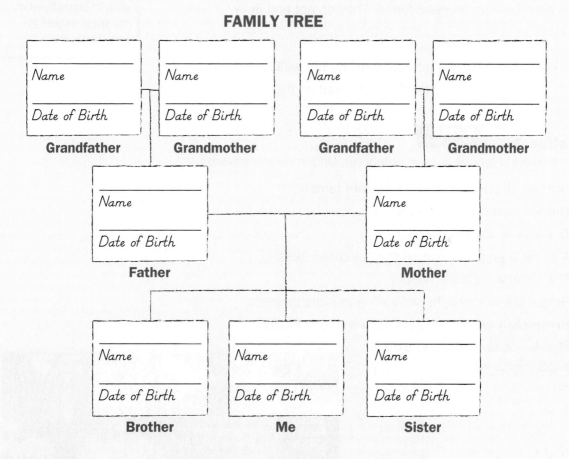

2. Write the names and birth dates of family members in the boxes. Ask people in your family questions to learn more about them. Write information about each family member. Leave places blank if you do not know the information.

3. Add a photo of your family or draw a picture.

4. Discuss your family tree with others. Compare information about your families. Answer your classmates' questions.

5. Display your family tree.

Grammar

Adverbs

Adverbs usually describe the action of verbs. They tell *how* an action happens. Many adverbs end in *-ly*.

> The sisters walked **quietly**.
>
> The scientist worked **carefully**.

Some adverbs have irregular forms. They do not end in *-ly*.

> The boys ran **fast**.
>
> John got 100 on the math test. He did **well**.
>
> Jane and I studied **hard**. We did **well** on the test.

Workbook Page 107

Practice

Write these sentences in your notebook. Underline the adverbs.

1. The two sisters missed their mother terribly.
2. The old man spoke carefully.
3. The sisters cried loudly.
4. A young farm girl answered the questions cleverly.
5. The sisters ran home happily.
6. Gregor Mendel thought seriously about the problem.
7. He carefully grew many generations of pea plants.
8. Mendel worked hard and did his experiments well.

> **Speaking SKILL**
>
> Remember that it is important to use adverbs correctly when you speak as well as when you write.

Writing

Write a Personal Letter

You write personal letters to your family members or close friends.

Read Sam's letter to his grandmother. Then discuss the questions.

January 10, 2012

Dear Grandma,

How are you? I am well.

My class learned about family history. We will make family trees. Can you tell me about our family history? Here is what I need to know. Who is in your family? What are your brothers' and sisters' names? Where were your brothers and sisters born? Where do they live now? Also, what are your parents' names? Where were they born? When did our family come to America? Why did we come here?

Please send me some family photos. I would really like one of you as a little girl. I will put the photos on my family tree. Will I see you soon? I hope so. I will show you my family tree.

Love,

Sam

1. What information does the writer need?
2. What are some questions the writer asks?
3. Find a sentence with an adverb in it. What verb does it describe?

Workbook
Pages 108–109

Practice

You will write a personal letter to a family member to learn about your family history.

1. Read Reread the letter on page 143. Notice how the writer asks questions.

Writing Strategy: Wh- Question Chart

A *wh-* question chart can help you list the questions you need to ask. Look at the chart Sam used before writing his letter.

Who:	Who is in your family?
What:	What are your brothers' and sisters' names? What are your parents' names?
Where:	Where were your brothers and sisters born? Where do they live now?
When:	When did our family come to America?
Why:	Why did our family come to America?

---

2. Make a chart Make a *wh-* question chart listing the questions you will ask a family member. What can he or she tell you about your family?

3. Write Write a personal letter like Sam's. Include the questions from your chart. Edit your work. Check your spelling. Make sure you use the possessive case correctly.

Prepare to Read

➤ BUILD BACKGROUND

You will now read two speeches about the same subject. The subject is daytime curfews for young people in school. A curfew is an order or law that requires people to be inside after a certain time. Some states have laws that say students under seventeen years of age have to be in school during school hours. The authors have different viewpoints about these laws.

Sometimes teenagers have a curfew at home, for example, they must be home by 11 p.m. Do you have a curfew? Share with the class.

What You Will Learn

Reading
- Vocabulary building: *Common sayings and expressions*
- Connect to reading: *Opinions and evidence*
- Text type: *Informational text (social studies)*

Writing
- Use feedback to revise writing
- Write a critique

BOOST YOUR LISTENING COMPREHENSION

Unit 4: Family Ties
Your teacher will play the DVD for this unit. After you listen, answer these questions.

1. What are some traits that people can inherit from their parents and grandparents?

2. What is *genetics*?

3. How did Gregor Mendel piece together the basic laws of heredity?

4. What are *genes*? What role do they play in heredity?

5. Explain the difference between dominant and recessive genes.

6. When Mendel presented his findings in 1865, they were largely ignored by the scientific world. Why? And why is this ironic?

► CONNECT TO VOCABULARY

Common Sayings and Expressions

All languages have special sayings and expressions. A common one in English is "The early bird catches the worm." These sayings and expressions can't be interpreted word for word. People use sayings like these to make a point. The expressions are used so much that they become common.

Look at some common sayings. Their meanings might surprise you.

Saying/Expression	Meaning
That test was a piece of cake.	piece of cake = very easy
I didn't study last night. The algebra quiz was all Greek to me!	all Greek to me = impossible to understand
Max wished his dad would hurry up and cut to the chase.	cut to the chase = get to the point
Too many cooks spoil the broth.	If too many people are involved in something, it won't turn out well.
Loose lips sink ships.	Telling secrets can create bad results.
Don't put all your eggs in one basket.	Don't rely too much on one plan.

Practice  **Workbook** Pages 111–112

Work in a small group. Explain the following common sayings.

1. Crime does not pay.

2. Experience is the best teacher.

3. A fool and his money are soon parted.

➤ CONNECT TO READING

Opinions And Evidence

Opinions are ideas that cannot be proven. Even though opinions are not facts, it is possible to back them up with facts. A **substantiated opinion** is one that is based on fact, evidence, and/or logical thinking. An **unsubstantiated opinion** is the opposite—it is not backed up by facts or evidence. Since substantiated opinions are based on facts, they are more **credible** (believable, reliable) than unsubstantiated ones.

Here are some examples of substantiated opinions and unsubstantiated opinions.

Type of Opinion	Example	Reason
Substantiated	*Dogs should be kept on leashes. According to the Centers for Disease Control and Prevention, 4.5 million dog bites are reported each year in the U.S. Leashes can help prevent dog bites.*	The writer uses a fact that supports the opinion.
Unsubstantiated	*All dogs bite. So they should all be kept on leashes. Dogs should not be allowed around kids.*	The writer has used the word "all." This is false. Also, there is no evidence to support the opinion.
Substantiated	*Only the students who ate pasta at Jennie's Diner on Friday got sick over the weekend. I think they probably got sick from something in the pasta.*	The writer uses logical thinking to support his or her opinion.
Unsubstantiated	*Students always hate doing homework on the weekend. Teachers should not assign it anymore.*	The writer has used the word "always" and this is probably false. Also, there is no evidence to support the opinion.

Workbook
Pages 113–115

Readers also have to decide whether someone's **evidence** is credible. Evidence is anything that helps prove that something is true. Credible evidence should directly support the writer's argument. It should also be logical. If facts are used, they should come from trustworthy sources.

Take a look at the sentences below from the first draft of Carmen's persuasive essay. She hopes to convince her parents to buy her younger sister a cell phone when she turns ten.

I think kids should get a cell phone when they turn ten. Cell phones are cool. They light up in the dark. They come in bright colors.

Carmen states a clear opinion. But she doesn't provide any evidence or reasons to support that claim. She only says why she likes cell phones.

Read how Carmen revised her essay. She has made her opinion more credible by including credible evidence.

I think it is a good idea for young people to have cell phones. Cell phones make it easy for parents to reach their children. They are great in emergencies and keep kids safe. One research survey says that kids who have cell phones talk more regularly with their parents. Cell phones can also make kids more responsible.

Practice

Work in a small group. Read the paragraph below. The writer hopes to persuade teenagers to watch less television. Then answer the questions.

I think teens shouldn't watch television during the school week. Their grades would improve. Teens should spend their free time learning new things instead of sitting around. Television never makes you think seriously about anything.

1. Is the writer's opinion substantiated or unsubstantiated?

2. Is the evidence trustworthy and logical?

3. Do you think most teens will be convinced? Why or why not?

Set a purpose for reading Remember to question evidence and opinions when you read or listen to a speech. Ask yourself: Have the authors used facts to form their opinions? Are the opinions substantiated or unsubstantiated? Is the evidence credible?

Daytime Curfew? *Audio*

SAY *YES* TO DAYTIME CURFEW

We need a daytime curfew for children and teenagers in school. Students should be in school during school hours. To get a good education, children and teens must attend classes. When students miss school, they miss important information. As one school official said, "Even if you are out of school for a good reason, you miss important things." My English teacher puts it this way: "Catching up is not the same as learning something the first time it's taught. Students do better when they attend school."

If we had a curfew, fewer teenagers would skip school. Parents would not schedule their kids' doctor's appointments during school hours anymore. A daytime curfew would make everyone more responsible.

Think about it. Last year, students missed thousands of school days. Yes, sometimes students have legitimate reasons for missing school. For example, kids should stay home if they are sick. However, the curfew is not for sick kids. It is for kids who can come to school but do not. A curfew would make us all a little smarter.

SAY *NO* TO DAYTIME CURFEW

Why do school kids need a daytime curfew? School kids know that they should be in school. If a student does not know that he or she should be in school, the student is foolish. The student will get bad grades or fail. Maybe summer school will teach the student a good lesson.

What about us good kids? Why should I have a curfew? A curfew is not fair. It makes me feel as if adults do not trust me. A curfew makes me feel trapped. Maybe I will start to dislike school. Maybe I will start to see school as a place I do not want to be. A curfew is not a good idea. It is only for students who do not care about school. I do care. I do not need a curfew.

SUPPORT YOUR READING EXPERIENCE

The more you read, the larger your vocabulary knowledge becomes. Now that you have read these speeches, go to www. LongmanKeystone.com and do the activity for this unit. You will learn ways to use kinesthetic visual support to develop vocabulary and structures and to build more background knowledge.

BEFORE YOU GO ON

1. Which speech is more convincing? Why?

2. Which speech has a more substantiated opinion? Why?

Writing

Ongoing Writing Skills Practice

Use Feedback to Revise Writing and Write a Critique

Most writers do not get everything right on their first try. They get feedback, or opinions and suggestions, from other people who read their work. You can, too. Ask your teachers and your classmates to read your writing. Ask them to suggest ways to make your writing better. Use them to improve your writing.

The student who wrote "Say No to Daytime Curfew" got feedback from his classmates. They said he needed to add evidence and use clearer words. Read his revision, and then answer the questions below.

Revision: Say No to Daytime Curfew

Most students are responsible people. They take school seriously.

In fact, the high school graduation rate has increased

again and again over the past five years. A curfew is a bad idea.

It might limit students' confidence and independence. A curfew

says that adults do not trust us. If adults believe in us, we will

do well. A survey was given to all the kids in my school. It asked

if kids felt better when their parents and communities trusted

them. Almost 90% of students said they felt better when they

were trusted. We know adults want us to do well in school.

However, a curfew is not the way to do it.

---

1. How has the student revised the essay?
2. How has the evidence improved?
3. How have the sentences changed?

Workbook
Pages 116–117

Practice
Workbook Page 118

You will write a critique of one of the speeches about daytime curfews. In a critique, you summarize the main ideas and details of another piece of writing. You also give your opinion about how good or bad the writing is.

1. **Read**   Reread the two speeches about daytime curfews. Pick one of the two to critique.

2. **Evaluate**   Answer the questions below to evaluate, or critique, the speech.

> *Is the author's opinion clear?*
>
> *Is the opinion supported by strong evidence?*
>
> *Is the evidence credible and logical?*
>
> *Is the language clear and well chosen?*

3. **Write**   Use your answers to the questions to write your critique. Tell whether you think the speech is good, and why.

4. **Get Feedback and Revise**   Ask your teacher or a classmate to read your critique. How can you improve it? Revise your critique to make it better.

5. **Share**   After you have finalized your critique, share it with your classmates. Consider posting your critique on a classroom bulletin board.

IMPROVE YOUR WRITING SKILLS

When you write, you write for a particular reader, or "audience." Good writers are careful about selecting the correct genre and determining an appropriate topic to write about. Go to www. LongmanKeystone.com and do the activity for this unit. You will learn strategies to help you convey meaning appropriately to different types of audiences.

Link the Readings

Make a chart like the one below to compare the readings in this unit. Look at each word in the column. Put an **X** under "The Clever Daughter-in-Law" if the word reminds you of the folktale. Put an **X** under "Family Traits" if the word reminds you of that selection. Put an **X** under "Daytime Curfew?" if the word reminds you of that selection. Put an **X** in all places if the word reminds you of all selections.

	"The Clever Daughter-in-Law"	"Family Traits"	"Daytime Curfew?"
fiction	_____	_____	_____
nonfiction	_____	_____	_____
traits	_____	_____	_____
lantern	_____	_____	_____
dominant	_____	_____	_____
recessive	_____	_____	_____
family	_____	_____	_____
social studies text	_____	_____	_____

Check Your Knowledge

Language Development
1. Did any of the people in the folktale remind you of yourself or your own family members? Explain.
2. How is the farm girl in "The Clever Daughter-in-Law" like Ali in the folktale "Jewel in the Sand"? In what ways were they both clever?
3. What is an adverb? Use an adverb in a sentence.

Academic Content
1. Why do some twins look so much alike?
2. What are some inherited traits?
3. Who was Gregor Mendel? What did his experiments with pea plants show?
4. What are the two kinds of opinions? Give examples.

THE POWER OF WORDS

The selection "Early Writing" tells how the people of ancient Sumer created the first known form of writing. Sometimes it is hard to understand another language. "The Great Minu" is a story about a man who hears a word from a different language and gets confused. Finally, you will read part of a famous speech by President Lyndon Johnson.

Reading

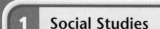

1 Social Studies	2 Folktale	3 Social Studies

"Early Writing"	"The Great Minu"	"The Great Society"
Reading Strategy: Take notes	**Reading Strategy:** Understand irony	**Connect to Reading:** Main ideas and details; Author's purpose; Speeches

Listening and Speaking

In this unit, you will summarize a social studies text and retell a story.

Writing

In this unit, you will create a subtopic web, write a report, and learn how to edit a draft.

Quick **Write**

Writing began in ancient Sumer in the Middle East. Write two or three sentences about an ancient civilization you know about.

VIEW AND RESPOND
Watch the Unit 5 DVD. As you watch,
answer the questions on page 175.
www.LongmanKeystone.com.

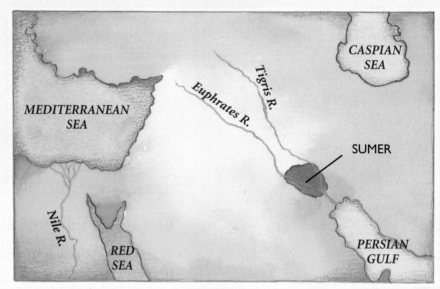

READING
1

Prepare to Read

What You Will Learn

Reading

- Vocabulary building: *Context; dictionary skills*

- Reading strategy: *Take notes*

- Text type: *Informational text (social studies); nonfiction*

Academic Content

- Social studies vocabulary

- Ancient Sumer

- Cuneiform

➤ BUILD BACKGROUND

"Early Writing" is nonfiction. It tells about real things, people, and events. Writing began thousands of years ago in different places. One of these places was Sumer. Sumer was a country in what is now Iraq, in the Middle East.

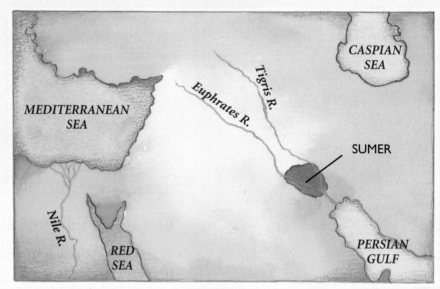

CASPIAN SEA

Tigris R.

Euphrates R.

MEDITERRANEAN SEA

SUMER

Nile R.

RED SEA

PERSIAN GULF

▲ The Tigris and Euphrates Rivers flowed through Sumer. The land was good for farming.

TRY TO PREDICT

Why do you think people began writing?

Workbook
Page 119

► VOCABULARY

Listening and Speaking: Key Words

Look at the pictures and the captions. They will help you learn the words in the box. Write the meaning of each highlighted word and say them aloud with a partner. Then check your work in a dictionary.

◄ People from ancient Sumer used a form of writing called cuneiform (kyoo-NEE-uh-form). Cuneiform was made of symbols shaped like wedges, or tiny triangles. Each symbol stood for a word.

▲ Some farmers in ancient Sumer grew grain. Grains are seeds that people eat, such as rice, wheat, and barley.

▲ Reeds are plants that grow in or near water.

Workbook
Pages 120–121

READING STRATEGY | TAKE NOTES

To **take notes** means to write down important ideas as you read. Taking notes can help you remember important facts from the text.

- Write only the most important words.
- You can shorten some words, such as *cune* for *cuneiform*.
- Reread your notes when you finish the text.

Workbook
Page 122

Set a purpose for reading "Early Writing" tells how an ancient form of writing began. As you read, look for important ideas. Write them in your notebook. Look at your notes after you finish reading.

EARLY WRITING

Why Did People Begin Writing?

Over five thousand years ago, people living in Sumer created the first known form of writing. What made these people begin to write?

Many Sumerians were farmers. Some farmers grew grain, such as barley, for food. Other farmers raised sheep for milk and wool. As Sumer got bigger, its people needed a way to record, or write down, facts about their **products**. For example, farmers needed to know how much grain or how many sheep they had. When farmers **traded** barley or sheep for other products, they needed a way to remember how much grain and how many animals they had traded.

Writing was a way for Sumerians to record facts and remember them. Perhaps writing began when a sheep farmer drew a picture of a sheep. Then he added marks next to it to show how many he had traded.

▲ This Sumerian clay tablet tells how many sheep and goats people had.

---

products, things people make or grow
traded, bought and sold

How Did the Sumerians Write?

The Sumerians did not have paper to write on as we do today. They wrote on clay tablets—flat pieces of clay. There was a lot of clay along the Tigris and Euphrates Rivers, where many Sumerians lived. Wet clay was soft and easy to write on. When the clay dried in the sun, it became hard and strong.

The Sumerians wrote on clay with reeds, plants that grew along the rivers. They pressed the end of a reed into the clay and made pictures and marks. The marks were shaped like wedges, or small triangles. We call these marks cuneiform. *Cuneiform* comes from two Latin words: *cuneus,* which means "wedge," and *forma,* which means "shape."

▲ Reeds grew along the Tigris and Euphrates Rivers.

▲ Sumerians wrote on clay with a reed. The reed made wedge-shaped marks in the clay.

BEFORE YOU GO ON

1. What kind of information did farmers in Sumer need to record?

2. Why did the Sumerians write on clay?

3. What does the word *cuneiform* mean?

Workbook Page 123

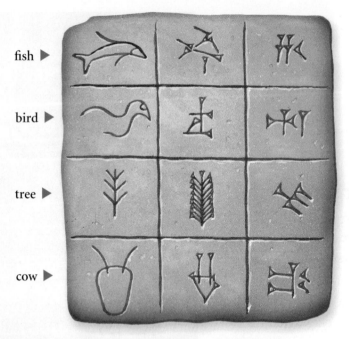

fish ▶

bird ▶

tree ▶

cow ▶

◀ This tablet shows how the pictures used in early Sumerian writing changed over time into wedge-shaped cuneiform.

How Did Sumerian Writing Change over Time?

The earliest Sumerian writing was made up of little pictures. The pictures stood for things and for the sounds of words for those things. For example, the symbol ≈ could mean the idea of water and the sound of the word for water in the Sumerian language.

Over time, the pictures changed to cuneiform. Cuneiform was easier and faster for people to write. Look at the tablet above. It shows how the pictures for *fish, bird, tree,* and *cow* changed over time.

▲ Cuneiform writing on a wall in the Palace of Darius I, Persepolis, Iran

How Did the Sumerians Write Numbers?

The Sumerians also used cuneiform to write numbers. One vertical, or up-and-down, wedge mark stood for the number 1, two vertical wedge marks stood for the number 2, and so on. One sideways wedge mark stood for the number 10.

Over time, trade in Sumer grew. The people needed to use larger numbers. People began to use the symbol 𒁹 to stand for both 1 and 60. How did they do this? A 𒁹 symbol on the left side of a number stood for 60. On the right side of a number, the same symbol stood for 1. For an example, see the number 201 in cuneiform below.

▲ This tablet tells how many workers were given certain jobs to do.

◀ The edge of the tablet shows the total number of workers: 201.

60 + 60 + 60 + 10 + 10 + 1 = 201

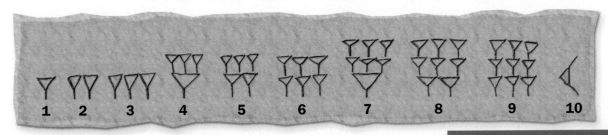

| 1 | 2 | 3 | 4 | 5 | 6 | 7 | 8 | 9 | 10 |

BEFORE YOU GO ON

1 How was cuneiform different from the earlier picture writing?

2 How did Sumerians change the way they wrote over time?

Reading 1 **161**

Review and Practice

▶ RETELL AND REVIEW

1. Tell a partner what you learned about early Sumerian writing and cuneiform. Use the headings and the pictures on pages 158–161 to help you. Use the Key Words. If you can't think of a word, describe it, use a synonym, or ask your teacher.

2. What important words and ideas did you write down as you read the text? Did you shorten words as you took notes?

▶ COMPREHENSION

**Workbook
Page 124**

Write the sentences below in your notebook. Write *Yes* if the statement is true. Write *No* if it is not true. Then rewrite the statement correctly. Reread pages 158–161 to find supporting evidence for your answers.

1. Sumerians used tree branches to write on clay. *No. Sumerians used reeds to write on clay.*

2. Sumerians first used writing to record facts about products they traded.

3. Farmers in Sumer grew barley, a kind of reed.

4. The earliest symbols used in Sumerian writing were little pictures.

5. In Sumer, people wrote on paper.

6. There were no rivers in Sumer.

7. Cuneiform symbols were shaped like wedges.

8. The same wedge-shaped symbol could stand for both the numbers 1 and 60.

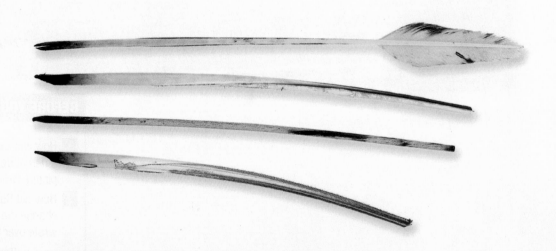

Extension

Other Early Writing

The Sumerians created one form of writing. Other ancient peoples wrote in other ways. They used different materials to write with and to write on. They used different symbols. Look at these examples:

▲ Ancient Egyptian writing

▲ Ancient Chinese writing

◀ Ancient Arabic writing

A. Talk about the early forms of writing in small groups.

   1. Describe the symbols. What shapes are they?

   2. What do you think the people wrote with?

   3. What material did they write on?

B. Find out more about early forms of writing.

   1. Use the library or the Internet to find information.

   2. Choose a place to read about, such as Sumer, Egypt, or China.

   3. Take notes as you read.

   4. Report what you have learned to a partner. Use formal language.

»)) *Listening* SKILL

Listen closely to your classmates. What points do they make? What details do they give to support their ideas?

Workbook
Page 125

What You Will Learn

Reading

- Vocabulary building: *Context; dictionary skills*

- Reading strategy: *Understand irony*

- Text type: *Literature (folktale and play)*

Grammar
Pronouns

Writing
Write notes for a report

➤ BUILD BACKGROUND

"The Great Minu" is a folktale from Ghana, a country in West Africa. Ghana has many regions, or parts. More than fifty languages were once spoken in these different regions. Today, children in Ghana learn English in school. It is now the main language in Ghana.

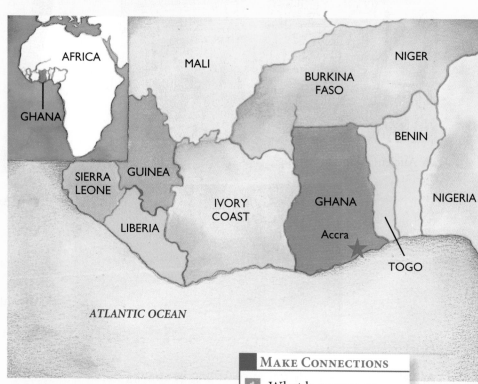

▲ Ghana is a country in West Africa. Accra is the capital city of Ghana.

MAKE CONNECTIONS

1. What language or languages do you speak?
2. How do you say "hello" in your home language?
3. Does your home language use the same alphabet as English?

Listening and Speaking: Key Words

Look at the pictures and the captions. They will help you learn the words in the box. Write the meaning of each highlighted word and say them aloud with a partner. Then check your work in a dictionary.

Key Words

coffin
funeral
port
sailor
village

▲ A West African village

▲ Many people walk behind the coffin during a funeral.

◄ The sailor works on a ship. The ship is in the port.

Workbook
Page 126

READING STRATEGY | **UNDERSTAND IRONY**

Sometimes in a story how things appear to be is very different from how they actually are. This is called **irony**. As you read, ask yourself:

- What does Akwasi think "Minu" means?
- What does the writer tell you "Minu" means?
- How does this irony make the story funny?

Workbook
Page 127

Set a purpose for reading This is a folktale about a man from a small village in Ghana. His name is Akwasi. Akwasi decides to travel to Accra, the capital city of Ghana. As you read, think about how the writer uses irony.

THE GREAT MINU

Adapted from *Folktales and Fairy Tales of Africa,* selected and retold by Lila Green

A long time ago, there was a young man named Akwasi (ah-KWAH-zee). Akwasi lived in a small village in Ghana. One day, Akwasi decided to travel to Accra, the capital city. It was a long way from his village. He had never been to Accra before. He did not know that the people of Accra spoke a different language.

Akwasi walked for many days. Finally, he arrived at the city of Accra. Just outside the city were hundreds of cows.

"Tell me, who owns all these cows?" he asked a young boy who was standing near the cows.

"Minu," the boy said, which in the language of Accra means, "I don't understand."

"Minu?" Akwasi said. "Minu must be a very rich man!"

Then Akwasi entered the city. He saw many big shops. The shops were full of beautiful things—rugs, gold jewelry, bells, lamps, and mirrors. In his small village, there were no shops like these.

Akwasi asked a woman, "Tell me, who owns all these beautiful shops?"

But the woman did not understand. "Minu," she said.

"Mr. Minu?" Akwasi said. "He owns all these shops, too? He really must be very, very rich!"

Next, Akwasi walked by some very large and fine houses.

"These houses are **magnificent**," he said. "They are not like the small **huts** in my village!"

Akwasi saw a young girl sweeping the steps of a big house.

"Tell me, who owns these houses?" he asked.

But the young girl did not understand. "Minu," she said.

"Minu," Akwasi repeated. "Of course, the great Mr. Minu!"

Then Akwasi arrived at the port. There were many ships. Akwasi could see that there were many boxes and bags of grain on the ships.

"Tell me, who owns all these ships?" Akwasi asked a sailor.

But the sailor did not understand. "Minu," he said.

"Is that so?" Akwasi said. "Mr. Minu owns these ships, too? Mr. Minu must be the richest man in the whole world!"

---

magnificent, grand, beautiful
huts, small houses with only one or two rooms

Workbook
Page 128

BEFORE YOU GO ON

1 Why is Akwasi confused?

2 Do you think Akwasi wants to be Mr. Minu? Why or why not?

Reading 2 **167**

After Akwasi had walked around Accra for a long, long time, he decided to go home. He wanted to be back in his own village. He began walking toward the edge of the city. Suddenly, he saw a long line of people. They were walking behind a coffin. Many of the people were crying.

"A funeral," Akwasi said to himself. "An important person must have died."

Akwasi stopped a woman who was in the long line of people. "Tell me," he said. "Who is the person who died?" But the woman did not understand.

"Minu," she said sadly.

"Oh, no!" Akwasi said. "The great Mr. Minu is dead! Can it be true? How sad! He owned hundreds of cows. He owned many beautiful shops. He owned magnificent houses. He owned many large ships. And now look at him! He is in a coffin. He has left all those fine things behind. He has died, just like any other person."

At that moment, Akwasi felt that it was not so bad to be just plain Akwasi, and not the great Mr. Minu. The more he thought about it, the more Akwasi understood that he had much to be thankful for. Akwasi felt that it was very good to be alive, even if he didn't own a lot of things. And so Akwasi walked back to his village, a happy man.

BEFORE YOU GO ON

Why was Akwasi happy to be himself and not Mr. Minu at the end of the story? How is this an example of irony?

The Great Minu ◆ A Play

Now read the same folktale as a play.
There are eight parts.

CHARACTERS

Narrator	**Young Girl**
Akwasi	**Sailor**
Young Boy	**Second Woman**
First Woman	**Chorus**

Narrator: A long time ago, a young man named Akwasi lived in Ghana.

Chorus: His home was in a village.

Narrator: One day, Akwasi decided to travel to Accra, the capital city. The people there did not speak his language, but Akwasi did not know this.

Chorus: He traveled for many days.

Narrator: Finally, he arrived at the city. Just outside the city were hundreds of cows.

Akwasi *(to boy):* Who owns these cows?

Young Boy: Minu.

Akwasi: Minu? Minu must be a very rich man!

Narrator: Then Akwasi entered the city.

Chorus: He saw many big shops full of beautiful things.

Akwasi *(to woman):* Look at all these beautiful shops! Who owns all these shops?

First Woman: Minu.

Akwasi: Mr. Minu, again? Does he own these shops, too? He really must be very, very rich!

Narrator: Next, Akwasi passed some large and fine houses.

Chorus: He had never seen anything like them in his own village.

Narrator: He saw a young girl sweeping some steps.

Akwasi *(to girl):* These houses are magnificent. Who owns these houses?

Young Girl: Minu.

Akwasi: Minu. Of course, it is the great Mr. Minu!

Narrator: Then Akwasi arrived at the port.

Chorus: He saw many ships full of grain.

Akwasi *(to sailor):* Who owns all these ships?

Sailor: Minu.

Akwasi: Can it be true? Mr. Minu must be the richest man in the world!

Narrator: Finally, Akwasi decided to go home to his village. As he was leaving Accra, he passed a long line of people.

Chorus: They were walking behind a coffin.

Akwasi *(to woman):* This must be a funeral. What important person died?

Second Woman: Minu.

Akwasi: Oh, no! Is the great Mr. Minu dead?

Narrator: Akwasi thought about all Mr. Minu had owned.

Akwasi: Now look! He is dead, just like any other person.

Chorus: Akwasi went home to his village.

Akwasi: I am happy to be who I am. I have many things to be thankful for. It is good to be alive.

Review and Practice

➤ RETELL AND REVIEW

1. Look back at the pictures in "The Great Minu" on pages 166–168. Cover the words on each page. Retell the events of the story to a partner, using only the pictures. Use the Key Words. If you can't think of a word, describe it, use a synonym, or ask your teacher.

2. How does the writer use irony in the story?

3. What do you think is the lesson of this folktale?

➤ COMPREHENSION  Workbook Page 129

Complete the sentences. Choose the correct word from the column on the right. Write the completed sentences in your notebook.

1. Accra is the _capital_ of Ghana.   things

2. The people of Accra did not speak Akwasi's _____.   village

3. Just outside the city, Akwasi saw hundreds of _____. grain

4. The shops were full of beautiful _____.   language

5. Akwasi talked to a young girl near one of the _____. coffin

6. There were many bags of _____ on the ships.   ~~capital~~

7. People in the funeral walked behind a _____.   cows

8. Akwasi traveled back home to his _____.   houses

Extension

Kente Cloth

Artists in Ghana make kente cloths for people to wear. These cloths have many different designs. Each design means something different. Look at the examples below.

"Babadua"
strength

"Mother Hen"
good mothers

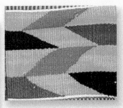

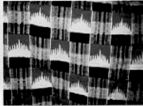
"Potsherd"
knowledge

"Rising Sun"
progress and energy

A. Talk about the kente cloths in small groups.

   1. What colors does each one include?

   2. What does each design mean?

   3. How are they the same? How are they different?

   4. Which is your favorite kente cloth? Explain why you like it.

B. Create your own kente cloth design.

   1. Choose three of four colors for your cloth. Create a pattern with the colors.

   2. Choose a meaning for your design.

   3. Draw your design on paper. The basic design should be 10 centimeters (4 in.) wide. Repeat the design to make the cloth wider.

   4. Share your kente cloth design with the class.

Grammar

Pronouns

Pronouns are words that take the place of nouns. A **subject pronoun** replaces a noun that is the subject of a sentence.

subject   subject pronoun

Akwasi left his village. **He** left his village.

An **object pronoun** replaces a noun that is the object of a sentence.

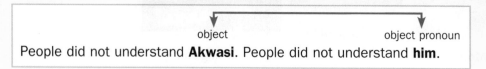

object   object pronoun

People did not understand **Akwasi**. People did not understand **him**.

Subject Pronouns	Object Pronouns
I	me
you	you
he, she, it	him, her, it
we	us
you	you
they	them

Speaking SKILL

Remember to use pronouns correctly when you speak as well as when you write.

Practice

Workbook Page 130

Copy these sentences in your notebook. Replace the <u>underlined noun</u> in the first sentence with a pronoun in the second sentence.

1. Akwasi traveled to <u>Accra</u>. _____*It*_____ is the capital city of Ghana.
2. Akwasi asked people <u>questions</u>. The people of Accra could not understand _____.
3. Akwasi saw a <u>girl</u> sweeping the steps. Akwasi asked _____ a question.
4. <u>Akwasi</u> decided to leave Accra. _____ thought it was time to go home.
5. <u>You and I</u> learned a lesson from Akwasi. _____ can explain it to the teacher.

Writing

Write Notes for a Report

A report gives information about a topic. To write a report, first choose a topic. Then find information about that topic. Suppose your topic is "Ancient Egyptian Writing." You can find information about ancient Egypt in books and on the Internet.

As you find information, you need to organize it, or put it in order. One way to organize information is to write notes. Write notes for each book or website you use.

- Write down important facts and ideas.
- Use your own words. Do not copy information from a source.
- Write the address of the website. For a book, write the title, author, publisher, place and date of publication, and page number.

Read notes that one student wrote. Then answer the questions.

Ancient Egyptian Writing

- *earliest form called hieroglyphs*
- *Egyptians began writing hiero around 3000 B.C.E.*
- *Most were pictures that stood for people, animals, & things*
- *Hiero were painted, carved, or written with brush and ink*

Source: Ancient Egypt, by George Hart, Dorling Kindersley, New York, 1990, p. 34

---

1. What is the topic of this report?
2. What source (book or website) did the writer use for the notes?
3. Where did the student write the source?

Workbook
Pages 131–132

Practice

You will write a report about an early form of writing.

1. **Read** Reread the student's notes on page 173. Think of a topic on early writing that you want to write about.

Writing Strategy: Subtopic Web

Think about your topic. What subtopics, or smaller topics, do you want to write about? Use a subtopic web to organize your ideas. Write your topic in the middle of a sheet of paper. Then think of some ideas to write about your topic. Look at this student's subtopic web.

Look for information about your subtopics in the library and on the Internet. Which ideas can you find the most information about? Choose these subtopics to write about.

---

2. **Make a subtopic web** Make a subtopic web for your topic in your notebook. Choose three subtopics. Then find information about them. Remember to write notes and be sure to include source information.

3. **Write** Use your notes to write your report. Edit your work. Make sure you vary your sentences. Use different lengths and types. Also check for pronoun agreement. Finally, use what you know about spelling patterns to check for misspellings.

Prepare to Read

▶ BUILD BACKGROUND

In 1964, President Lyndon Johnson made a speech explaining how he wanted to make the country a better place. He said he wanted to create the "Great Society." The two main goals of President Johnson's Great Society were to get end poverty and racial injustice. He also wanted new programs to improve education, medical care, and transportation. In this section, you will read part of his speech to the American people.

▼ President Johnson signing the Civil Rights Act of 1968

What You Will Learn

Reading
- Vocabulary building: *Connotation*
- Connect to reading: *Main ideas and details; Author's purpose; Speeches*
- Text type: *Informational text (social studies)*

Writing
- Editing a draft
- Editing

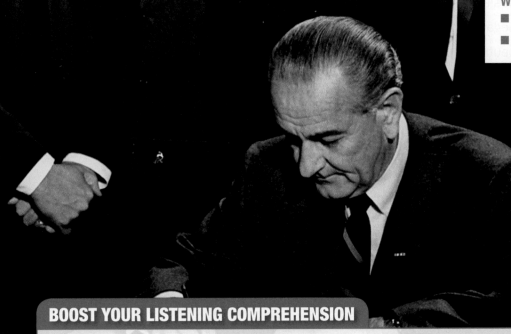

BOOST YOUR LISTENING COMPREHENSION

Unit 5: The Power of Words
Your teacher will play the DVD for this unit. After you listen, answer these questions.

1. Where is Ghana?

2. Where do the people of Ghana go to buy, sell, and trade goods?

3. For what other reasons do people go to the market?

4. What is bargaining?

5. What are some items you can buy at a typical market in Ghana?

6. Why are words so powerful at a market in Ghana?

► **CONNECT TO VOCABULARY**

Connotation

Most words have both a denotation and a connotation. **Denotation** is the dictionary definition of a word. **Connotation** is the feeling that goes along with a word. Sometimes, you can tell the connotation of a word by its context. That means the way it is used in a sentence. Words with positive connotations send a positive message. Words with negative connotations send a negative message. Words with neutral connotations do not express positive or negative feelings.

Words can have similar denotations but different connotations. Read the examples below. All the words mean "having little body fat." However, their connotations are different.

Word	Connotation (Feeling)
slender	positive
skinny	negative
lean	neutral or positive

Practice Workbook Pages 134–135

Read the paragraph. Use a dictionary to find the denotation of the word *stingy*. Use the meaning of the paragraph to figure out the connotation of *stingy*.

Many people are careful with money. They think before they spend. However, some people are too careful with money. These people are *stingy*. They don't buy gifts for people, they never lend money to friends, and they never give money to people in need.

➤ CONNECT TO READING

Main Ideas and Details

The **main idea** of a piece of writing makes a point about the subject. The main idea is usually big, or general. **Details** explain the main idea. Details are usually small, or specific. Read the paragraph. Look for the main idea and details.

Summer

Often, summer is a happy time for children. The weather is usually good. The sun shines, and children can play outside. They can go swimming. If they have a pool, they can use it. Otherwise, they can go to the beach. They can also ride their bikes. Another reason summer is a happy time for children is this—in the summer, many children don't have to attend school.

Summer is the subject of the paragraph. The first sentence is the main idea. It makes a point about summer. The point is that summer is often a happy time for children. Many details explain the main idea:

- The weather is usually good.
- The sun shines.
- Children can play outside.
- They can go swimming.
- They can swim in a pool or go to the beach.
- They can ride their bikes.
- Many children do not have to go to school.

Some details are more important than others. For example, "They can go swimming" is more important than "They can swim in a pool." Why? Because "They can go swimming" has a broader meaning. It is a detail that can be broken down into smaller details. "They can swim in a pool" is a good detail, but it cannot be broken down into smaller details, so it is not as important.

Practice

What are the most important details in the paragraph? Work with a partner. Discuss your ideas.

Author's Purpose

An **author's purpose** is his or her reason for writing. These are the three main purposes for writing:

- to inform readers, or explain a subject
- to entertain readers, or engage them
- to persuade readers, or make them do something

Source	Passage	Author's Purpose
Encyclopedia	"Many Sumerians were farmers. Some farmers grew grain, such as barley, for food. Other farmers raised sheep for milk and wool."	To inform: This paragraph gives facts about Sumerians.
Play	"'Minu,' the boy said, which in the language of Accra means, 'I don't understand.' 'Minu?' Akwasi said. 'Minu must be a very rich man!'"	To entertain: This passage makes people laugh. It is just for fun.
Book review	"Everyone should read the folk tale 'The Great Minu.' It uses humor to teach a powerful lesson about life."	To persuade: This passage makes people want to read "The Great Minu."

Practice  **Workbook** Pages 136–137

Identify the purpose of the paragraph below. Then find the main idea.

"The earth's crust is a layer of rock that covers the earth. It is underneath all the land and water on the earth. The crust is made of huge pieces of rock called plates. The plates move very slowly."

Speeches

A **speech** is a talk given by a speaker to an audience. A good speech makes people sit up and listen. It uses clear, interesting language. It is easy to understand. Good speakers use language devices to help them make their point. A **device** is a tool. Look at the language devices used in the examples below.

Device	Definition	Example
repetition	repeating words	The only solution is change; change that will help us all; change that will bring about a new vision of our future.
alliteration	repeating the first consonant sound in a string of words	I am offering you—kind members of this community—my creativity and courage.
allusion	making a hint about something or someone	This is the home of the brave; we need to show that bravery by voting against this unfair policy.

Practice

Work with a partner. Write a short speech about school. Use one or more of the speech devices.

Set a purpose for reading As you read part of President Johnson's speech, look for the main idea and important details. Also look for any devices Johnson used to strengthen his speech.

Audio

from "THE GREAT SOCIETY"

▲ President Lyndon Johnson

I have come today from the turmoil of your Capital to the tranquility of your campus to speak about the future of your country. The purpose of protecting the life of our Nation and preserving the liberty of our citizens is to pursue the happiness of our people. Our success in that pursuit is the test of our success as a Nation.

For a century we labored to settle and to subdue a continent. For half a century we called upon unbounded invention and untiring industry to create an order of plenty for all of our people.

The challenge of the next half century is whether we have the wisdom to use that wealth to enrich and elevate our national life, and to advance the quality of our American civilization.

. . . [I]n your time we have the opportunity to move not only toward the rich society and the powerful society, but upward to the Great Society.

SUPPORT YOUR READING EXPERIENCE

The more you read, the larger your vocabulary knowledge becomes. Now that you have read this speech, go to www.LongmanKeystone.com and do the activity for this unit. You will learn ways to use kinesthetic visual support to develop vocabulary and structures and to build more background knowledge.

Workbook
Pages 138–139

BEFORE YOU GO ON

1 What is the purpose of Lyndon Johnson's speech? How can you tell?

2 Reread the first sentence of the speech. What device is used?

3 The phrase "pursue the happiness" is an allusion to the Declaration of Independence. Why do you think Johnson made this allusion?

Writing

Edit a Draft

In this lesson, you will learn to edit a draft. When you edit, you check for mistakes in spelling, grammar, and punctuation. You also check to see that the writing is organized. Is there a main idea? Are there details to support the main idea?

Read the paragraph a student wrote. Then answer the questions.

> Playing tennis is my favorite exersise. To play good, I have to use most of the muscles in my body. I have to use my leg muscles to move forwurd and backward I have to use my arm muscles to serve and hit the ball. After a match, I feel great. Do you like to have fun. I suggest you play tennis.

1. What spelling mistakes did the student make?
2. What grammar mistake did the student make in the second sentence?
3. Where did the student forget to put a period? A question mark?

Workbook
Pages 140–141

Practice

1. **Read** Reread the student's paragraph. Do you like sports or dislike sports?

2. **Write** Write a paragraph. Give your opinion of sports. Explain your opinion with reasons.

3. **Edit** After you finish writing your paragraph, edit it. Use the checklist below. It will help you find any mistakes, and will remind you to include a main idea and supporting details.

EDITING CHECKLIST	
I have spelled all words right. If I have used a computer spell-check program, I have double-checked my paragraph.	
My paragraph is free of errors in grammar. I have used verb tenses correctly. All pronouns refer to the correct nouns.	
My draft is free of errors in punctuation. I have used correct end punctuation.	
My paragraph is organized. I have a main idea, and I have included details that support it.	

4. **Share** After you have edited your draft, trade paragraphs with a partner. Look over each other's writing. Did you find and fix all the mistakes? If not, fix them now.

Link the Readings

Make a chart like the one below to compare the readings in this unit. Look at each word in the column. Put an **X** under "Early Writing" if the word reminds you of that text. Put an **X** under "The Great Minu" if the word reminds you of the folktale. Put an **X** under "The Great Society" if the word reminds you of the speech. Put an **X** in all places if the word reminds you of all selections.

	"Early Writing"	"The Great Minu"	"The Great Society"
grain	_____	_____	_____
reeds	_____	_____	_____
village	_____	_____	_____
speech	_____	_____	_____
wedges	_____	_____	_____
symbols	_____	_____	_____
funeral	_____	_____	_____

Check Your Knowledge

Language Development

1. Look at your notes from "Early Writing." Use your notes to tell a friend what you learned.
2. What is a pronoun? Say a sentence with a subject pronoun. Say a sentence with an object pronoun.
3. Describe the irony in the folktale "The Great Minu."

Academic Content

1. What modern country is located where ancient Sumer once was?
2. Why did the people of Sumer need writing?
3. How did the Sumerians write numbers?
4. What were the goals of President Johnson's "Great Society"?

Exploring The Senses

Sometimes we learn the truth about something by thinking about it in different ways. The fable "The Blind Men and the Elephant" is a story that teaches a lesson about "seeing" and understanding. Animals use their senses to survive, or stay alive. Read "Animal Senses" to learn about some interesting ways animals use their hearing, smell, sight, and touch. Finally, you will read a poem inspired by nature.

Reading

1 Fable	2 Science	3 Poem

"The Blind Men and the Elephant"	"Animal Senses"	"Tiny Giant"
Reading Strategy: Make inferences	**Reading Strategy:** Find main ideas	**Connect to Reading:** Structure and elements of poetry

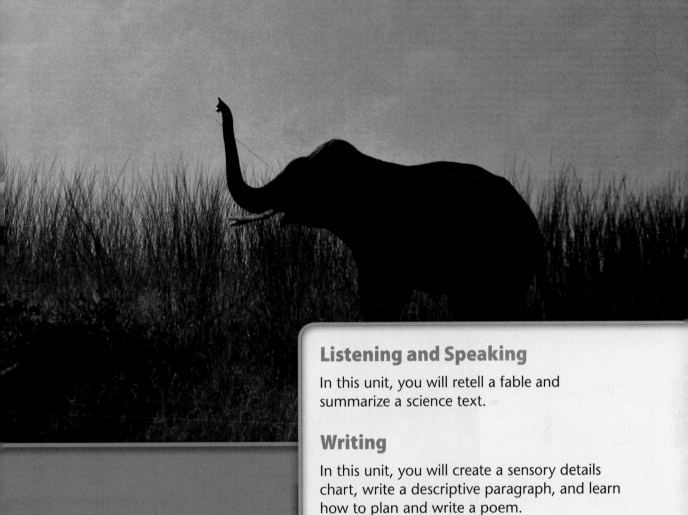

Listening and Speaking

In this unit, you will retell a fable and summarize a science text.

Writing

In this unit, you will create a sensory details chart, write a descriptive paragraph, and learn how to plan and write a poem.

Quick Write

We have five senses: hearing, sight, touch, smell, and taste. Write two or three sentences about the sense that is the most important to you.

VIEW AND RESPOND
Watch the Unit 6 DVD. As you watch, answer the questions on page 205.
www.LongmanKeystone.com.

185

Prepare to Read

What You Will Learn

Reading

- Vocabulary building: *Context; dictionary skills; similes*

- Reading strategy: *Make inferences*

- Text type: *Literature (fable and play)*

➤ **BUILD BACKGROUND**

"The Blind Men and the Elephant" is a fable. A fable is a story that teaches a moral, or a lesson about life. This fable is from India.

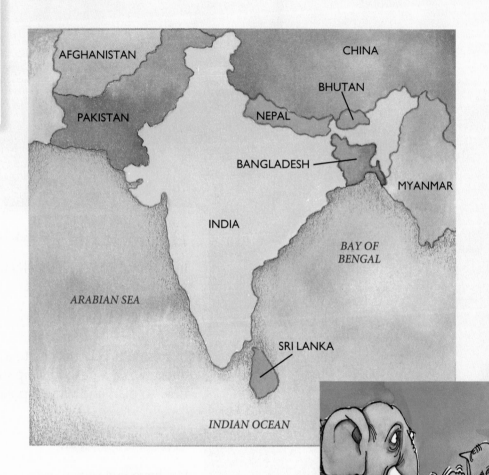

TRY TO PREDICT

Why do you think the man is touching the elephant? Explain.

Workbook
Page 142

➤ VOCABULARY

Listening and Speaking: Key Words

Look at the pictures and the captions. They will help you learn the words in the box. Write the meaning of each highlighted word and say them aloud with a partner. Then check your work in a dictionary.

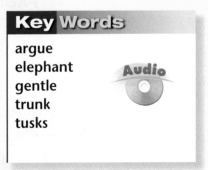

Key Words

- argue
- elephant
- gentle
- trunk
- tusks

Audio

▲ An elephant is a large animal. It has two long front teeth called tusks and a long nose called a trunk. The elephant in the story is a gentle animal. It does not hurt people.

▲ When people have different ideas, they sometimes argue about which idea is right.

Workbook
Pages 143–144

READING STRATEGY | MAKE INFERENCES

Sometimes writers do not tell you what a story means. They give clues about the story's meaning. These clues can be things that the characters do and say. The reader uses the clues to **make inferences** about, or guess, the story's meaning.

- Look for clues in the story.
- Think about what the characters do and say.
- Use these clues to guess the meaning of the story.

Workbook
Page 145

Set a purpose for reading "The Blind Men and the Elephant" is a fable from India. Like most fables, it has a moral, or a lesson about life. As you read, make inferences and guess the moral of the story.

The Blind Men and the Elephant

Once upon a time, six blind men were walking down a road in India. They met an old man leading an elephant. They stopped to speak to the old man. One of the blind men said, "Sir, what kind of animal do you have? It is making a **strange** noise."

The old man said, "It is an elephant."

"An elephant?" said one of the blind men. "I don't know what an elephant is."

"May we touch it?" asked the second blind man. "We want to know what an elephant is like."

"Of course," said the old man. "This elephant is gentle. It will not hurt you."

One by one, the blind men began to touch the elephant. The first blind man touched one of the elephant's tusks. It was long and smooth. The tip was pointed and sharp. He said, "An elephant is like a spear."

---

strange, not usual

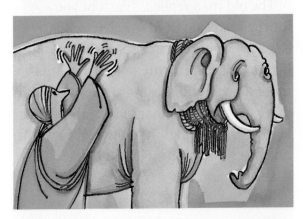

Then the second blind man touched the elephant's trunk. It was long and very strong. It moved up and down and from side to side. He cried, "Brothers, an elephant is not like a spear. It is like a snake!"

Next, the third blind man touched one of the elephant's legs. It felt thick and rough. It was very tall. "No, you are wrong, my brothers. An elephant is not like a spear. It is not like a snake, either. It is like a large tree."

After that, the fourth blind man touched the elephant's side. Then he said, "Are you crazy? An elephant is not like a spear. And it is not like a snake. It is not like a tree, either. It is hard and wide and flat. I cannot find the end of it. An elephant is like a great wall."

At that moment, the elephant lowered its head. The fifth blind man reached out and touched one of the elephant's ears. It felt big and soft and flat. It flapped and made a **breeze**. He said, "No, my brothers. An elephant is not like a spear or a snake or a tree or a wall. It is like a huge fan."

---

breeze, gentle wind

BEFORE YOU GO ON

1. Why did the blind men want to touch the elephant?

2. What did the blind men think the elephant felt like?

3. Have you ever touched something that you couldn't see? Describe your experience.

Finally, the sixth blind man touched the elephant's tail. It was long and thin. It had hair on the end. He said, "You are all wrong. An elephant is not like a spear or a snake or a tree or a wall, or even a fan. An elephant is like a rope."

Now, the blind men started to argue. Each one thought that his idea about an elephant was correct.

"Wait," said the old man with the elephant. "You are all right. But you are also all wrong."

The six men were confused. "How can we be right—and wrong?" they asked.

The old man replied, "Each of you touched only a part of the elephant. An elephant is more than a spear. It is more than a snake. It is more than a tree. It is more than a wall. It is more than a fan. It is more than a rope. **Imagine** an animal that is all of those things put together. Can you imagine something huge and strange? *That* is an elephant."

---

imagine, see in your mind, picture

BEFORE YOU GO ON

1 Why did the men argue about what an elephant is?

2 How does the old man describe the elephant?

3 Do you think elephants are strange? Why or why not?

The Blind Men and the Elephant
A Play

Now read the fable as a play. There are nine parts.

CHARACTERS

Narrator
First Blind Man
Elephant Keeper
Second Blind Man
Third Blind Man

Fourth Blind Man
Fifth Blind Man
Sixth Blind Man
Chorus

Narrator: Once upon a time, six blind men were walking down a road in India. They met an old man leading an elephant.

First Blind Man: Sir, what kind of animal do you have? It is making a strange noise.

Elephant Keeper: It is an elephant.

First Blind Man: An elephant? I don't know what an elephant is.

Second Blind Man: May we touch it? We want to know what an elephant is like.

Elephant Keeper: Of course. This elephant is very gentle. It will not hurt you.

Narrator: The blind men began to touch the elephant.

Chorus: The first blind man touched a tusk.

First Blind Man: It is long and pointed! This animal is like a spear.

Chorus: The second blind man touched the trunk.

Second Blind Man: It is long, and it moves up and down and from side to side! Brothers, this elephant is like a snake!

Chorus: The third blind man touched one of the elephant's legs.

Third Blind Man: It is thick and rough. No, brothers, an elephant is like a large tree.

Chorus: The fourth blind man touched the elephant's side.

Fourth Blind Man: Are you crazy? This animal is hard and wide and flat. An elephant is like a great wall.

Chorus: Then, the elephant lowered its head. The fifth blind man touched one of the elephant's ears.

Fifth Blind Man: It is big and flat. It makes a breeze. An elephant is like a fan.

Chorus: The sixth blind man touched the elephant's tail.

Sixth Blind Man: It is long and thin. It has hair on it. An elephant is like a rope.

Narrator: The blind men started to argue. Each one thought his idea about the elephant was right.

Elephant Keeper: Wait! You are all right. But you are also all wrong. Each of you touched only a part of the elephant.

Chorus: An elephant is more than a spear. It is more than a snake. It is more than a tree. It is more than a wall. It is more than a fan. It is more than a rope.

Elephant Keeper: Can you imagine an animal that is all of those things put together? Can you imagine something huge and strange? *That* is an elephant.

Review and Practice

► RETELL AND REVIEW

1. Look back at the pictures in "The Blind Men and the Elephant" on pages 188–190. Cover the words on each page. Retell the events of the story to a partner, using only the pictures. Use the Key Words. If you can't think of a word, describe it, use a synonym, or ask your teacher.

2. What is the moral of this fable? Explain how clues from the story helped you understand the moral.

► COMPREHENSION

Workbook Page 147

Complete the sentences. Choose the correct word from the column on the right. Write the completed sentences in your notebook.

1. This fable takes place in the country of _India_.   fan
2. The six blind men did not know about _____.   ~~India~~
3. The first blind man thought the tusk was like a _____.   wall
4. The second blind man thought the trunk was like a _____.   snake
5. The third blind man thought the leg was like a _____.   rope
6. The fourth blind man thought the side was like a _____.   spear
7. The fifth blind man thought the ear was like a _____.   elephants
8. The sixth blind man thought the tail was like a _____.   tree

Extension

Similes

A simile shows how two things are alike, or similar. In a simile, you use the word *like* to compare two things.

The elephant's tail was *like* a rope.
(The simile compares the elephant's tail to a rope.)

A. Look at your completed Comprehension sentences from page 192. Find the similes in sentences 3–8. Then write in your notebook the two things that each simile compares.

The first blind man thought <u>the tusk was like a spear.</u>
The simile compares an elephant's tusk to a spear.

B. Read the poem. Then complete the activity.

Rain Poem

The rain was like a little mouse,
quiet, small and gray.
It pattered all around the house
and then it went away.

It did not come, I understand,
indoors at all, until
it found an open window and
left tracks across the **sill**.

—Elizabeth Coatsworth

sill, bottom of a window

1. Underline the simile in the poem.
2. What two things are being compared?
3. Name three words that show how the two things are alike.

What You Will Learn

Reading

■ Vocabulary building: *Context; dictionary skills; sensory images*

■ Reading strategy: *Find main ideas*

■ Text type: *Informational text (science)*

Academic Content

■ Science vocabulary

■ Animal senses

Grammar
Adjectives

Writing
Write a descriptive paragraph

► BUILD BACKGROUND

"Animal Senses" is a nonfiction text. It tells about the ways animals see, hear, smell, and touch.

Elephants cannot see very well. But they have good senses of smell, touch, and hearing. ►

DISCUSS

In what ways do elephants "talk" to each other?

► VOCABULARY

Listening and Speaking: Key Words

Look at the pictures and the captions. They will help you learn the words in the box. Write the meaning of each highlighted word and say them aloud with a partner. Then check your work in a dictionary.

▲ Bees live in a hive.

▲ Owls see well. Their good vision helps them find food to survive, or stay alive.

◄ Owls eat mice. Owls are predators. Mice are their prey.

Workbook Page 149

READING STRATEGY | FIND MAIN IDEAS

The **main ideas** are the most important ideas in a text. Each paragraph usually has one main idea. The main ideas help you remember the important parts of the text.

- Notice headings and titles. They are clues to main ideas.
- Remember that the first sentence of a paragraph often tells the main idea.
- Look for facts that support the main idea in each paragraph.

Workbook Page 150

Set a purpose for reading "Animal Senses" is a nonfiction text. It explains how three kinds of animals use their senses. As you read, look for main ideas in each section. What details support each main idea?

Audio

Animal Senses

Why Are Senses Important?

Animals use their senses to survive in nature. Animals' abilities to see, hear, smell, taste, and touch help them find food. Animals also use their senses to avoid, or stay away from, their enemies.

Animals **adapt** to their specific environments, or surroundings. As a result, most animals have one or two senses that are more important than the others. These senses help animals survive.

▲ A baby elephant feels safe holding onto its mother's tail. What conclusion can you draw about elephant families?

How Do Elephants Use Their Senses of Smell and Touch?

Elephants have small eyes, and they cannot see well. They use their senses of smell and touch to find food, water, and other animals. Elephants breathe and smell with their trunks. They use their trunks to smell the air

Elephants use their trunks to smell the air and the ground. ▼

---

adapt, change to fit a specific situation better

and the ground. Sometimes they can smell other animals or water from miles away.

Elephants also touch each other with their trunks to **communicate**. Friendly elephants touch trunks as a greeting. Mother elephants touch new baby elephants with their trunks to welcome them. When a baby elephant is afraid, the mother strokes it with her trunk. Sometimes a baby elephant holds its mother's tail with its trunk. That makes the baby feel safe.

How Do Elephants Feel with Their Feet?

Scientists think that elephants' feet can feel **vibrations** in the ground. For example, when thunder makes the ground shake far away, elephants feel the direction of the thunder with their feet. Then the elephants know where to find rainwater.

▲ Elephants' big ears can hear sounds that people's ears cannot hear.

How Do Elephants Use Their Sense of Hearing?

Elephants use their sense of hearing to avoid danger. Elephants can hear low sounds that human ears can't. They can also make special low sounds with their trunks to communicate with other elephants far away. For example, elephants make sounds to tell other elephants about dangerous animals, such as lions. Baby elephants make special sounds when they are afraid. When a mother elephant hears the sounds, she goes to help her baby.

▲ Elephants make sounds with their trunks to communicate with other elephants.

---

communicate, give or share information
vibrations, shaking movements

Workbook
Page 151

BEFORE YOU GO ON

1 Why don't elephants use their sense of vision to find food and water?

2 Name two ways elephants communicate with each other.

Reading 2 **197**

What Is Special about an Owl's Eyes?

Owls have excellent vision. At night, they fly and look for prey—small animals to eat, such as mice, rabbits, frogs, and birds. When owls see an animal move, they fly down and catch it.

Owls are predators—they catch and eat other animals. Their large eyes are specially adapted for **hunting** at night. Most birds have eyes on the sides of their head. These birds see well on the sides, but they do not see well in front of themselves. Owls are different. They have eyes in the front of their head, which makes them good hunters. Their eyes are good at following and catching prey.

hunting, catching and killing animals for food

▲ "Eyes in front, likes to hunt." Predators, such as owls, have eyes in the front of their head. Their front-facing eyes help them find and catch prey.

◀ "Eyes on the side, likes to hide." Many animals, such as this sparrow, have eyes on the sides of their head. Sparrows can see left and right, so they can escape from predators.

▲ Owls catch and eat mice, frogs, rabbits, and birds.

Why Do Honeybees Dance?

Honeybees live together in large groups in hives. Honeybees travel to different flowers to get food and **nectar**. They use the nectar to make honey inside the hive. Honeybees cannot hear very well, and it is dark inside the hive. As a result, they touch each other and use their senses of touch and smell to communicate.

A scientist named Karl von Frisch studied honeybees. He saw that honeybees move back and forth in a kind of "dance" when they return to the hive. They dance in different ways to tell other honeybees where to find food. Frisch saw that honeybees dance in a circle to show that food is near. They dance in a figure eight (∞) and **wiggle** to show that food is far away. The other honeybees in the hive use their senses of smell and touch to learn the **location** of the food from the dancing bees.

▲ Honeybees get food and nectar from flowers.

nectar, a sweet liquid found inside flowers
wiggle, to move and shake the body
location, place

▲ Honeybees use touch and smell to communicate with each other.

BEFORE YOU GO ON

1. How are the dances of honeybees like a language?
2. Can you think of another bird or animal that has eyes in front?
3. In English, the sound an owl makes is, "Whooo!" What sound does an owl make in your first language?

Reading 2 **199**

Review and Practice

► RETELL AND REVIEW

1. Tell a partner the main ideas you learned about elephants, owls, and honeybees. Use the headings and pictures on pages 196–199 to help you.

2. What facts do you remember about each animal? Explain.

»)) *Listening* SKILL

Listen carefully to your partner for ideas that are not stated directly.

► COMPREHENSION  **Workbook** Page 152

Write the sentences below in your notebook. Use the words in the box to complete the sentences.

smell	survive	vibrations	touch
avoid	predators	vision	nectar

1. Animals use their senses to __survive__ in nature.

2. To survive, animals need to find food and _____ danger.

3. Owls have very good _____

4. Mother elephants _____ new babies with their trunks to welcome them.

5. Scientists think that elephants can feel _____ with their feet.

6. Elephants breathe and _____ with their trunks.

7. _____ catch and eat other animals.

8. Honeybees tell one another where to find _____ by dancing.

Extension

Sensory Images

Poems often have sensory images. Poets use sensory images so readers can see, hear, taste, touch, or smell things as the poet does. Read this poem.

Wings

If I had wings
I would touch the fingertips of clouds
and glide on the wind's breath.

If I had wings
I would taste a chunk of the sun
as hot as peppered curry.

If I had wings
I would listen to the clouds of sheep bleat
that graze on the blue.

If I had wings
I would breathe deep and sniff
the scent of raindrops.

If I had wings
I would gaze at the people
who cling to the earth.

If I had wings
I would dream of
swimming the deserts
and walking the seas.

—Pie Corbett

»)) Listening SKILL

Play the Audio CD. Listen for patterns of intonation. Listen to the rhythm of the words and the way the voice rises and falls. Intonation gives clues to the meaning of the poem.

What can you see, hear, touch, taste, and smell in the poem? Copy the chart. Complete it with a partner.

See	Hear	Touch	Taste	Smell
people who cling to the earth				

Grammar

Adjectives

Adjectives describe nouns—people, places, and things.
Adjectives can come after the verb *be*.

>   *be* adjective
> An elephant is **gentle.**
> A lion   is **dangerous.**

Adjectives usually come before nouns.

>   adjective noun   adjective   noun
> An owl has **large** eyes and **excellent** vision.
> adjective   noun
> **Friendly** elephants touch each other with their trunks.

Do not add -s to adjectives that describe more than one noun.

> Elephants have **long** tusks.

Speaking SKILL

Remember to use adjectives correctly when you speak as well as when you write.

Practice

Use the words to make sentences in your notebook. Put the adjectives in the right place.
Example: sounds / hear / low / elephants

Elephants hear low sounds.

1. live / animals / environments / in / specific
2. long / elephant / tusks / the / has
3. trunk / strong / is / its
4. dance / honeybees / different / in / ways
5. dangerous / lions / are
6. dark / is / hive / a / honeybee's

Writing

Write a Descriptive Paragraph

Use adjectives and sensory images when you write a **description**. Then your reader can see, hear, taste, smell, or feel what the person, place, or thing you are describing is like.

Read this description that Carlos wrote about his dog. Then answer the questions.

Carlos Salgeras

My Dog Blue

My dog Blue has a long body and short legs. Blue's skin is very loose. When you pull his skin gently, it stretches like a rubber band! His ears are very long. Sometimes they fall into his food. Then his ears smell like dog food! Blue makes a loud, strange sound when he drinks water, "Thuk-a-thuk-a-thuk-a-thuk!" When he wants to go for a walk, he howls, "Ah-h-o-o-o-o-w!" Blue has a big head and a long nose. His face is wrinkled, and his eyes are sad. I named him "Blue" because "blue" means sad. Blue looks sad, but he's a very funny dog!

1. Which adjectives describe what Blue looks like?
2. What sensory images does Carlos use? Which senses do they describe?
3. How do Carlos's words and images make you feel about Blue? Explain.

Workbook
Pages 153–154

Practice

Workbook Page 155

You will write a descriptive paragraph about an animal. You can describe a pet, an animal you have seen at the zoo, or any animal you like.

1. **Read** Reread "Animal Senses" on pages 196–199 and Carlos's description of his dog on page 203. What descriptive words and images do the writers use?

Writing Strategy: Sensory Details Chart

A sensory details chart can help you describe how things look, smell, sound, taste, and feel. Carlos used this chart to write his description.

What I See	What I Smell	What I Hear	What I Feel
long body, nose, ears short legs big head, wrinkled face, sad eye	dog food on his ears	"Thuk-a-thuk-a-thuk-a-thuk!" when he drinks water "Ah-h-o-o-o-o-w!" when he howls	his loose skin stretches like a rubber band

---

2. **Make a chart** In your notebook, make a sensory details chart about your animal. Write words that describe what you see, smell, hear, and feel when you are near the animal.

3. **Write a descriptive paragraph** Use your chart to write a descriptive paragraph about your animal. Edit your work. Make sure you combine sentences correctly. Check your work for errors in spelling.

Prepare to Read

➤ BUILD BACKGROUND

In this section, you will read a poem inspired by nature. You will also learn about the different tools poets use to write poems. Poems can be short or long. Some poems are just a few lines. Other poems are many pages long. Have you ever written a poem about nature? What inspired you to write the poem? Share with the class.

What You Will Learn

Reading
- Vocabulary building: *Analogies*
- Connect to reading: *Structure and elements of poetry*
- Text type: *Literature (poetry)*

Writing
- Plan a poem
- Write a poem

BOOST YOUR LISTENING COMPREHENSION

Unit 6: Exploring the Senses
Your teacher will play the DVD for this unit. After you listen, answer these questions.

1. What is the largest land animal in the world?

2. How did many of Africa's highways begin?

3. What do elephants eat?

4. What can elephants do with their trunks?

5. What are some unusual things about the baobab tree?

6. Why do elephants need to eat a lot? Why is this a problem?

► CONNECT TO VOCABULARY

Analogies

An **analogy** compares two sets of words that are related in the same way. Look at the analogy below.

> **More** is to **less** as **loud** is to **soft**.

To understand the analogy, you must see how the two sets of words relate to each other. Ask yourself: How are *more* and *less* related? The answer is that they are opposites. How are *loud* and *soft* related? They, too, are opposites.

Now, try to complete the analogy below.

> **Nose** is to **smell** as **ear** is to _____.

The word *smell* tells what you do with your nose. To complete the analogy, find a word that tells what you do with your ear. The correct answer is *hear*. You use your nose to smell, and you use your ear to hear. The two sets of words are related in the same way.

Practice

Workbook
Pages 156–157

Work with a partner. Choose the word that best completes each analogy.

1. **Pencil** is to **write** as **knife** is to _____.
2. **Shovel** is to **dirt** as **fork** is to _____.
3. **Rock** is to **hard** as **blanket** is to _____.
4. **Glove** is to **hand** as **sock** is to _____.
5. **Candy** is to **sweet** as **lemon** is to _____.

➤ CONNECT TO READING

Structure and Elements of Poetry

To understand a poem, you may have to read it several times. The first few times, try to understand what the poem is about. Ask yourself: What is the subject of this poem? What does the poem say about this subject?

Once you can answer those questions, think about *how* ideas are expressed in the poem. Ask yourself how elements in the poem help shape the poem's meaning. The chart below describes some common elements of poetry.

Element	Definition	Example
Diction	The words a poet chooses to use in a poem. Diction helps express ideas, set a mood, and create rhythm and sound.	*"The **bleak** night brought Only the **wail** of wind, The shadows, like **ghosts,** rose beyond the window."*
Understatement	Expressing less emotion than one would normally expect. Understatement creates a sense of surprise or irony.	*"**Her love was nothing** to me. I could have tossed it like a stone into the river."*
Overstatement	Expressing more emotion than one would normally expect.	*"I did not just love her, I worshipped her. So I lay a **thousand kisses** upon her brow."*
Irony	The poet writes something that is the opposite of what the reader might normally expect.	***"Water, water every where** And all **the boards did shrink; Water, water, every where, Nor any drop to drink."***
Sarcasm	The poet states one thing, but means the opposite.	*"I was awoken by the sound Of two cats yowling. **What music to my ears!**"*
Paradox	A statement that doesn't seem to make sense, but which is still true.	*"She has **eyes, yet she cannot see.**"*

Use your imagination when you read a poem. As you read, try to picture the people, places, and things that are described. Look for **imagery**, or descriptions that help you form pictures in your mind. See whether the poem has a **controlling image**, or main "word picture" that is repeated. For example, in the poem "The Rime of the Ancient Mariner," Samuel Taylor Coleridge describes the sea many times. These descriptions are the controlling image.

Figurative language is another imaginative element of poetry. The chart below explains different kinds of figurative language.

Figurative Language	Definition	Example
Simile	Using the word *like* or *as* to compare two things that are similar in some way.	*"Do we run away,* **Like frightened rabbits?***"*
Metaphor	Directly comparing two things without using the word *like* or *as*.	*"The* **moon was a misty eye** *Looking down on us Through the night sky."*
Personification	Giving human qualities to ideas or objects.	**"Stalks of corn greeted us** *As we walked in the field."*

Also think about how a poem is organized. Many poems are organized into stanzas. A **stanza** is a group of lines that go together. It is similar to a paragraph in a story.

Structural Element	Definition	Example
Couplet	A stanza of two lines, which usually rhyme.	*"In sunny fields we run, Hands linked; hearts as one."*
Tercet	A stanza of three lines. If all three lines rhyme, the stanza is called a *triplet*.	*"Though my head aches, And my spirit quakes, I will do what it takes."*
Quatrain	A stanza of four lines.	*"Roses are red, Violets are blue, Sugar is sweet; And so are you."*

Workbook
Pages 158–159

Read this poem, "The Wayfarer," by Stephen Crane. (A *wayfarer* is someone who walks from place to place.) As you read, think about what you have just learned about the structure and elements of poetry. Reread the first two paragraphs on page 207, and keep those questions in mind as you read.

The Wayfarer

The wayfarer
Perceiving the pathway to truth,
Was struck with astonishment.
It was thickly grown with weeds.
"Ha," he said,
"I see that none has passed here
In a long time."
Later he saw that each weed
Was a singular knife.
"Well," he mumbled at last,
"Doubtless there are other roads."

Practice

Work in a small group. Reread "The Wayfarer." Then answer the questions.

1. What is the subject of the poem?
2. What point does the poem make about the subject?
3. What is the controlling image in the poem?
4. Where is a metaphor used in the poem?
5. What two things are compared in the metaphor?
6. How would you describe the poet's diction, or choice of words? Why?

Set a purpose for reading You will read a poem about someone who had an unexpected encounter while viewing a field of flowers. As you read, think about the structure and elements of poetry that are used in this poem.

Tiny Giant

Audio

Along a road
I stopped to see
a parade of bluebonnets
marching there.

All yellow and violet
eyes met me
and watched me stoop
to kindly stare
upon their fluffy heads of bloom.

A bee buzzed near,
a burglar, he!
Legs heavy
with their tons of dust.

The tiny giant
rattled me,
reduced me to a swatting fuss.

Thinking only of the sting,
I flailed back to my waiting car.
So brave I am!
Such might! Such nerve!
Admiring that giant from afar.

SUPPORT YOUR READING EXPERIENCE

The more you read, the larger your vocabulary knowledge becomes. Now that you have read this poem, go to www.LongmanKeystone.com and do the activity for this unit. You will learn ways to use kinesthetic visual support to develop vocabulary and structures and to build more background knowledge.

BEFORE YOU GO ON

1 Which words in the second stanza help you imagine how the flowers look?

2 The description "tiny giant" is an example of which poetic element? Explain.

3 Which lines in the poem show sarcasm? Explain.

Workbook
Pages 160–161

Writing

Ongoing Writing Skills Practice

Plan a Poem

When you plan a poem, you think about these things:

- The subject, or what you will write about
- The theme, or what point you will make about the subject
- The descriptions you might use, including figurative language
- The structure of the poem, or what type of poem you will write

Many poems follow a set structure. In an English sonnet, the first three stanzas contain four lines each. In each stanza, the last word of the first and third lines rhymes, and the last word of the second and fourth lines rhymes. The last two lines of the poem rhyme with each other. (See the definition for *quatrain* and *couplet* on page 208.) A haiku poem has only three lines. The first line has five syllables, the second has seven syllables, and the third line has five syllables. Free verse, another kind of poem, does not follow a set pattern.

Below is the plan a student used to write "Tiny Giant."

> Subject: Bees
>
> Theme: It is a little silly to be afraid of a tiny bee.
>
> Descriptions
>
> — might describe tiny bee as a frightening animal (irony)
>
> — might describe bee as a burglar
>
> — might describe how I reacted to the bee: reduced me to
>
> a swatting fuss, flailed back, brave (sarcasm)
>
> — fear of bee contrasts with pleasant field of flowers
>
> Structure: Free verse

1. What things do you need to include in a plan for a poem?
2. Why is it helpful to make a plan?

Workbook
Page 162

IMPROVE YOUR WRITING SKILLS

Now that you have practiced writing a poem, go to www. LongmanKeystone. com and do the activity for this unit. You will find suggestions for planning future written works, including how to determine appropriate topics through a range of strategies.

1. **Read** Reread the poem "Tiny Giant," on page 210. Compare the poem to the student's plan. Think about how the writer used the plan to write the poem. Did she follow her plan, or did she make changes to it?

2. **Make a Poetry Chart** Make a poetry chart for your poem. Use the chart below as a model.

Writing Strategy: Writing a Poem

<u>What is my subject?</u>
<u>What is my theme?</u>
<u>What descriptions do I think I might use?</u>
<u>What structure will I use?</u>

---

3. **Write** Use the chart to write your poem.

Link the Readings

Make a chart like the one below to compare the readings in this unit. Look at each word in the column. Put an **X** under "The Blind Men and the Elephant" if the word reminds you of the fable. Put an **X** under "Animal Senses" if the word reminds you of that selection. Put an **X** under "Tiny Giant" if the word reminds you of the poem. Put an **X** in all places if the word reminds you of all selections.

	"The Blind Men and the Elephant"	"Animal Senses"	"Tiny Giant"
trunk	_____	_____	_____
vision	_____	_____	_____
spear	_____	_____	_____
bee	_____	_____	_____
prey	_____	_____	_____
fan	_____	_____	_____
snake	_____	_____	_____

Check Your Knowledge

Language Development
1. What is a fable? How is it different from a legend?
2. What inferences did you make about the moral of "The Blind Men and the Elephant"?
3. What is a simile? Give an example of a simile and use it in a sentence.
4. What is an adjective? Give an example using an adjective and the verb be.

Science Content
1. What senses does an elephant use to survive?
2. How do owls use their sense of vision to hunt?
3. How do honeybees use their senses of touch and smell to communicate?

The World of Plants

Plants give us food and oxygen. How do they do it? Find out when you read "Amazing Plants." The myth "Apollo and Daphne" is an ancient Roman story. Read it to learn how the beautiful laurel tree came to be. Finally, you will read a play.

Reading

1 Science	2 Myth	3 Play

"Amazing Plants"	"Apollo and Daphne"	"The Horse's Friend"
Reading Strategy: Use diagrams	**Reading Strategy:** Visualize	**Connect to Reading:** Archetypes; motifs

Listening and Speaking

In this unit, you will summarize a science text, retell a myth, and sing a folk song.

Writing

In this unit, you will create a Venn diagram, write a comparison, learn how to plan theme and mood, and write a script for a short play.

Quick Write

Do you have a favorite tree or flower? Write two or three sentences about a plant you like.

DVD

VIEW AND RESPOND
Watch the Unit 7 DVD. As you watch, answer the questions on page 235.
www.LongmanKeystone.com.

Prepare to Read

What You Will Learn

Reading

- Vocabulary building: *Context; dictionary skills*
- Reading strategy: *Preview*
- Text type: *Informational text (science)*

Academic Content

- Science vocabulary
- Parts of a plant
- Photosynthesis

► BUILD BACKGROUND

"Amazing Plants" is a nonfiction science text. It tells how plants make their own food, make seeds, and help make new plants.

▲ Giant redwood trees

TRY TO PREDICT

1 How old do you think these trees are?
2 How do you think insects, birds, and other animals help plants?

▲ Hummingbird eating the sweet liquid inside a flower

Workbook
Page 164

➤ VOCABULARY

Listening and Speaking: Key Words

Look at the pictures and the captions. They will help you learn the words in the box. Write the meaning of each highlighted word and say them aloud with a partner. Then check your work in a dictionary.

Key Words

absorb
oxygen
pollen
pollination
release
reproduce
roots
stem

Audio

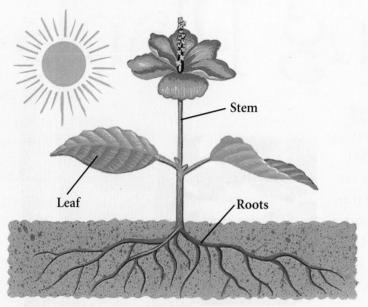

Stem

Leaf

Roots

▲ The roots of a plant absorb, or take in, water from the ground. The stem holds up the plant. The leaves absorb sunlight and release, or give off, oxygen (OX-ih-jin), an important gas.

▲ During pollination (pol-ih-NAY-shun), bees carry pollen between many different flowers. Pollen, made of tiny grains, helps plants reproduce, or make seeds for new plants.

Workbook
Pages 165–166

READING STRATEGY | USE DIAGRAMS

The **diagrams**, or labeled drawings, in a science text give you important information.

- Look at each diagram carefully.
- Read all the labels.
- How does the diagram make ideas in the text clearer?

Workbook
Page 167

Set a purpose for reading "Amazing Plants" is a nonfiction science text that tells about plants and how they grow. As you read, look carefully at the diagrams that go with the text.

Audio

Amazing Plants

Why Are Plants Amazing?

Plants are an amazing form of life. Scientists think there are about 300,000 different kinds of plants. Some plants are huge and old, like the giant redwood tree. Other plants, such as algae, are tiny and live in water. Some plants, like orchids, have beautiful flowers. Other plants, like the saguaro cactus, have sharp spines instead of leaves.

Without plants, most other forms of life on Earth could not live. Plants are an important food for many living things. People and many animals eat different parts of plants, including fruits, nuts, leafy vegetables, and seeds like grains. Plants also release oxygen into the air. People and animals need oxygen to live.

▲ Orchids have beautiful flowers.

▶ The saguaro cactus grows in the desert.

▲ Apples are a major fruit crop in the United States.

Photosynthesis

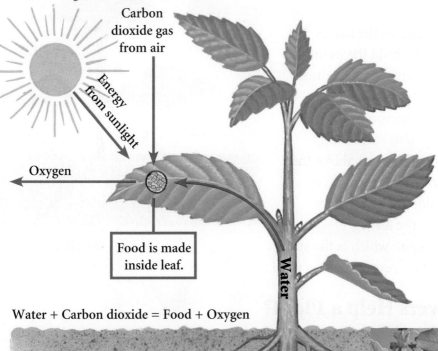

Carbon dioxide gas from air

Energy from sunlight

Oxygen

Food is made inside leaf.

Water

Water + Carbon dioxide = Food + Oxygen

▲ Plants make their own food through a process called photosynthesis.

▲ Photosynthesis happens in the leaves of plants.

How Do Plants Get Energy?

Living things need energy to grow and reproduce. People and animals get energy from food. Most plants get energy from sunlight. Plants use sunlight to make food. This process is called photosynthesis (foe-toe-SIN-thih-sis). In Greek, *photo* means "light" and *synthesis* means "put together," or "combine."

Photosynthesis happens in the leaves of plants. In photosynthesis, sunlight provides the energy needed to combine water with carbon dioxide gas from the air. This process makes food for the plant. It also releases oxygen into the air, as shown in the diagram above.

Workbook
Page 168

BEFORE YOU GO ON

1 Give examples of two different kinds of plants.

2 Name two ways that plants are important to other living things.

3 What happens in the process of photosynthesis?

What Does Each Part of a Plant Do?

The roots, the stem, and the leaves help a plant grow. Roots hold the plant in the ground. They support the plant under the ground. Hairs on the roots absorb water and minerals. Some roots—like carrots and potatoes—also store food.

The stem supports the plant above the ground. The stem connects the roots to the leaves. Tubes inside the stem carry water and minerals to the leaves.

Leaves absorb sunlight, which is the start of photosynthesis, the process of making food.

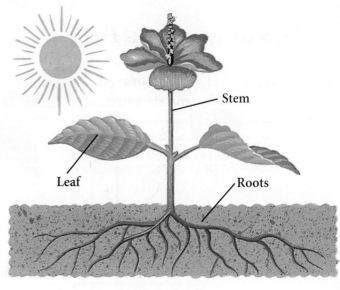

▲ Parts of a plant

How Do Flowers Help a Plant?

Flowers help a plant reproduce, or make new plants. Some plants have big, colorful flowers. The color and sweet smell attract insects, birds, and other animals. When insects and animals touch a flower, they often touch the pollen inside the flower. The pollen sticks to their bodies. Then, when the insect or animal moves to another flower, the pollen passes to that flower. This process is called pollination.

◀ Butterflies pass pollen from flower to flower in a process called pollination.

How Does a Fruit Form?

When pollen reaches the **ovary** in the center of the flower, the plant can reproduce. Parts of the pollen and ovary combine, and the ovary grows larger. It becomes a fruit with seeds inside. The fruit protects the seeds as they grow. The seeds will later become new plants. Some fruits, such as peaches, have only one large seed inside. Others, like lemons, have many seeds.

▲ A peach has one large seed.

What Is the Plant Life Cycle?

When seeds fall to the ground, they begin a new **cycle** of plant life. Rain makes the seeds soft, and roots start to grow out of the seed and into the ground. New leaves and stems form and grow above the ground. The plants produce flowers. Insects pollinate the flowers, and seeds form again. This process is called the plant life cycle. The plant life cycle is one of many cycles in nature.

▲ A lemon has many small seeds.

---

ovary, place inside a flower where fruit and seeds form
cycle, events that happen again and again in the same order

PLANT LIFE CYCLE

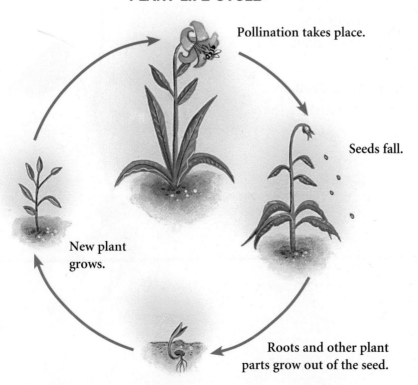

Pollination takes place.

Seeds fall.

New plant grows.

Roots and other plant parts grow out of the seed.

◀ Each event in the life cycle of flowering plants happens in the same order, year after year.

BEFORE YOU GO ON

1. What happens in a plant after pollination?

2. Explain the plant life cycle. Why is it shown as a circle?

3. What flowers grow in your home country? What do they look like? What do they smell like?

Review and Practice

▶ RETELL AND REVIEW

1. Tell a partner what you learned about plants. Use the headings and the pictures on pages 218–221 to help you. Use the Key Words. If you can't think of a word, describe it, use a synonym, or ask your teacher.

2. How did the diagrams and labels help you understand the text?

3. Explain the diagram of photosynthesis on page 219.

▶ COMPREHENSION  Workbook Page 169

Write the sentences below in your notebook. Write *Yes* if the statement is true. Write *No* if it is not true. Then rewrite the statement correctly. Reread pages 218–221 to find supporting evidence for your answers.

1. Plants make their own food. *Yes*

2. Insects, birds, and other animals pass energy from flower to flower.

3. The hairs on plant roots absorb water and minerals.

4. The stem supports the plant under the ground.

5. Photosynthesis happens in the roots of a plant.

6. Flowers help a plant reproduce.

7. A seed begins to grow in a flower after pollination.

8. The plant life cycle is the only cycle in nature.

Extension

This is a folk song about planting rows of seeds. The rhythm of the song makes it a good work song. Read the words. Then listen and sing along with the music.

Garden Song

Chorus

Inch by inch, row by row, gonna make this garden grow
All it takes is a rake and a hoe and a piece of **fertile** ground
Inch by inch, row by row, someone **bless** these seeds I **sow**
Someone warm them from below
'Till the rain comes tumbling down.

Pulling weeds and pickin' stones;
We are made of dreams and bones
I feel the need to grow my own 'cause the time is close at hand.
Grain for grain, sun and rain, I'll find my way in nature's chain
Tune my body and my brain to the music of the land.

Chorus

Plant your rows straight and long,
Temper them with prayer and song.
Mother Earth will keep you strong if you give her love and care.
An old crow watching hungrily from his **perch** in **yonder** tree.
In my garden I'm as free as that feathered thief up there.

Chorus

—David Mallett

fertile, able to grow a lot of plants
bless, say a prayer for
sow, place in the ground
temper, help, give treatment to
perch, branch, place where a bird stands
yonder, over there

Prepare to Read

What You Will Learn

Reading

- Vocabulary building: *Context; dictionary skills*

- Reading strategy: *Visualize*

- Text type: *Literature (myth and play)*

Grammar
The comparative form of adjectives

Writing
Write a comparison

➤ BUILD BACKGROUND

"Apollo and Daphne" is a piece of classical literature. It is an ancient Roman myth. In ancient times, people made up myths, or stories, to try to explain things in nature. This myth explains how the laurel tree came to be.

TRY TO PREDICT

1 What kind of arrow do you think the boy is shooting?

2 Why do you think the girl is running?

➤ VOCABULARY

Listening and Speaking: Key Words

Look at the pictures and the captions. They will help you learn the words in the box. Write the meaning of each highlighted word and say them aloud with a partner. Then check your work in a dictionary.

Key Words

arrows
bark
bow
crowns
forest

▲ Winning athletes sometimes wear crowns of laurel leaves.

◀ Many trees grow in a forest. Trees are covered with bark.

▲ Cupid played with his bow and arrows.

Workbook
Page 171

READING STRATEGY | VISUALIZE

To **visualize** means to picture people, places, or things in your mind. Visualizing helps you understand the events in a story.

- As you read, look for words that describe the characters.
- Look for details about the story's setting (time and place).
- Look for words and details that describe events and actions.

Workbook
Page 172

Set a purpose for reading Myths come from many different cultures. "Apollo and Daphne" started as a Greek myth. Then the Romans changed it a little. As you read, visualize the people, places, and events.

Apollo and Daphne

One day, Cupid, the young god of love, was playing with his little bow and arrows. The arrows were a gift from his mother, Venus. She was the goddess of love and beauty. Cupid's arrows were small, but they were powerful. They could make people fall in love.

Cupid wanted to be a hunter like Apollo, his uncle. However, Apollo didn't think Cupid was big and strong enough. One day, Apollo saw Cupid playing with his bow and arrows. "Put away your little arrows, Cupid," he said. "You can't be a hunter. You need to be bigger and stronger."

Apollo's words made Cupid angry. "You and your arrows are bigger," Cupid said, "but my arrows are more powerful." Cupid shot one of his arrows at Apollo and hit him. Cupid's arrow made Apollo fall in love with Daphne, the daughter of the river god, Peneus (puh-NEE-us).

Daphne was very beautiful. She had long hair and fair skin. Daphne was also very shy. She did not like talking to people, so she lived alone in the forest.

As soon as Apollo saw Daphne in the forest, he fell in love with her. He wanted to talk to her, so he followed her. Daphne was afraid and ran away from Apollo. She did not love him.

Apollo ran after her. "Daphne! Please, wait!" Apollo cried. "I love you. I am not your enemy." But Daphne did not stop. She ran farther into the forest.

They ran and ran. Daphne was fast, but Apollo was faster. Soon Daphne was tired, and Apollo came closer. Daphne called to her father, Peneus. "Father! I'm tired! You must help me!" The river god heard his daughter's voice.

"Don't worry, Daphne," he cried. "I am here. I will help you!"

BEFORE YOU GO ON

1. What did Cupid's arrow do to Apollo?
2. Are there forests in your home country? Explain.
3. Do you know any myths? Talk about them.

Reading 2 **227**

Suddenly, Daphne began to change. Her feet became roots, and they grew into the earth. Her arms became branches, and her hair became leaves. Daphne's body became covered in bark. She was now a beautiful laurel tree.

Apollo was amazed. He touched her branches and leaves. "You cannot be my wife," Apollo said sadly, "but you will always be my special tree. I will wear your leaves as my crown forever."

From that day, Apollo gave laurel crowns to all the great musicians, poets, and athletes in honor of Daphne, his one great love.

Even in our time, we still give laurel crowns to honor great athletes.

BEFORE YOU GO ON

1 What happened to Daphne?

2 What do laurel crowns mean today?

3 Have you read any books or seen any movies about classical mythology? Share with the class.

Apollo and Daphne
❦ A Play ❦

Now read the same myth as a play.
There are seven parts.

CHARACTERS

Narrator	**Daphne**
Venus	**Peneus**
Cupid	**Chorus**
Apollo	

Narrator: One day, Cupid was playing with his little bow and arrows. They were a gift from his mother, Venus. She was the goddess of love and beauty.

Venus: Be careful, Cupid. Those are special love arrows. They're very powerful.

Cupid *(aiming his bow and arrow):* I want to be a hunter like Uncle Apollo.

Apollo *(laughing):* You can't be a hunter, Cupid. You're too small. You need to be bigger and stronger.

Cupid *(angrily):* Your arrows are bigger than mine, Uncle Apollo. But my arrows are more powerful!

Chorus: Cupid shot one of his arrows and hit Apollo.

Venus: Oh, no! Now Apollo will fall in love.

Narrator: Apollo was walking in the forest. Suddenly, he saw a beautiful young woman.

Apollo: It's Daphne, daughter of Peneus. She is very beautiful.

Chorus: Apollo wanted to talk to Daphne. He followed her.

Daphne: Go away, Apollo! Don't follow me.

Narrator: Daphne was afraid, and she ran away.

Apollo: Daphne! Please, wait! I love you. I am not your enemy.

Chorus: They ran and ran. Daphne was fast, but Apollo was faster.

Daphne: Father! I'm tired! You must help me!

Peneus: Don't worry, Daphne. I'm here. I will help you!

Narrator: Suddenly, Daphne began to change.

Chorus: Her feet became roots. Her arms became branches, and her hair became leaves.

Narrator: Daphne's body became covered in bark.

Chorus: She had become a beautiful laurel tree!

Apollo: You will always be my special tree. I will wear your leaves as my crown forever.

Narrator: From that day forward, Apollo always wore a crown of laurel leaves. And he gave crowns of laurel leaves to all the great musicians, poets, and athletes.

Review and Practice

➤ RETELL AND REVIEW

1. Look back at the pictures in "Apollo and Daphne" on pages 226–228. Cover the words on each page. Retell the events of the story to a partner, using only the pictures. Use the Key Words. If you can't think of a word, describe it, use a synonym, or ask your teacher.

2. Did you visualize the myth the way the artist who drew the pictures did? Explain.

3. Draw a picture that shows how you visualized Daphne turning into a tree.

➤ COMPREHENSION

Workbook Page 174

Complete the sentences. Choose the correct word from the column on the right. Write the completed sentences in your notebook.

1. Cupid was playing with his bow and _arrows_ .   Peneus

2. Venus was the goddess of love and _____.   athletes

3. Cupid shot an arrow at _____.   river god

4. Daphne was the daughter of _____.   laurel tree

5. When Apollo called out to Daphne, she _____.   ~~arrows~~

6. Daphne's father was the _____.   Apollo

7. Suddenly, Daphne began to change into a _____.   ran away

8. Apollo gave laurel crowns to great musicians,   beauty
   poets, and _____.

Song

Scientists think that an ancient redwood tree in California is about
12,000 years old! This song tells about some events in history that
happened during the life of this amazing tree.

Giant Silent Redwood

Chorus

Giant Silent Redwood tell me what you know
Giant Silent Redwood tell me what you know
Stand and tell me what you know

Antony and Cleopatra kissed upon the Nile
You stood there Giant Redwood,
Tell me, did they smile?
Tell me, did they smile?

Chorus

Marco Polo walked to China, worked for
    Kublai Khan
You stood there Giant Redwood
Tell me how to move on
Tell me how to move on

Chorus

By, of, and for the people, Lincoln made
    a speech
You stood there Giant Redwood
Tell me how to teach
Tell me how to teach

Chorus

Loggers in the woods got their eye on you
You stand yet Giant Redwood
Tell me what to do
Tell me what to do
You stand yet Giant Redwood
Tell me what to do
Tell me what to do

—Dan Scanlan

Grammar

The Comparative Form of Adjectives

Use the **comparative form** of an adjective to compare two people, places, or things.

For most one-syllable adjectives, add -er + than.

adjective	comparative
Cupid was **young**.	Cupid was **younger than** Apollo.
Daphne was **fast**.	Apollo was **faster than** Daphne.

For two-syllable adjectives that end in -y, change the y to i and add -er + than.

adjective	comparative
Cupid was **angry**.	Cupid was **angrier than** Apollo.

For most adjectives with two or more syllables, use more + adjective + than.

Cupid's arrows were **more powerful than** Apollo's.

Daphne was **more tired than** Apollo.

Practice  **Workbook** Page 175

Copy these sentences in your notebook. Complete each sentence with the comparative form of the adjective in parentheses.

1. Cupid's arrows were _____*smaller*_____ than Apollo's. (small)

2. Venus was _____ than Daphne. (beautiful)

3. Apollo was _____ than Cupid. (strong)

4. Lions are _____ than elephants. (dangerous)

5. My Spanish homework is _____ than my English homework. (easy)

6. A peach seed is _____ than a lemon seed. (large)

7. Apollo was _____ than Peneus. (famous)

8. My science class is _____ than my social studies class. (difficult)

Writing

Write a Comparison

A comparison tells how two people, places, or things are alike and different. In a two-paragraph comparison, explain how the things are alike in the first paragraph. Then tell how they are different in the second paragraph. Use the word *both* to show how the things are alike. Use the comparative form of adjectives to show how they are different.

Read this two-paragraph comparison. Then answer the questions.

Eddie Monroy

Two Amazing Plants

A giant redwood and a saguaro cactus are alike in some ways. They both grow in the United States. Both are very tall plants. Both plants live to be very old. A redwood can live more than 3,000 years, and a saguaro can live to be 200 years old.

The giant redwood and the saguaro cactus are also different in many ways. The giant redwood grows taller and lives longer than the saguaro cactus. The giant redwood is covered with strong bark. The saguaro cactus is covered with sharp spines. The giant redwood needs a lot of rain and fog. The saguaro cactus needs little rain and lots of sun.

1. What two things does the writer compare?
2. What does the writer explain in the first paragraph? In the second paragraph?
3. What comparative forms does the writer use? What do they show?

Workbook
Pages 176–177

Practice

Workbook Page 178

You will write a two-paragraph comparison of two plants.

1. Read Reread the comparison on page 233. How does the writer show that the two kinds of plants are alike and different?

Writing Strategy: Venn Diagram

A Venn diagram shows how two things are alike and different. Eddie made this Venn diagram to compare a giant redwood and a saguaro cactus. The middle of his diagram shows how both plants are alike. The left and right parts of his diagram show how the plants are different.

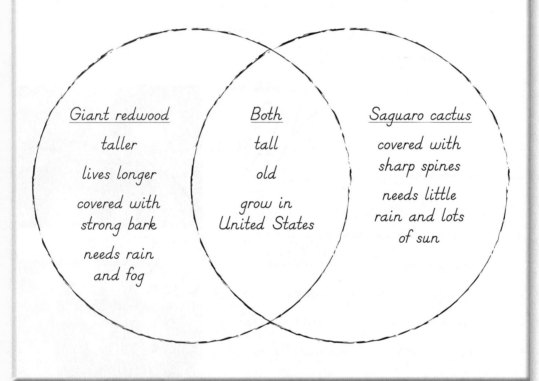

Giant redwood
taller
lives longer
covered with strong bark
needs rain and fog

Both
tall
old
grow in United States

Saguaro cactus
covered with sharp spines
needs little rain and lots of sun

---

2. Make a Venn diagram Draw a Venn diagram in your notebook. List ways your two plants are alike and different.

3. Write Use your Venn diagram to write two paragraphs comparing your plants. In the first paragraph, explain how the plants are alike. In the second paragraph, tell how they are different. Edit your work. Make sure you use compound subjects correctly.

Prepare to Read

► **BUILD BACKGROUND**

You will read a short play about a boy's special connection to the natural world. Billy surprises his workmates when he tames a wild horse. Have you ever ridden a horse? Share your experience with the class.

What You Will Learn

Reading

■ Vocabulary building: *Roots from other languages*

■ Connect to reading: *Archetypes; Motifs*

■ Text type: *Literature (play)*

Writing

■ Plan theme and mood

■ Write a script

BOOST YOUR LISTENING COMPREHENSION

Unit 7: The World of Plants

Your teacher will play the DVD for this unit. After you listen, answer these questions.

1. What do we call the stem of a tree?

2. What is the function of a tree's bark?

3. What is photosynthesis? Describe the process.

4. What is the main difference between deciduous and evergreen trees?

5. How long do trees live?

6. Why are trees an important part of our habitat?

➤ CONNECT TO VOCABULARY

Roots from Other Languages

Many English words used in your classes come from Latin and Greek roots. If you know what the roots, or main parts of a word, mean, you can figure out the meaning of the whole word more easily. Look at the example below. Can you guess what the word *autograph* means?

autograph = *auto* ("self") + *graph* ("write")

Use the following roots to understand words in your English, math, social studies, and science classes.

Root	Language It Comes From	Meaning
bio	Greek	life
therm	Greek	heat
junct	Latin	join
meter	Greek	measure

Many English words also have prefixes and suffixes from other languages. A prefix comes before a root. A suffix comes after a root.

Prefix or Suffix	Language It Comes From	Meaning
anti-	Latin	against
pre-	Latin	before
-ful	Old English	full of
-less	Old English	without

Practice  **Workbook** Pages 179–180

Use roots, prefixes, or suffixes to figure out the meaning of each underlined word. Then check your work in a dictionary.

1. Miguel is studying the <u>antislavery</u> movement in history class.

2. Maya had a <u>wonderful</u> time at the concert last week.

3. The <u>thermometer</u> outside our back door reads 78 degrees Fahrenheit.

4. The <u>speedometer</u> said we were going 45 miles per hour.

Archetypes

An **archetype** is an original model or pattern that other people copy. An archetype can be a kind of character or a situation. Archetypes from long ago still appear in stories, plays, poems, and movies today. Below are some examples:

Archetype	Description	Examples
Hero	Someone who is very brave	Odysseus (*Odyssey*, 8th century B.C.E.), Superman (comic-book hero, 1930s)
Wise Person	Someone very smart	Merlin (wizard in legends of King Arthur), Obi-Wan Kenobi (Jedi teacher in *Star Wars*, 1977)
Innocent Person	Someone pure, simple, trusting, and honest	Jane Eyre (novel by Charlotte Brontë, 1847), The Little Prince (novella by Antoine de Saint-Exupéry, 1943)
Tragic Lovers	Sweethearts who are doomed or who are separated	Romeo and Juliet (Shakespearean characters, 1595), Rose and Jack (*Titanic*, 1997)
Outsider or Outcast	Person who is not part of society or a main social group	Oedipus (character in Sophocles' plays, 5th century B.C.E.), Ugly Duckling (fairy tale character, 1843)

Here are some examples of situation archetypes:

Archetype	Description	Examples
Quest	A long, hard search for something precious	Gilgamesh's journey to find eternal life (Sumerian myth, 2000 B.C.E.), Jason's search for the golden fleece (Greek myth, 8th century B.C.E.)
Task	A difficult job that must be done to earn something precious	The ten labors of Hercules (ancient Roman myth, 2nd century B.C.E.)
Triumph of Good over Evil	Good characters winning out over bad characters	Dorothy and her friends (*The Wizard of Oz*, 1900), Despereaux Tilling (*The Tale of Despereaux*, 2003)

Motifs

A **motif** is a repeated idea or description. Writers use motifs to express important ideas. For example, the jewel in "Jewel in the Sand" in Unit 1 is a motif. The word *jewel* is repeated many times. It develops the idea that a good character is more valuable than "precious" gems.

Animal motifs are also common in stories, especially folktales. In these tales, owls often represent wisdom. Foxes and coyotes often represent slyness, or the ability to trick others.

Many motifs are used over and over again. For example, many stories are about the difference between truth and lies or the difference between darkness and lightness. Look at the chart for more examples of motifs.

Motif	Description
wishes	People make silly or thoughtless wishes that come true.
night and day	Bad things happen at night; good things happen in the light of day.
revenge	Someone is hurt by another person. He or she then tries to hurt that person in return.

Archetypes and motifs often work together to express an important idea. In "Jewel in the Sand," for example, there is a quest for love from a beautiful and kind princess. The jewel motif adds a new idea to the quest. Just as the princess generously gives her jewels to the old woman, the sheik selflessly gives the princess back to her intended groom.

Practice  Workbook Page 182

In a small group, talk about the archetypes in the charts. Answer the following questions.

1. What are some other archetypes from stories you have read or movies you have seen?

2. Are there any motifs in stories you have read or movies you have seen?

Then discuss whether there are any motifs in the stories or movies.

Set a purpose for reading The Horse's Friend is a short play. As you read the play, notice the stage directions. They tell you what the actors should do and how they should do it.

Characters: Billy, Mr. Hernández, Juan, Ben

The Horse's Friend

The play takes place on a ranch. It is morning. Billy is a new worker at the ranch. He is wearing new clothes that are too big.

Billy: *[Walks up to Mr. Hernández and shakes his hand.]* Good morning, Mr. Hernández. I am ready to work.

Mr. Hernández: Follow me. *[Walks to the stable, Billy behind him.]* Juan! Ben! Come out here! *[Walking away]* Good-bye, Billy.

Juan: *[Walks from stable towards Billy.]* Howdy.

Billy: *[Holds out his hand for a handshake, but Juan does not shake his hand.]* Nice to meet you, Juan.

Juan: *[Shouts to Ben.]* Get out here!

Ben: *[Walks to Billy.]* You are just a kid. Can you do a man's work? You do not even fit in those men's clothes. They are too big for you.

[Before Billy can answer, a loud noise comes from the stable. All three turn and hurry in. A horse rears and kicks at its stall.]

Billy: *[Directly approaches the horse. Whispers as he grabs her lead.]* It is all right, girl. Settle down. You are okay. I am your friend.

Ben: Get out of the way, boy! That horse is crazy! Let me at her!

Juan: *[To Billy]* Look out! You are going to get kicked!

Billy: *[Does not listen to Ben and Juan. Keeps whispering to horse.]* Easy, girl. I am Billy. I am your friend. Do not be afraid.

Juan: *[With a look of surprise as the horse quiets]* I cannot believe my eyes!

Ben: I guess you are not as inexperienced as you look, Billy. I am sorry about what I said. Your clothes may be too big, but you can sure do a man's work.

Juan and Ben: *[Together]* Good to work with you, Billy.

"Get out of the way, boy! That horse is crazy!"

SUPPORT YOUR READING EXPERIENCE

The more you read, the larger your vocabulary knowledge becomes. Now that you have read this play, go to www.LongmanKeystone.com and do the activity for this unit. You will learn ways to use kinesthetic visual support to develop vocabulary and structures and to build more background knowledge.

Workbook
Pages 183–184

BEFORE YOU GO ON

1. Who are the characters in the play?

2. How do the stage directions help you understand what happens?

3. Do you think Billy fit the archetype of the Innocent Person? Why or why not?

Writing

Plan Theme and Mood and Write a Script

Every play has a theme and at least one mood.

A **theme** is the main idea of a play. Sometimes, the theme of a play is stated, or spoken. For example, Akwasi states the theme of "The Great Minu," in Unit 5, when he says, "I have many things to be thankful for. It is good to be alive."

Other times, the theme is not stated. To find an unstated theme, think about what the characters learn from their experiences. For example, Juan and Ben in "The Horse's Friend" learn that it is wrong to judge someone by his age or looks. That is the theme.

The **mood** of a play is the feelings it creates in the audience. A play can make people feel happy, sad, fearful, or cheerful. The mood of a play may change. For example, the mood is tense and fearful in the middle of "The Horse's Friend." At the end of the play, the mood is happy.

Here are a student writer's notes for a play.

Notes for a Play

My play will be about two sisters. One night, they are baby-sitting. They hear strange noises. They are scared. Is a stranger in the house? No, it is just the wind. From this experience, the sisters learn to be more confident. They learn that it is good to be careful but not fearful. I want my play to be scary. At the end, though, everyone should feel happy.

1. What will the theme of the play be?

2. What moods will it create in the audience?

Workbook
Page 185

You will write a script for a short play.

1. **Read** Reread the student writer's notes on page 241. Think of something you would like to write about.

2. **Make a script chart** Make a script chart for your play. Use the chart on this page as a model.

Writing Strategy: Writing a Script

Think about your play. Who will be in it? What will happen to them? Use a script chart like the one below to organize your ideas as you plan your play.

What happens? (plot)
What do the characters learn? (theme)
How does the audience feel? (mood)

---

3. **Write** Use your chart to write a script for a short play. Be sure to include a character list, dialogue, and stage directions. Remember to use brackets or parentheses to offset your stage directions.

IMPROVE YOUR WRITING SKILLS

When you write, you write for a particular reader, or "audience." Good writers are careful about selecting the correct genre and determining an appropriate topic to write about. Go to www.LongmanKeystone.com and do the activity for this unit. You will learn strategies to help you convey meaning appropriately to different types of audiences.

Link the Readings

Make a chart like the one below to compare the readings in this unit. Look at each word in the column. Put an **X** under "Amazing Plants" if the word reminds you of that selection. Put an **X** under "Apollo and Daphne" if the word reminds you of the myth. Put an **X** under "The Horse's Friend" if the word reminds you of the play. Put an **X** in all places if the word reminds you of all selections.

	"Amazing Plants"	"Apollo and Daphne"	"The Horse's Friend"
fiction	_____	_____	_____
nonfiction	_____	_____	_____
photosynthesis	_____	_____	_____
roots and leaves	_____	_____	_____
laurel tree	_____	_____	_____
giant redwood	_____	_____	_____
pollination	_____	_____	_____
character	_____	_____	_____

Check Your Knowledge

Language Development
1. How can diagrams help you understand a nonfiction text?
2. What does visualize mean?
3. What is the comparative form of the adjective *short*?
4. What is the comparative form of the adjective *dangerous*?

Science Content
1. Name three parts of a plant. What does each part do?
2. How do insects and animals help with pollination?
3. Why is photosynthesis important to a plant?
4. Explain what happens in the plant cycle.

Wings

In this unit, you will learn about Bessie Coleman. Bessie Coleman dreamed of flying and worked hard to make her dream come true. You will also read a poem about dreams and flying. Then you will read a story about a boy who rescues a pigeon with a broken wing. You will also read about a bird that saved the lives of American soldiers. Finally, you will read a short story about a boy who learns to spell new words in a surprising way.

Reading

1 Social Studies	2 Poem	3 Short Story

"Bessie Coleman, American Flyer"	"This Big Sky"	"Aaron's Gift"
Reading Strategy: Summarize	**Reading Strategy:** Summarize	**Reading Strategy:** Understand an author's purpose

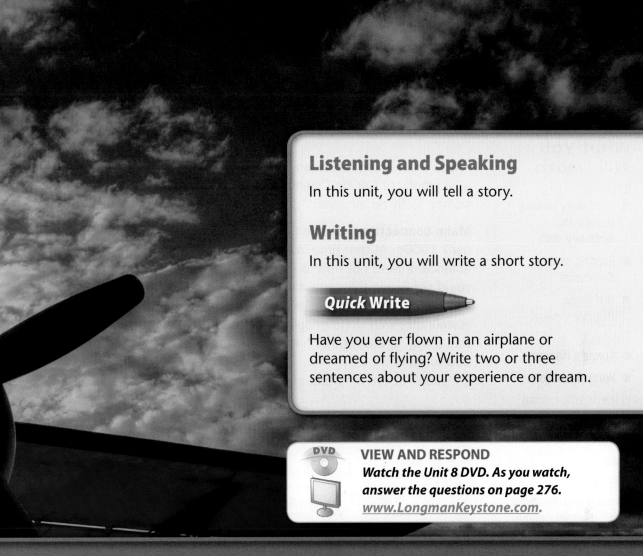

Listening and Speaking

In this unit, you will tell a story.

Writing

In this unit, you will write a short story.

Quick Write

Have you ever flown in an airplane or dreamed of flying? Write two or three sentences about your experience or dream.

DVD

VIEW AND RESPOND
Watch the Unit 8 DVD. As you watch, answer the questions on page 276.
www.LongmanKeystone.com.

| 4 | Social Studies | 5 | Short Story |

"Cher Ami—World War I Hero"

Reading Strategy:
Understand an author's purpose

"The Goat and the Bee"

Connect to Reading:
Figurative language; Procedural texts; Genres

What You Will Learn

Reading
- Vocabulary building: *Visual cues, dictionary skills*
- Reading strategy: *Summarize*
- Text types: *Biography, poem*

Writing
- Create a diagram
- Write instructions

Listening/Speaking
- Group discussion
- Poetry

Grammar
Imperatives

Viewing/Representing
Maps, diagrams, photos

Academic Content
- Social studies vocabulary
- Bessie Coleman
- Early aviation

▶ BUILD BACKGROUND

"Bessie Coleman, American Flyer" is a nonfiction text. It is a biography of Bessie Coleman, the first African-American woman to fly an airplane.

Make connections Bessie Coleman grew up in Texas in the early 1900s. At that time in the American South, African Americans were not free to live as they wished. Black people could not live in the same neighborhoods or go to the same schools as white people. They could not even eat in restaurants with white people. For Bessie Coleman, there was a way to escape her hard life and feel free. That way was to fly.

Look at the map and answer the questions.

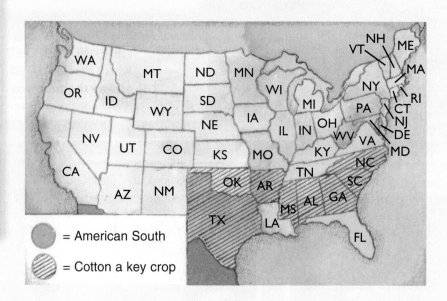

1. Which states are part of the American South?
2. In which states was cotton a key crop?
3. What inference can you make about cotton and the American South?

Workbook
Page 187

246 Unit 8

► VOCABULARY

Listening and Speaking: Key Words

Look at the pictures and the captions. They will help you learn the words in the box. Write the meaning of each highlighted word and say them aloud with a partner. Then use a dictionary, the glossary, or a thesaurus to determine or confirm your answers.

Key Words

encouraged
famous
publisher
thrilling
toured

Audio

▲ Bessie toured the country in her plane. She did flying tricks and put on thrilling, or exciting, air shows.

◄ Robert Abbott was a newspaper publisher, or owner. He encouraged Bessie to go to France.

BLACK HERITAGE

USA 32

BESSIE COLEMAN

◄ Bessie Coleman is famous. This U.S. postage stamp was made in her honor.

Workbook
Pages 188–189

READING STRATEGY | SUMMARIZE

To **summarize** means to state or write the main ideas of a text in your own words.

- As you read, summarize each section.
- Keep your summaries simple. Include only important facts.
- After you finish reading the text, review your summaries. This will help you understand and remember the main ideas.

Workbook
Page 190

Set a purpose for reading "Bessie Coleman, American Flyer" is a biography of the first African-American woman pilot. As you read, summarize each section.

Audio

BESSIE COLEMAN
AMERICAN FLYER

Bessie Coleman was the first African American to get an international pilot's **license**. She was also the first African-American woman to fly an airplane. Bessie was brave, smart, and determined to do something special with her life. She did not let **prejudice** stop her.

Bessie's Childhood

Bessie Coleman was born into a large family in Atlanta, Texas, on January 26, 1892. She grew up in a time of **discrimination**. In the South, African Americans couldn't go to school with white people. They couldn't eat at the same table or ride in the same train car. Life was very hard.

Bessie's parents were hard-working cotton farmers. They moved the family to the small city of Waxahachie, Texas. The whole family worked in the cotton fields at harvest time. When not helping out in the field, Bessie and her brothers and sisters went to a one-room schoolhouse for African-American children.

▲ Bessie Coleman

▼ Picking cotton at harvest time

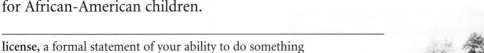

---

license, a formal statement of your ability to do something
prejudice, an unfair dislike of someone who is of another race or religion
discrimination, treating one group of people in an unfair way

◀ An African-American schoolroom in the early 1900s

The school had few supplies. Sometimes there were not enough books, pencils, or paper to go around. But that didn't stop Bessie from walking four miles there and four miles back. Bessie loved school and was a great reader. She was also very good at math and soon became the family's bookkeeper. Bessie completed all eight grades at her school and wanted to learn more. She saved her money and went to an African-American college for one year. Then her money ran out, and she went back home to work.

▲ Chicago in the 1920s

The Beginning of a Dream

When she was twenty-three, Bessie moved to Chicago to live with her brother. She hoped to find a better life there. Soon her mother and three younger sisters moved to Chicago, too. Bessie loved the excitement of the big city. She watched the great musician Louis Armstrong and other talented African-American performers play jazz. Chicago was an exciting place to be.

Bessie soon got a job at a barber shop. There, she listened to men tell stories about World War I. Some of them had been pilots in France. Bessie decided that she wanted to become a pilot, too. But who would teach her? Flight schools were all-white and all-male. There were no African-American instructors then. Bessie had to find a way to make her dream come true.

BEFORE YOU GO ON

1 How did Bessie Coleman spend her days as a child?

2 What was Bessie Coleman's dream?

How About You?
Do you like small towns or big cities? Explain.

◀ Bessie flew a Curtiss JN-4 biplane.

Bessie's friend Robert Abbott was the publisher of the *Chicago Defender,* a newspaper that wrote about African Americans at a time when other papers did not. He encouraged Bessie to go to flight school in France. First, Bessie studied French. Then she sailed on a ship to France.

The flight training was difficult and dangerous. Sometimes the 27-foot **biplanes** they used had accidents, and some pilots were killed. But Bessie did not give up. On June 15, 1921, she received her international pilot's license. Bessie was finally a pilot!

Returning Home

Bessie returned to the United States in September 1921. Many newspaper reporters came to meet her. Bessie dressed like a pilot. She wore tall, shiny boots and a helmet with goggles. Large crowds watched her thrilling air shows.

Bessie became famous. She was the guest of honor at an African-American musical. The audience stood up and clapped and clapped for her. Bessie was proud of her own accomplishments, and she was proud to be an African American.

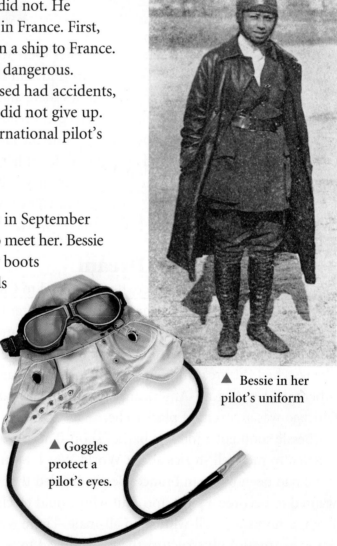

▲ Bessie in her pilot's uniform

▲ Goggles protect a pilot's eyes.

---

biplanes, airplanes with two main supporting panels

Free to Fly

For the next five years, Bessie toured the country. Thousands of people came to watch her perform thrilling stunts at her air shows. Bessie encouraged other African Americans to fly. "The air is the only place free from prejudices," she said. Bessie wanted to start a flight school for African Americans. To gain support for the school, she traveled across the country to give flying shows.

Bessie practiced before each show. Her last performance—and her last flight—was on April 30, 1926. Her plane went into a **tailspin**, and Bessie fell to her death.

Bessie's body was brought home to Chicago. Many, many people went to her funeral. They wanted to honor the woman who had the courage to follow her dream.

Bessie Remembered

Bessie Coleman's flying career was short, but her skill and love of flying are still remembered. She has **inspired** countless young African Americans to become pilots. Many flying clubs are named for her. A street in Chicago is now called Bessie Coleman Drive. In 1995, a U.S. postage stamp was made in her honor. Every spring, African-American pilots fly over "Brave Bessie's" grave in Chicago. They drop flowers on the grave in honor of the little girl with a big dream.

BLACK HERITAGE
USA 32
BESSIE COLEMAN

---

tailspin, an uncontrolled fall of a plane through the air
inspired, encouraged someone to do something good

They Can't Keep Us Down

◀ This cartoon celebrated Bessie's success as a pilot. What does the caption mean?

BEFORE YOU GO ON

1 Why was Bessie Coleman an unusual pilot?

2 Describe how people remember Bessie.

💡 **On Your Own**
Bessie's dream was to become a pilot. What is your dream?

➤ **COMPREHENSION**  **Workbook** Page 191

The list of events below from "Bessie Coleman, American Flyer" are out of order. Reread the biography on pages 248–251. Copy the chart below in your notebook. Then put the events in their correct time order.

Events: Bessie got her pilot's license.
Bessie returned to the United States.
~~Bessie worked hard in school.~~
Bessie listened to Louis Armstrong and other Chicago jazz musicians.
Bessie went to France.
Bessie toured the country in air shows.

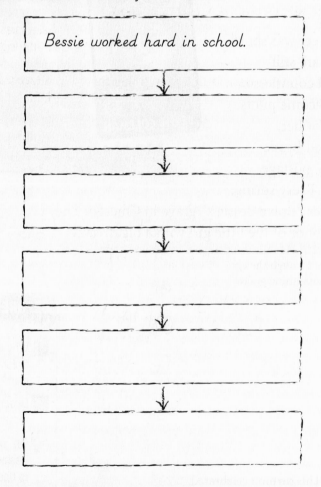

Bessie worked hard in school.

Compare charts with a partner.

► EXTENSION

Find out about some other famous pilots. Examples include the Wright brothers, Charles Lindbergh, and Amelia Earhart. Use the following sources:

- biographies
- books about the history of aviation
- the Internet
- encyclopedias

Write a short report telling what you learned about the pilot. Share your report with your classmates.

► DISCUSSION

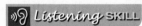
Listening SKILL

Implicit ideas are ideas that are not stated directly. Listen to your classmates carefully for implicit ideas. Listen for clues, such as examples, word choice, or intonation.

Discuss in pairs or small groups.

1. Why do you think Bessie Coleman wanted to become a pilot?
2. Why was it difficult for her to become a pilot?
3. How did Bessie use her fame to help others?
4. What conclusions can you draw about Bessie Coleman's desire for freedom?

▼ Charles Lindbergh

THIS BIG SKY

This sky is big enough
for all my dreams.

Two **ravens** burst black
from a piñon tree
into the blare
of blazing sun.

I follow their wide **ebony** flight
over **copper** hills,
down canyons **shimmering** gold
autumn leaves.

Two ravens spread their wings, rise
into **whispers**
of giant **pines**, over mountains blue
with **memories**.

This sky is big enough
for all my dreams.

—**Pat Mora**

---

ravens, large black birds
ebony, black
copper, orange-brown
shimmering, shining and shaking
whispers, soft sounds
pines, trees with green needles
memories, things you remember

Reading Skill

Poets choose their words carefully to convey specific ideas. Which words seem important to you as you read the poem? What ideas do they convey? Discuss with a partner.

BEFORE YOU GO ON

1 What did you visualize as you read the poem?

2 What idea is repeated in the poem?

On Your Own
How do you feel when you watch a bird flying? Explain.

Link the Readings

► REFLECTION

Reread the selections on pages 248–251 and page 254. Then copy the chart in your notebook and complete it.

Title	Type of Text	What It's About	Main Idea
"Bessie Coleman, American Flyer"			
"This Big Sky"			

► DISCUSSION

Speaking SKILL

If you make a mistake as you are speaking, stop and correct yourself.

Discuss in pairs or small groups.

1. How are the ideas about flying alike in both selections?
2. Do you think Bessie Coleman would like the poem "This Big Sky"? Explain.
3. Have you ever flown in a plane? If so, tell about it.

Grammar

Imperatives

Use **imperatives** to give instructions, directions, or orders. The subject of an imperative sentence is usually *you*. The subject is usually not stated.

subject	verb	
	Open	your books to page 24.
(You)	**Turn**	right on Main Street.
	Finish	your homework.

Reading **Skill**

Imperatives appear routinely in classroom materials. They also appear in cookbooks, instruction manuals, and user guides.

Use *please* to make an imperative more polite. *Please* can come at the beginning or the end of a sentence. Use a comma when *please* comes at the end.

> **Please** eat your breakfast.
> Wash the dishes, **please**.

Practice  Workbook Page 192

Read the eight examples. In your notebook, write an imperative sentence for each example.

1. John wants Sam to stop talking. John should say:
   Please stop talking, Sam.

2. It might rain, so Dana wants her daughter Angela to take an umbrella. Dana should say:

3. Luke the dog is about to grab Molly's sandwich. Molly should say:

4. Steve is at track practice. Paula wants to meet him afterward. Paula should say:

5. Ahmed loves milk shakes. Ahmed's dad makes great milk shakes. Ahmed should tell his dad:

6. Irina has a bad cold. Nicolo wants her to feel better. Nicolo should say:

7. Lee wants her brother Tim to feed her bird. Lee should say:

8. Jake can't answer the phone. His sister Sally is sitting right next to the phone. Jake should say:

Writing

Write Instructions

Instructions should be easy to understand. Here are some ways to write good instructions:

- Organize your instructions in numbered steps.
- Make sure that each step is simple and clear.
- If possible, include a diagram to show each step.
- Ask a classmate to read your instructions. Can he or she follow them easily?

How to Make a Paper Airplane, by Kevin Eng

1. Fold the paper in half. Open the paper and fold the top corners down.

2. Fold each side across the dotted lines to make wings.

3. Bring the wings together. Then fold each wing down along the dotted lines.

1. How are the instructions organized?
2. How does Kevin make the instructions simple and clear?
3. How do the diagrams make the instructions easier to understand?

Workbook
Page 193

Practice

Workbook Page 194

You will write instructions that explain how to do or make something. Here are some ideas:

- how to make scrambled eggs
- how to make your bed
- how to send and receive e-mail
- how to wash and dry clothes
- how to teach a dog to catch a ball

1. Read Look back at the model on page 257. Are the instructions easy to understand?

Writing Strategy: Draw Diagrams

Diagrams can help make instructions easier to understand and follow. On page 257, Kevin's diagrams show what the paper airplane looks like as you do each step. The diagrams show information that Kevin does not need to include in his writing. You can use similar diagrams to make your instructions easier to understand.

---

2. Draw diagrams Draw a picture of each step of your instructions.

3. Write Write step-by-step instructions for the process you are going to describe. When you finish, reread your instructions. Are they clear? Are they easy to follow? Are they complete? Be sure you have included all the necessary information. Read your instructions aloud to a partner. See whether he or she can follow them. Ask your partner for feedback about how to clarify your instructions.

Check Your Knowledge

► LANGUAGE DEVELOPMENT

1. How did summarizing the biography in Reading 1 help you remember the main ideas?

2. Write an imperative sentence. What is the subject of your sentence?

3. What is a good way to organize instructions? How can drawing diagrams help make your instructions easier to understand?

► ACADEMIC CONTENT

1. What social studies words did you learn in Reading 1? What do the words mean?

2. Who was Bessie Coleman?

3. How did Bessie Coleman inspire other people?

4. What visual images do you remember from the poem "This Big Sky"? Explain.

Prepare to Read

What You Will Learn

Reading

- Vocabulary building: *Visual cues, dictionary skills*

- Reading strategy: *Understand an author's purpose*

- Text types: *Short story, social studies text*

Writing

- Create an outline

- Write a review

Listening/Speaking

- Retell a story

- Discussion

Grammar
Subject-verb agreement

Viewing/Representing
Charts, photos, illustrations, maps

Academic Content

- Social studies vocabulary

- World War I

- Eastern European history

➤ BUILD BACKGROUND

"Aaron's Gift" is a short story. It takes place in New York City in the 1940s. The main character is a boy named Aaron, who lives with his parents and grandmother. In the story, Aaron remembers his grandmother's story about something that happened to her as a girl in Ukraine. When the story was written, Ukraine was called "the Ukraine." In the early 1900s, soldiers called Cossacks persecuted Jewish people in Russia and Ukraine—they treated them cruelly because of their religious beliefs. Cossacks sometimes destroyed villages and killed many people. Over time, many Jews left Ukraine and Russia and came to the United States.

Make connections Aaron's grandmother lived through a Cossack attack as a young girl. In the story, Aaron uses the name "Cossacks" to describe some boys who are cruel.
    Look at the map and answer the questions.

1. Is Ukraine east or west of the major part of Russia?
2. What three countries are south of Russia?

► VOCABULARY

Listening and Speaking: Key Words

Look at the pictures and the captions. They will help you learn the words in the box. Write the meaning of each highlighted word and say them aloud with a partner. Then use a dictionary, the glossary, or a thesaurus to determine or confirm your answers.

Key Words

broken
grabbed
leaped
soothe
wounded

Audio

▲ The wounded pigeon did not move. Its left wing was broken.

▲ Aaron gently picked up the bird and tried to soothe, or comfort, it.

▲ Aaron leaped up and grabbed the bird with his hands.

Workbook
Page 195

READING STRATEGY | UNDERSTAND AN AUTHOR'S PURPOSE

Authors write fiction for different purposes, or reasons. For example, sometimes an **author's purpose** is to entertain the reader. Sometimes his or her purpose is to teach the reader something. An author may have more than one purpose for writing.

- As you read, think about the author's purpose for writing the story.
- Write down words and details that show the author's purpose.
- Reread the story. Do you think the author had one—or more than one—purpose?

Workbook
Page 196

Set a purpose for reading "Aaron's Gift" is a short story about a boy who finds a hurt pigeon. By helping the bird, he learns an important lesson. As you read, think about the author's purpose for writing this story.

Aaron's Gift

Adapted from the story by Myron Levoy

Aaron went to Tompkins Square Park to roller-skate because the streets around his house were too crowded with children and dogs and traffic. He skated back and forth, pretending he was in a race. Then he noticed a pigeon on the grass.

The pigeon looked hurt. It tried to fly, but its left wing wouldn't flap. Aaron thought the wing looked broken. He took a cookie from his pocket and tossed some crumbs on the ground. "Here pidge, here pidge," he said.

The pigeon strutted over to eat the crumbs. Aaron pulled off his shirt. Moving slowly, he covered the wounded pigeon with his shirt and captured it. "Good pidge," he said softly. "That's your new name. Pidge."

The pigeon **struggled**. Aaron stroked the bird and tried to soothe it. "I'm going to take you home, Pidge," he said. "I'm going to fix you up. Easy, Pidge. "

---

struggled, moved wildly

Aaron skated out of the park and headed for home. He held the pigeon in his hands. When he reached his house, he saw his friend Noreen on the stoop. "Is he sick?" asked Noreen.

"Broken wing," Aaron responded. "I'm going to fix it. Want to help?"

"Yes, I'll help," said Noreen.

Aaron and Noreen began to fix the pigeon's wing. They used two ice-cream sticks and strips of cloth to hold the wing in place. Pidge did not move while the children fixed his broken wing. He seemed to know they were trying to help him.

Aaron wasn't sure what his mother would say about his new pet. But he knew his grandmother would be happy for him.

She liked to feed crumbs to the birds on the back fire escape. Sometimes Aaron heard her talking to the birds about her childhood in the Ukraine. Aaron knew she would love Pidge.

To his surprise, Aaron's mother told him he could keep Pidge temporarily. That meant he could keep Pidge for a while. But when Aaron's father came home, he stared at the pigeon with the bandaged wing. "Who did this?" he asked.

"Me," said Aaron. "And Noreen."

"You're a genius!" his father said. "You're only a kid and you fixed a bird's wing. Just like a real doctor." Aaron could tell that his father would let him keep Pidge.

Workbook
Page 197

BEFORE YOU GO ON

1 What was wrong with the pigeon?

2 How did Aaron help the pigeon?

On Your Own
Did you ever find an animal athat was hurt? Explain what happened.

Aaron decided to train Pidge to be a **carrier pigeon**. He tied a little cardboard tube to Pidge's left leg. Inside the tube he put secret messages. Then he had Pidge walk across the living room toward a pile of crumbs. "When your wing is stronger," Aaron told Pidge, "you can fly with messages like a real carrier pigeon."

Aaron told all his friends about Pidge. Soon the whole neighborhood was talking about him. But it was a mistake to let everyone know about Pidge. A gang of older boys lived in the neighborhood. They had their own clubhouse. Aaron wanted to join the gang more than anything else. He wanted to learn their secret words. He wanted to belong. Carl, the gang leader, said Aaron could be a member if he brought Pidge to the clubhouse. Aaron couldn't believe it! He raced home to tell his mother.

But his mother didn't like the boys. She told Aaron to keep away from them. Then she asked him to make something special for Grandma's birthday. That way he would be too busy to think about the gang.

Aaron wanted to give Grandma something special for her birthday. He thought about what it could be. All at once, he knew. Pidge would be her present! Pidge could carry messages for her. Maybe Pidge could even make her feel better about something that happened a long time ago.

Aaron remembered the story Grandma had told him many times. When she was a little girl in the Ukraine, she had a pet goat. She loved the goat more than anything. Aaron thought she must have loved the goat as much as he loved Pidge.

---

carrier pigeon, a bird that is trained to carry messages

One day, the people in Grandma's village got some terrible news. They knew the **czar** hated all the Jewish people. Now, he had ordered his soldiers, the Cossacks, to attack their village. The Cossacks were coming! Grandma's family had to hide quickly in the cellar. Grandma had to leave her goat upstairs. If it made a sound, the soldiers would find their hiding place.

Soon Grandma and her family heard the sound of horses galloping into the village. Then the Cossacks were in their house, breaking furniture and smashing all of their things. Grandma thought the terrible noise would never end, but finally the house was quiet. The family came out of the cellar.

The first thing Grandma saw was her goat. It was on the floor, dead. Grandma was heartbroken. She cried for days for her lost pet. Aaron knew that even now, she was still sad about her goat. But maybe Pidge could somehow replace Grandma's long-lost pet. Wouldn't that be the best gift he could give her?

Aaron was excited that he had thought of just the right present for Grandma. But he hadn't forgotten about wanting to join the gang. A few days later, he met Carl in the street again. "Bring the pigeon to our clubhouse," Carl said. "We've got a new kind of **badge** for you. A membership badge."

---

badge, a small piece of paper, plastic, or fabric that shows you belong to a special group

---

czar, a Russian ruler before 1917

BEFORE YOU GO ON

1 Why did Aaron want to join the gang of older boys?

2 What happened to Grandma's goat?

On Your Own
Did you ever want to join a club or a special group?

Aaron raced home to get Pidge. Gently, he removed the strips of cloth and the sticks. Pidge's wing seemed to be completely healed. With Pidge in his arms, Aaron ran to the clubhouse. Carl came out. "Give me the bird," he said.

"Be careful," Aaron warned. "I just took the bandages off."

"Oh sure, don't worry," said Carl. Then he turned to one of the other club members. "Give Aaron his special badge," Carl said. "And light the fire."

"What fire?" Aaron asked.

"Hey!" said Carl. "Don't ask questions. I'm the leader here. Now light the fire, Al."

The boy named Al struck a match. Soon the fire was glowing with a bright yellow-orange flame.

"Get the rope," Carl said. Another boy brought a rope, and Carl tied it around the bird.

"What . . . what are you doing?" shouted Aaron. "You're hurting his wing!"

"Don't worry about his wing," said Carl. "We're going to throw him into the fire, and you're going to pledge an oath to—"

"No!" shouted Aaron.

"Grab him!" Carl said to the other boys.

Aaron acted quickly. He leaped across the fire at Carl and **punched** him in the face. Carl slid to the floor and dropped Pidge. Aaron grabbed Pidge and raced out of the clubhouse. But before he could get very far, the boys were on top of him. He fell to the ground. Pidge slipped out of his hands. The rope came loose from around the bird's wings, and Pidge flew away.

At that moment Aaron hated the gang more than he had ever hated anyone in his life. He thought of the worst, the most terrible thing he could shout at them. "Cossacks!" he screamed. "You're all Cossacks!" Then he broke away and started running.

---

punched, hit with fists

When Aaron got home, his parents and Grandma saw his bloody face and torn shirt. "What happened?" they asked. **Sobbing**, Aaron told them about the gang, the clubhouse, and the fire. He told them how he had planned to give Pidge to Grandma as a gift. He told them how he thought Pidge was the best present he could ever give her.

Aaron's grandmother looked lovingly at her grandson. Then she kissed him and thanked him for his present. Aaron didn't understand. What was she talking about? Pidge was gone. Aaron didn't have any present for Grandma at all.

---

sobbing, crying with short, quick breaths

Later that night, before he fell asleep, Aaron thought about Pidge. He knew Grandma would have loved Pidge. She would have loved talking to him and taking care of him. But then Aaron realized something else. Grandma would have loved Pidge so much that she would have wanted Pidge to be free. She would have let Pidge go.

And then Aaron knew what Grandma meant when she thanked him for her present. Pidge's freedom was the best gift she could have had. For her, it was as if her goat had escaped from the Cossacks. It was as if her goat were free. Then Aaron fell asleep with a smile on his face.

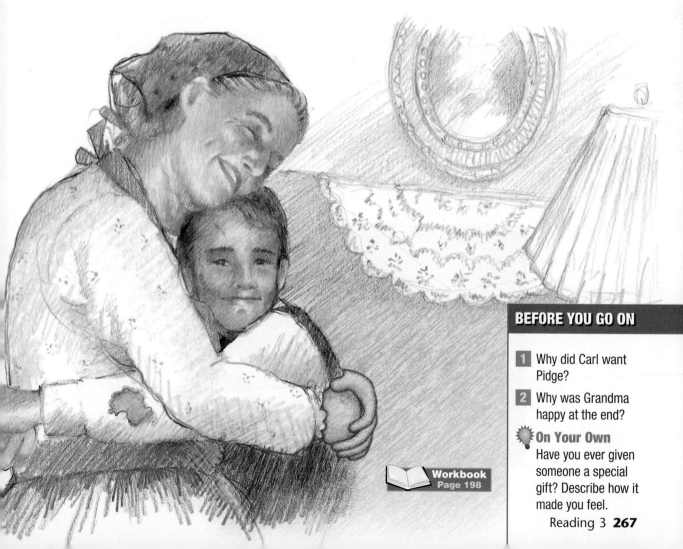

Workbook
Page 198

BEFORE YOU GO ON

1 Why did Carl want Pidge?

2 Why was Grandma happy at the end?

On Your Own
Have you ever given someone a special gift? Describe how it made you feel.

Reading 3 **267**

Review and Practice

► COMPREHENSION  **Workbook** Page 199

The characters in the story "Aaron's Gift" face many problems. Each problem has its own solution. Read the sentences in the boxes below. Then write a solution for each problem.

Problem	Solution
The bird has a broken wing.	*Aaron fixes it using ice-cream sticks.*
Aaron wants to train Pidge to be a carrier pigeon.	
Aaron wants to join the gang.	
Aaron needs a gift for Grandma.	
Carl tries to hurt Pidge.	
Pidge flies away. Aaron has no gift for Grandma.	

Use your finished chart to retell the events of the story.

➤ EXTENSION

What should you do if you find a hurt animal? To find out, contact or go to one or more of the following sources for information.

- park ranger
- library
- nature center
- animal shelter
- zoo
- Internet

Use the information you find to make a poster that tells how a park ranger or other adult would treat an injured animal. Present your poster to the class and give a brief talk. Use formal language.

➤ DISCUSSION

Discuss in pairs or small groups.

1. How did Aaron's mother feel about Carl's club? Was she right about the club? Explain.

2. Why did Aaron think that Pidge would be a good gift for Grandma?

3. Why was Aaron's grandmother happy even though Aaron had no gift for her?

4. Why did Aaron call the gang of boys "Cossacks"?

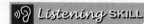

»🎧 Listening SKILL

Listen to your classmates carefully to understand the general meaning of what they are saying.

Set a purpose for reading In this nonfiction text, you will read about a special pigeon named Cher Ami. In French, cher ami means "dear friend." Look at the pictures. Why do you think Cher Ami was special?

Cher Ami—World War I Hero

During World War I (1914–1918), American soldiers used radios to talk to each other. The radios often broke. Carrier pigeons were another way for soldiers to communicate. Soldiers put a message in a small metal tube. They tied it to the leg of a pigeon. Then the pigeon carried the message to soldiers in another place.

Cher Ami was a famous carrier pigeon in World War I. He carried twelve messages in France. His last message saved many American soldiers. In 1918, enemy German soldiers **surrounded** a **battalion** of American soldiers. The battalion's radio broke. Later, another group of American soldiers thought the battalion was German and started shooting at them. German *and* American soldiers were attacking the battalion!

The battalion had three carrier pigeons. Two pigeons flew with messages to the American soldiers. German soldiers shot them. Cher Ami was the last pigeon. He was shot in the chest and leg, but he carried a message to the American soldiers. The shooting stopped, and 194 soldiers in the battalion were saved.

The French government gave Cher Ami a medal of honor. He was a hero.

▲ Cher Ami

BEFORE YOU GO ON

1 How did soldiers use carrier pigeons in World War I?

2 How did Cher Ami save soldiers' lives?

How About You?
Can other animals be heroes? Explain.

---

surrounded, were all around
battalion, a large group of soldiers

Link the Readings

▶ REFLECTION

Reread the story on pages 262–267 and the selection on page
270. Then copy the chart in your notebook and complete it.

Title	Type of Text	What It's About	Main Idea
"Aaron's Gift"			
"Cher Ami—World War I Hero"			

▶ DISCUSSION

Discuss in pairs or small groups.

1. How are Pidge and Cher Ami alike? How are they different?

2. Do you think soldiers use carrier pigeons today? Why or why not?

3. Have you ever had a pet that was special to you? Explain.

Grammar

Subject-Verb Agreement: Simple Present

In the simple present, the subject and the verb of a sentence must agree.
When the subject is a singular noun or *he, she,* or *it,* add -s or -es to the verb.
When a verb ends in -*y,* change the *y* to *i* and add -es.

> **Aaron finds** a pigeon in the park.
> **He fixes** the pigeon's wing with Noreen.
> **She helps** him.
> **The pigeon carries** messages.

When the subject is a plural noun or *I, you, we,* or *they,* use the base form of the verb. Do not add -s or -es.

> **We have** a clubhouse.
> **You read** every night.
> **Carrier pigeons help** people communicate.

Practice  **Workbook Page 200**

Copy the sentences in your notebook. Choose the correct subject or verb.
Read the completed sentences aloud with a partner.

1. Mike (find/finds) a baby bird.
2. The cars (move/moves) slowly along the highway.
3. The (dog/dogs) catches the ball.
4. (He/They) listen carefully to the teacher.
5. The monkey (eat/eats) fruit.
6. (Plant/Plants) need water and sunlight.

> ### 🔊 Speaking SKILL
> Make sure your subjects and verbs agree when you speak as well as when you write.

Writing

Ongoing Writing Skills Practice

Write a Review

A review gives the writer's opinion about a book, a story, a movie, or a show. A review includes:

- information about the work: the title, the author, what the work is about
- the writer's opinion: how he or she feels about the work
- reasons and examples that support the writer's opinion
- the writer's recommendation: advice about whether or not to see or read the work

Read the review. Then discuss the questions below.

Shonna Reese

"Aaron's Gift"

The story "Aaron's Gift" by Myron Levoy is very exciting. It's about a boy named Aaron who finds a pigeon with a broken wing. He calls the bird "Pidge" and fixes its wing. Aaron decides to give Pidge to his grandma for her birthday. When Grandma was a child in Ukraine, she had a pet goat. But the Cossacks killed it, and Grandma was very sad. Aaron thinks she will be happy to have a pet again. But Aaron also wants to join a gang of boys. The boys want Pidge, too. I can't tell you what happens because it would spoil the ending. All I can say is I really liked the story. It seemed like real life. I think you should read "Aaron's Gift."

1. How does the writer feel about the story?
2. What details does she give about the story?
3. What advice does she give her readers?

Workbook Page 201

Practice

Workbook Page 202

You will write a review of a favorite book, story, movie, or show.

1. **Read** Reread the model on page 273. What kind of work would you like to review? Make a list of ideas.

2. **Make a chart** To write her review, Shonna used the outline below. In your notebook, make an outline to organize your ideas for the review you are going to write.

Writing Strategy: Outline

Shonna organized her review around three main topics. Then she listed details to support each main idea.

I. Introduction
    A. Title, author, and description
    B. Opinion
II. The story
    A. Characters: Aaron, Pidge, Grandma, and gang
    B. Plot
        1. Aaron fixes Pidge's broken wing.
        2. Aaron wants to give Pidge to Grandma.
        3. The gang wants Pidge, too.
III. My recommendation: You should read this story.

---

3. **Write** Use your outline as a guide when you write your review. Edit your work. Check for correct subject-verb agreement. Make sure you use contractions correctly.

Check Your Knowledge

> ## LANGUAGE DEVELOPMENT

1. What was the author's purpose for writing "Aaron's Gift"? What details and words helped you to understand his purpose?

2. What lesson does Aaron learn at the end of the story?

3. Write a sentence in the simple present with *I, we,* or *they* as the subject. Write the same sentence with *he, she,* or *it* as the subject. How does the verb for the second sentence change?

4. What is a review? What does it include?

> ## ACADEMIC CONTENT

1. What new social studies words did you learn in Reading 4? What do the words mean?

2. What terrible thing happened to Aaron's grandmother when she was a little girl in Ukraine? Explain.

3. What connection do you see between flight and freedom? How do the selections in Reading 1 and Reading 4 show this connection?

What You Will Learn

Reading

- Vocabulary building: *Foreign words*

- Connect to reading: *Figurative language; Procedural texts; Genres; Comparing works of different genres; Fiction; Point of view*

- Text type: *Literature (short story)*

Writing

- Plan plot and characters

- Write a short story

➤ **BUILD BACKGROUND**

In this section, you will learn how to read and evaluate instructions. You will learn about figurative language, different kinds of readings, and story parts. Finally, you will read and write a short story. You have already read some short stories in this book. Authors write different kinds of stories, such as mystery, adventure, horror, and love stories. What are your favorite kinds of stories?

BOOST YOUR LISTENING COMPREHENSION

Unit 8: Wings

Your teacher will play the DVD for this unit. After you listen, answer these questions.

1. What fifteenth-century artist's drawings and notes are an important part of the history of flying?

2. What happened on December 17, 1903?

3. How were planes used in World War I?

4. Who was the first person to fly across the Atlantic Ocean? How long was the flight?

5. What important change took place in aviation in the early 1930s?

6. How did the *Enola Gay* help to end World War II?

➤ CONNECT TO VOCABULARY

Foreign Words

You may see foreign words in English texts. Social studies books often use French words. Health books may have Latin or Greek words. Stories and poems may have Spanish words.

The chart below lists some foreign words and expressions. The chart also shows how to pronounce the words, what language each word comes from, and what the words mean.

Word or Expression	Language	Meaning
aficionado (ah FIS ee uh NAH doh)	Spanish	true fan
bona fide (BOH nah fiyd)	Latin	real, genuine
carte blanche (kart blahnsh)	French	full power or authority
caveat emptor (KAH vey aht EMP tor)	Latin	buyer beware
quid pro quo (kwid proh kwoh)	Latin	something given or received in exchange for something else

Sometimes you can figure out the meaning of a foreign expression by using context, or words and sentences near the unfamiliar word.

Practice
Workbook Page 203

With a partner, choose a word from the chart to complete each sentence. Write the completed sentences in your notebook.

1. Blanca is a real soccer _____. She never misses a game.

2. When I tried to return the watch, the store owner said, "_____."

3. Call me at work only for _____ emergencies, not small or petty problems.

4. The chef has _____ in hiring and firing. Nobody tells her what to do. If she likes you, you are hired.

5. My father and I have a _____ arrangement. I cook, and he washes the dishes.

► CONNECT TO READING

Figurative Language

Figurative language is not literal. It does not mean exactly what it says. For example, someone might say, "That test was a bear!" This does not mean the test was a big, hairy animal. It means that passing the test was as hard as fighting a bear.

A writer's figurative language can give clues about his or her **culture**, or background. It can also tell what time period he or she lived in.

Read the lines below. The lines are from a poem by Robert Frost, called "The Road Not Taken." Do you think this poet comes from the city or the country? Which word or words give you a clue?

> Two roads **diverged** in a wood, and I
> I took the one less traveled by,
> And that has made all the difference.

---

diverged, moved apart

This chart has lines from Pat Mora's poem "This Big Sky" (page 254). Mora grew up surrounded by mountains and desert. Read the figurative language Mora used in her poem and the possible meanings.

Figurative Language	Possible Meaning
"This sky is big enough for all my dreams."	Looking at this big sky makes me feel free to daydream and imagine.
". . . whispers of giant pines . . ."	The wind blowing through the pine trees makes a whispering sound that speaks to me.
". . . mountains blue with memories."	The rock of the mountain is old and seems sad.

Practice  **Workbook Page 204**

Work in a small group. Reread the lines from "This Big Sky." Answer the questions below.

1. Which words give the reader a clue to Mora's background?

2. What type of scenery would reflect your creative self?

Procedural Texts

Procedural texts are texts that tell you how to do or make something. Examples include a recipe for macaroni and cheese, a set of instructions for how to play backgammon, an instruction manual for how to use your new digital camera, or a set of directions to get you from your home to the nearest public library. Some sets of instructions are better than others. Below are instructions for doing something simple: changing a light bulb. Imagine yourself following these instructions. Think about what is good and bad about these instructions.

How to Change a Desk-Lamp Light Bulb

1. Unplug the lamp.
2. Do not step on the top step of the ladder.
3. Make sure the old light bulb is cool. Then remove it.
4. Insert the new light bulb.
5. Turn on the light.

You may have noticed that step #2 seems out of place. In addition, the instructions do not tell you to plug the lamp back in. These instructions might confuse someone who does not know how to change a light bulb.

Good instructions for riding a bicycle, for example, would be important. Sometimes people ride safely. Sometimes they do not. Imagine that you have to explain safe ways of riding a bicycle. List ideas you would need to include in your safety instructions. Here are some suggestions:

- what to wear
- how and where to ride
- what dangers you may come across
- what laws you should know

After you make your list, read the draft of the Cruz Bicycle Company's "Guide to Riding Safely" on the next page. Then answer the questions at the bottom of the page.

Cruz Bicycles' Guide to Riding Safely

1. **Know local laws regarding bicycle riding.** Each city and state has laws for cyclists. Some basic rules of cycling are as follows:

   - Ride defensively. Do not expect car drivers to see you.

   - Ride in single file with other cyclists.

2. **Watch the road.** Look for potholes, drains, sand, gravel, and other dangers. Cross railroad tracks at a 90-degree angle. Walk your bike if you suspect that riding conditions are dangerous.

3. **Pass parked cars cautiously.** If someone opens a door or the car pulls out, you could be hurt badly. Cruz recommends putting a bell on your handlebars so that people will hear you coming.

4. **Night riding.** Cruz also recommends wearing a reflective vest so that people can see you in the dark.

5. **Storage.** You may need to store your bicycle for a long period of time. Make sure your bicycle is clean and well-oiled.

6. **Wet-weather riding.** Allow a longer breaking distance in wet weather. Also remember that rain causes reduced visibility. Turn corners more slowly. Look out for wet leaves and slippery manhole covers.

Practice

Compare the list of ideas you made with your partner to the set of instructions above. Then answer these questions:

1. What important riding-safety instructions are not included in the guide?

2. Is any information in the guide unrelated to safe riding? Explain.

Genres

Genres are different kinds of writing. Poetry, short stories, novels, biographies, and informational articles are different genres.

Writers choose different genres depending on their purpose. For example, if an author wanted to describe a moment in time that made a deep impression because of things he or she saw, heard, smelled, and felt, the author might choose to write a poem called a haiku. Here is an example:

The air smells of rain.
Gray clouds linger in the trees.
Cold drops sting my skin.

Writers use different tools depending on the genre they choose. In the haiku above, for example, the writer includes sensory details so that the reader can see, feel, and smell what is being described.

Genre	Purpose	Writers' Tools
Poetry	To convey images, ideas, and feelings	Poetic devices, figurative language, sensory details
Informational articles	To inform	Main ideas, explanations, facts, details, statistics
Short stories and novels	To tell a story that entertains and/or teaches a lesson	Characters, plot (beginning, middle, and end)

Sometimes, reasons for writing in different genres overlap. For example, some poems might express feelings and ideas *and* tell a story.

"Bessie Coleman, American Flyer" (page 248) is an informational article. "This Big Sky" (page 254) is a poem. Both are about the same subject. The diagram below compares the two texts. The information in the outer edges shows the differences. The information in the overlapping area shows the similarities.

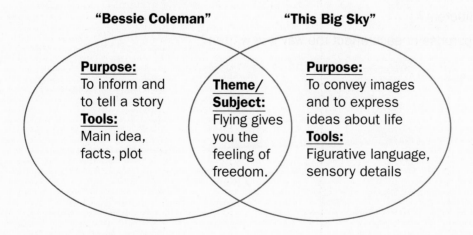

"Bessie Coleman" **"This Big Sky"**

Purpose:
To inform and to tell a story
Tools:
Main idea, facts, plot

Theme/ Subject:
Flying gives you the feeling of freedom.

Purpose:
To convey images and to express ideas about life
Tools:
Figurative language, sensory details

Comparing Works of Different Genres

The following excerpts are from works of different genres. However, both selections are about pigeons. Read the excerpts:

Short Story:
From "Aaron's Gift"

Aaron and Noreen began to fix the pigeon's wing. They used two ice-cream sticks and strips of cloth to hold the wing in place. Pidge did not move while the children fixed his broken wing. He seemed to know they were trying to help him.

Informational Text:
From "Cher Ami—World War I Hero"

During World War I (1914–1918), . . . [c]arrier pigeons were another way for soldiers to communicate. Soldiers put a message in a small metal tube. They tied it to the leg of a pigeon. Then the pigeon carried the message to soldiers in another place.

Cher Ami was a famous carrier pigeon. . . . He carried twelve messages in France. His last message saved many American soldiers.

Practice
Workbook
Pages 207–208

Work with a partner. Compare the two selections. Then answer the questions below.

1. How are these two selections similar?

2. How are they different?

3. How does the purpose of each affect the way it is written?

Fiction

Legends, folktales, short stories, and novels belong to the larger genre of *fiction*. **Fiction** is imaginative writing. Fictional writing has a **plot**, or series of events. Most plots have a similar structure.

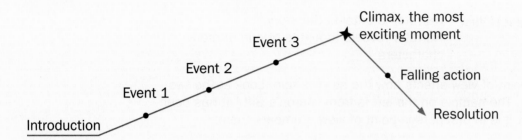

The folktale "The Great Minu" (page 166) follows this plot structure.

Introduction	Reader is introduced to main character and conflict. **Main character:** Akwasi
Conflict/ Problem	• He asks who owns things in the city. • "Minu" ("I don't understand") is the reply. • He thinks *Minu* is the name of a rich man.
Climax	Akwasi sees a funeral and asks people who died. People answer "Minu." He thinks that "Minu" has died.
Falling action	Akwasi decides that Minu's wealth didn't mean much in the end. His wealth could not keep him from dying.
Resolution	Akwasi returns to his small village, poor but contented.

Not all stories are told in a straight line from beginning to end. A **flashback** tells the reader something that happened before the story started. A flashback helps the reader know more about the characters and their experiences. In "Aaron's Gift," Aaron remembers when his grandmother told him about the Cossacks. This is an example of a flashback.

Point of View

Every story has a **narrator**. The narrator tells the story. Every narrator has a **point of view**. Here are two types of point of view:

First-Person Point of View	Narrator is a character in the story. Narrator uses *I* and *we* to tell the story.
Third-Person Point of View	Narrator is outside the story. Narrator reveals thoughts of one or more characters.

The narrator's point of view affects how the story is told. Look at the two examples below. The sample on the left is from "Aaron's Gift." It has been rewritten so that it is in first-person point of view. Compare them:

Third-Person Point of View	First-Person Point of View
"When Aaron got home, his parents and Grandma saw his bloody face and torn shirt."	"When I got home, my parents and Grandma saw my bloody face and torn shirt."

Developing Characters

Writers have several tools that help them make characters seem real.

Writer's Tools	Example from "Aaron's Gift"
Description of action	"Aaron raced home to get Pidge."
Dialogue	"Be careful," Aaron warned.
Inner thoughts	"Aaron hated the gang more than he had ever hated anyone in his life."
Character foils (contrasting characters)	Carl is very unlike Aaron—he wants to hurt Pidge.

Practice

In a small group, complete the activities below.

1. For "Aaron's Gift," make a chart like the one for "The Great Minu."

2. Rewrite part of "Aaron's Gift" from Grandma's point of view.

3. Find other examples of each of the following in "Aaron's Gift": dialogue, description of action, a character's inner thoughts.

Set a purpose for reading Think about the events in the story. What is the main problem, or conflict? How does the conflict get resolved?

The Goat and the Bee

My eyes snap open when I hear the alarm clock. I get up quickly, dress, and make my bed. I take a quick look over the shelves in my room. My collections—the baseball cards, the shells, and the books—are all in neat rows. At the breakfast table, I sit down to my usual breakfast: corn flakes with banana slices and orange juice. While I eat, I scan a list of words: *incessant, incommunicado, indefensible* . . .

I collect words like I collect baseball cards and seashells. I organize them and rearrange them. I make lists and charts and flashcards of words. There is a reason, though. I am preparing for the regional spelling bee. It is tomorrow, in Nashville. The winner of this spelling contest gets to go to Washington, D.C., for the national spelling bee. I really want to be there. For the next fourteen hours, I'm going to study words.

BEFORE YOU GO ON

1 What is the author preparing for?

2 From what point of view is this story told?

This is probably my last chance, since I turn sixteen this month. That's the cut-off age for the National.

Rrrring. It's the doorbell. I look through the peephole. It's Javier. I've known him since we were both in kindergarten. We're totally different. Besides being an excellent speller, I'm a pretty good student all around. I do my homework. I turn in my assignments on time. Javier is the opposite. He doesn't study as much as he should. He is not the most organized person in the world. And, boy, is he a terrible speller. But he has his own talents. He is really good with animals. He's in FFA. That's Future Farmers of America. It's a club in our high school. FFA and his goat, Capi, are his life.

He named her after the constellation Capricornius— *la cabra,* the goat. He says she's good luck. But if you ask me, Capi has been a lot of trouble. Last week, Javier's neighbor called the police to complain about a goat in her yard. That is typical Javier: He goes and adopts a goat with no way to keep it safe or away from the neighbors. The police officer said Javier would have to build a special pen immediately. So I took Javier to the library. We spent hours finding out about the rules for animal pens.

Suddenly, Javier knocks on my door, looking worried. He's holding Capi in his jacket. Two horns stick out of the zippered front.

"You've got to help me. It's Capi. She's been hit by a car. We've got to get her to the vet," says Javier.

"Oh, no," I say. "Not today. You take her."

"Ray, I need you. I can't sneak her on to the bus without your help."

I hear Capi crying inside Javier's jacket, "Baaa-aaa-aaa." "Javier, I'm studying for the spelling bee. It's tomorrow. I can't spend all day running around with you and your goat."

"Maybe your mom can give us a ride?" asks Javier.

My mother comes down the stairs. "I'll see you after work, Ray. Study hard, Sweetie."

> **"You've got to help me. It's Capi. She's been hit by a car."**

"*Mamá*, can you take Javier and his goat to the vet?"

"*Pobrecita!*" she says, noticing the goat. "OK, Javier, I'll drop you and Ray off at Dr. Limón's on my way to work."

"But, *Mamá*, why do I have to go?"

"Ray, you must help your friend."

I throw up my hands. "*Vámonos*," I say.

My mom lets us out at the curb and zooms away. She hates to be late. We turn to the door. A sign says, "Closed Sundays."

"Oh, great," I say. "*Cerrado!*"

"But look here," says Javier. "It says 'For bo-na-fee-day emergencies, call 555–1267.'"

"Bo-na what? Let me see." Sure enough, there is a new, interesting word: *bona fide*. I take a mental photograph of it. At the same time, I remember how much I want to be studying.

"What's that mean?" says Javier.

"It probably means, 'real,' like, 'real emergencies.' There's a phone booth." I pull coins out of my pocket and call. A voice on the other end tells me Dr. Limón is not available. She says we have to go to the 24-hour emergency animal clinic or to the Nashville Zoo.

"Are those places more expensive?"

The woman said, "Well, yes, they might be more expensive. But at least the zoo is close to Dr. Limón's office. Take the bus east."

Finally, after the bus ride, we arrive at the zoo. Javier unzips his coat a little to let Capi breath better. He had been hiding her from the bus drivers. We show Capi to the cashier. She makes us wait in the lobby. I survey the gift shop. A magazine called *Big Cat Aficionado* catches my eye. This sounds crazy, but I think the tiger on the cover winks at me. "Aficionado." I tell myself, "A-F-I-C-I-O-N-A-D-O."

A kind-looking woman in a lab coat comes in. "Hi, boys, I'm Dr. Huggins. Let's see your goat." She leads us to a clean, white room.

"Ray, you must help your friend."

"Tell me what happened," Dr. Huggins says. She starts examining the small brown and white animal.

"She got out of her pen and a car hit her," says Javier.

"Hmmm, she may have an internal hemorrhage."

"Heh-mor-ej?" says Javier, "What's that?"

"I think it means 'bleeding.' How do you spell that?" I ask. Then I feel ashamed. This is no time to worry about spelling.

Dr. Huggins gives me a funny look. "H-E-M-O-R-R-H-A-G-E," she says. "And you're right. It does mean bleeding. But I think she has a very good chance. Her pulse is strong. We'll have to watch her. With luck, you can pick her up tomorrow. Now, as for payment . . . how about this? We need volunteers to work with the zookeepers. Can you each volunteer one hour a week all summer?"

"I can volunteer *two* hours a week!" Javier practically shouts.

It is dark when we leave the zoo. On the bus home, Javier nudges me. "Hey, you want me to ask you spelling words?"

"No, *hombre*, that's OK. I left the list at home." I close my eyes and think of my new words: *bona fide, aficionado, hemorrhage.*

The next day, at the regional spelling bee, I feel unprepared. But the first round goes well. The boy ahead of me misspells *celestial.* But my word is *bona fide.* I remember it from Dr. Limón's sign.

It's the second round. The girl ahead of me stumbles over *presbytery.* But *my* next word makes me think Javier may be right about Capi. Maybe she *is* good luck. My word is *hemorrhage.* H-E-M-O-R-R-H-A-G-E. I spell it perfectly.

The final round is brutal. It is between me and another fifteen-year-old from Nashville's best high school. She has not missed a word or broken a sweat. I have not missed a word either. But I can feel sweat on the back of my legs, trickling down into my socks. The announcer says the word. The girl

"I can volunteer *two hours a week!*" Javier practically shouts.

pauses. Her forehead wrinkles. She asks to hear the word in a sentence. She misspells it.

Then the same word goes to me. I ask to hear it again. I want to make sure I'm not dreaming.

"*Aficionado!*" says the announcer.

I look out into the audience. Javier is in the front row, in his baggy jacket. It's the same one he always wears. Javier gives me a thumbs-up sign. I say the word: "*Aficionado*. A-F-I-C-I-O-N-A-D-O."

The audience cheers. I jump up and hoot. And from down front I hear, very clearly, "Baaa-aaa-aaa!"

> "I want to make sure I'm not dreaming."

BEFORE YOU GO ON

1. What happens in the story? Retell the story in your own words.

2. What are some examples of figurative language in the story?

3. What is the most exciting point, or climax, of this story?

Workbook
Page 209

Writing

Plan Plot and Characters and Write a Short Story

Short story writers create exciting plots and believable characters. They use dialogue to make the story life-like and interesting.

Conflict   Conflict is what makes stories interesting. There are different types of conflicts that occur in stories. Usually, a conflict has something to do with what one or more characters want. For example, in "The Goat and the Bee," Ray wants to spend his time studying for the spelling bee. But Javier's goat is hurt, and he wants Ray to help him. This creates an interesting conflict.

Characters   Interesting stories usually have believable characters. Before you start writing, think about your characters. What are they like? What do they care about? What is important to them?

Dialogue   Good dialogue should reveal information about the characters' situations. It should also help the reader understand the characters' personality and attitude.

Here is an excerpt of the first draft of a student writer's short story.

> "Mom, can I please, please go to the concert on Friday night?" asked Carmen nervously. All her friends were going. She knew her mother would say, "No, absolutely not!" because Carmen hadn't done her chores last week. She'd also been rude to her younger brother. And she'd gotten a C on her quiz, too. But maybe, just maybe, Carmen could persuade her mother.

1. What is the conflict?
2. What does the dialogue tell us about the main character?
3. Does Carmen seem like a realistic and interesting character? Why or why not?

Practice  **Workbook Page 210**

You will write a short story that has a well developed plot and interesting, believable characters.

1. Read Reread the student writer's first draft on page 290. Think of something you would like to write about.

Writing Strategy: Writing a Story

Think about your story. Who will be in it? Who will tell the story? What will happen? Ask and answer the questions below to help you plan your story.

Who will be in my story? (characters)
How will I make my characters seem real? (dialogue, description)
Who will tell the story? (narrative point of view)
What will happen in the story? (plot)

2. Make a story chart Make a story chart for your story. Use the chart on this page as a model.

3. Write Use your chart to write a short story.

IMPROVE YOUR WRITING SKILLS

Now that you have practiced writing a short story, go to www.LongmanKeystone.com and do the activity for this unit. You will find suggestions on various aspects of the writing process, such as how to generate ideas for a first draft, how to develop a thesis or controlling idea, and how to select the correct genre.

Put It All Together

LISTENING & SPEAKING WORKSHOP

Tell a Story

You will tell a story about a person who had a problem and found a solution.

1 **THINK ABOUT IT** Think about people you know or have read about who had a problem and solved it. Choose one person to write about. You could also write about a character you create.

   Make an idea map. First, draw a circle and write the person's name inside it. Next, draw lines coming out of the circle. On one line, write the problem the person had. On another line, write how the person solved it. Write details about the person and the problem on the other lines:

2 **ORGANIZE** A story has a beginning, middle, and end. Use your idea map to make note cards for your story.

- *On card 1:* Write one or two facts to describe the person. This is the beginning of your story.

- *On card 2:* Write the problem he or she had. This is the middle of your story.

- *On card 3:* Write how he or she solved the problem. This is the end of your story.

- You may wish to use pictures to help you tell your story. If so, find or draw them.

3 **PRACTICE** Use your note cards to practice telling your story. Then, put the cards away and tell your story from memory.

4 **PRESENT AND EVALUATE** Tell your story to the group. When each person finishes, evaluate the story. What did you like about it? Do you have any questions or ideas for how it might be better?

> **Speaking SKILL**
> - Look at your audience.
> - If you make a mistake, stop and correct yourself.

> **Listening SKILL**
> - Look at the speaker as he or she tells the story.
> - If you have a question, write it down and wait until the speaker is finished to ask it.

WRITING WORKSHOP

Short Story

A short story is a short work of fiction. The writer's purpose is to entertain and to teach the reader something about life. Most short stories are about characters that writers invent, or make up, using their imagination. However, some stories are based on real people. Writers imagine what these people said and did. Characters in short stories usually have problems. As a character tries to solve a problem, he or she learns something about life.

A short story usually includes:

- one or more characters
- a setting—when and where the story happens
- a series of events, including a problem that one or more characters tries to solve
- a beginning, a middle, and an end

Write a short story about a character who learns something by solving a problem. Read the model that begins on the next page. Follow the steps below and on page 295.

1 PREWRITE Think about the stories you told in your group. What did each person learn by solving a problem? In this unit, think about what Bessie Coleman learned from flying. What did Aaron learn from taking care of Pidge?

Make a list of new ideas for a story. Discuss your ideas with a partner. Do you want to base your story on something that happened to someone you know? Do you want to write a story from your imagination?

Choose a story idea. Look at the outline on page 274. Make an outline to plan your story. For your main ideas (I, II, III), use number I for the beginning of your story, number II for the middle, and number III for the end. For details (A, B, etc.), include the setting, the character, the problem, other events, how the character solves the problem, and what he or she learns.

WRITING TIPS

Use dialogue to make your story more interesting to read.

- Remember to put dialogue in quotation marks. Here is an example: "Be careful," Aaron said. "I just took the bandages off."
- Use different verbs, such as *shouted* and *asked,* in your dialogue.
- Write dialogue that sounds natural—the way people really talk.

Before you write your story, read this model.

Haley Coy

The Summer of Friends

Maureen hung up the phone with her friend Tina. ← Beginning
When school was finished, Tina would be moving to New
York. "It's going to be a long, lonely summer," Maureen
thought sadly. ← Problem: Maureen's friend moves away.

A few days after Tina moved, Maureen saw something
in her backyard. Hiding near the fence was a gray kitten
with white paws. Maureen saw a tag around the kitten's
neck. It read: "My name is Socks. Please return me to the
Larsons."

Mrs. Larson lived on Maureen's street. She never spoke
to anyone. "Mrs. Larson's not very friendly," Maureen
thought. But she picked up the kitten and brought him to ← Middle
Mrs. Larson's home anyway.

"Thanks for finding Socks!" said Mrs. Larson with a
big smile. "Come in, Maureen. Have some cookies. I just
made them for my grandchildren. They're coming
tomorrow for the summer. You should come and meet
Gina. She's just about your age."

"Thanks, Mrs. Larson," Maureen said, taking a cookie.
"I'd love to meet Gina." Later, as she walked home,

Maureen thought, "I was wrong about Mrs. Larson. She's really nice."

The next day Maureen met Gina. They went swimming together and rode their bikes in the park. They became best friends.

Maureen had lost one friend, but she gained two— Mrs. Larson and Gina.

←— **End**

←— **Solution: Maureen makes new friends.**

2 **DRAFT** Use the model and your outline to help you write your story.

3 **REVISE** Work with a partner. Trade papers and read each other's stories. Use the Revising Checklist below to evaluate your work.

> ### REVISING CHECKLIST
> #### Does your story . . .
> ▶ have a beginning, middle, and end?
> ▶ have a character with a problem?
> ▶ include dialogue in quotation marks?

4 **EDIT** Write a new draft of your story that includes your revisions. Correct mistakes in spelling and punctuation.

5 **PUBLISH** Obtain feedback from your teacher and classmates. Then prepare your final draft. Share your story with the class.

Media Literacy & Projects

Work in pairs or small groups. Choose one of these projects.

1 Use the library or the Internet to research different ways to make an airplane out of paper, oak tag, or cardboard. Choose one way and make a paper plane. Write the steps for how you made your plane. Share your work with the class.

2 Bessie Coleman felt free when she flew her airplane. What makes you feel free? Make a collage of things that make you feel free. A collage is a kind of art you make by cutting and pasting pictures, photos, and other materials together. Share your collage with the class.

3 Cher Ami was a carrier pigeon who saved many American soldiers in World War I. Make a poster about another special animal. Use the library or the Internet to find information about your animal. Here are some interesting topic ideas:
- Belka and Strelka (two dogs who traveled into space)
- Koko (gorilla who learned American Sign Language)
- Fungie (wild dolphin who likes people)

4 The famous Greek myth of Daedalus and Icarus is about flight and freedom. Find this story in the library or on the Internet. Read the story. Then draw a comic strip that retells the story. Share your comic strip with the class.

5 Go to LongmanKeystone.com for links to articles or websites about flight and flying. Follow the online instructions to analyze how each medium changes when addressing different audiences. Describe how the tone and the level of formality change for audiences of different age groups, interests, professions, and levels of language proficiency.

Further Reading

Choose from these reading suggestions. Practice reading silently for longer and longer periods.

***Amelia and Eleanor Go for a Ride,* Pam Muñoz Ryan** This book tells about an event that really happened. On April 20, 1933, First Lady Eleanor Roosevelt and pilot Amelia Earhart left a formal dinner party at the White House to enjoy a plane ride around Washington, D.C. Then, before they returned to the White House, they took the same tour by car.

***Talkin' about Bessie: The Story of Aviator Elizabeth Coleman,* Nikki Grimes** The author imagines the story of Bessie Coleman's life as told by people who knew her, including her parents, her sisters and brothers, a teacher, a newspaper publisher, a flight instructor, and two reporters. As each person gives a new point of view about Bessie, the reader learns about what a special person she was.

***This Big Sky,* Pat Mora** This collection of fourteen poems celebrates the American Southwest. Pat Mora's poetry is spare; the words are simple. Yet the images her poetry evokes range from playful to deeply mysterious. The poems in this book are sure to delight readers of varying ages and reading abilities.

***Apollo 13,* Dina Anastasio** It is April of 1970, and Jim Lovell, Fred Haise, and Jack Swigert are flying the *Apollo 13* spaceship to the moon. Suddenly something goes wrong. They hear a loud noise. Then the ship starts to lose oxygen and power. The astronauts cannot fly the ship without power, and they cannot live without air. Will they get home to Earth? Read this book to find out.

***Bird,* David Burnie** Among the many topics you will learn about in this book are how birds' bodies are designed for flight, why their wings are different shapes and sizes, and how many feathers birds have and what each one does. The book contains hundreds of colorful photos and illustrations about the history, behavior, and life cycle of birds.

Test Preparation

UNIT 1 PRACTICE

Read the following test sample. Study the tips in the boxes. Work with a partner to answer the questions.

Traveling Across the United States

(1) Many people travel across the United States each year. (2) Some of these travelers stay in hotels. (3) Many others stay at campgrounds as they move from state to state. (4) There are many fine campgrounds across the United States.

(5) Most campgrounds have showers for campers. (6) Some even have small stores that sell food and other items you may need. (7) Camping costs less money then a hotel. (8) Staying at a campground in a national park can be an adventure. (9) If you decide to travel across the United States, try campgrounds instead of hotels.

1　What change, if any, should be made to sentence 7?
    A　Change *then* to *than*.
    B　Change *less* to *fewer*.
    C　Delete the sentence.
    D　Make no change.

2　Which sentence could be added after sentence 9?
    F　Hotels can be fun to stay at, too.
    G　Campgrounds are often close to parks.
    H　You will be glad you did.
    J　Hotels are more comfortable.

Taking Tests
You will often take tests to show what you know. Study the tips below to help you improve your test-taking skills.

Tip
Every sentence in a paragraph should connect to the sentences before and after it. Some sentences are special, like the first and last sentence. They should make the reader think about what is going to be said or what has been said.

Tip
It is important to read the whole passage before you answer questions. This helps you know where to look for the information you are being asked about.

Workbook
Pages 213–214

UNIT 2 PRACTICE

Read the following test sample. Study the tips in the boxes. Work with a partner to answer the questions.

Being Prepared for an Earthquake

Earthquakes can happen anywhere. However, they are more common in certain areas than in others. People living in areas where earthquakes happen more often should be prepared for an earthquake. You can do certain things before an earthquake happens that will keep you safe.

The first thing is to make sure that items in your home are secure. Things can fall off of shelves and bookcases during an earthquake and might hit you. You should also make sure your closet doors have locks so things can't fall out. Many injuries during earthquakes are caused by falling objects. Also be sure to check your gas lines for cracks. Escaping gas can cause fires during earthquakes. A few simple repairs can help keep you safe. If an earthquake occurs and you're indoors, get under a table. That's the safest place to be.

1 Why should closets have locks on them?
   A   So no one will steal things from them
   B   So important things will not break
   C   So no one will hide inside
   D   So falling objects will not hit you

2 Based on the information in the passage, where is the safest place to go during an earthquake?
   F   Under a shelf
   G   Under a table
   H   Near a tree
   J   Near a tall building

Taking Tests
You will often take tests to show what you know. Study the tips below to help you improve your test-taking skills.

Tip
Sometimes the correct answer uses different words than those used in the passage. You have to find the information in the passage and decide which answer makes sense.

Tip
Look for key words in questions to help locate the information you need. In question 1, you should look for the words *closet* and *lock* to find the answer in the passage.

Workbook
Pages 215–216

Taking Tests

You will often take tests to show what you know. Study the tips below to help you improve your test-taking skills.

Read the following test sample. Study the tips in the boxes. Work with a partner to answer the questions.

The Aztecs Play Ball

The ancient Aztec people played a ball game much different from the ones played today. The Aztec game was very close to a ball game played by other early cultures. However, the Aztec game was very difficult to play.

Using a ball called an *ulli*, players on each team had to get the ball through a tiny hole in a stone disk. Unlike the baskets and goals today, the hole was not much bigger than the ulli. While the players tried to get the ball through the hole, they had to keep the ball from hitting the ground. They could not touch the ball with their hands or feet, though. They had to use their elbows, head, hips, and knees. Because of this, the games were very fast-moving and fun to watch. Some games lasted for hours.

Tip

Very few tests have "trick" questions. Usually when you think a question is tricky, you have misunderstood the question.

1 How was the Aztec game different from games played in other cultures?
  A   It was more difficult.
  B   It used a ball.
  C   It had teams.
  D   It was fast-moving.

Tip

If you aren't sure which answer is correct, go through each one and ask yourself if it makes sense based on the information in the passage.

2 Why was it hard to get the ulli through the stone disk?
  F   The disk was guarded by a goalie.
  G   The players were very skilled.
  H   Players had to use their feet.
  J   The hole was very small.

Workbook
Pages 217–218

UNIT 4 PRACTICE

Read the following test sample. Study the tips in the boxes. Work with a partner to answer the questions.

The Tale of the Wasteful Son

There once were two brothers who worked on their father's farm. Their father was very rich and had many workers, herds, and much land. One day, the younger brother said to his father, "Father, when you die, I will receive half of what you own. Give me that money now, so that I can go out and see the world." The father was very hurt, but gave his son as he asked. The older son remained at the farm and continued to work.

The younger brother wandered around the world, wasting his money until he had none left. He wound up sleeping with animals in the fields. He decided to go to his father and apologize for what he had done. "If my father forgives me, maybe he will give me a job as a worker," he thought. When the younger son approached the house, his father saw him. His father ran to him with tears in his eyes and called for a party to welcome him home. The older brother who had stayed behind was angry because he had done as he was told. But the father explained that the older son already had everything the father had. It was time to celebrate the son who had been lost and was finally found.

1 Why was the father hurt when his son asked for the money?
  A   The son wanted to travel the world.
  B   The son always did what he was told.
  C   The son asked for his money before his father died.
  D   The son told the father he would never return.

2 What emotion caused the older brother to complain about the welcome party?
  F   Jealousy
  G   Excitement
  H   Worry
  J   Hope

Taking Tests
You will often take tests to show what you know. Study the tips below to help you improve your test-taking skills.

Tip
Some test questions ask you to decide what caused characters to act the way they did. To help you decide, think about your own life and experiences. How would you feel in the same situation?

Tip
When questions ask about characters, look for clues. What do the characters say to one another? How are they acting? What emotion seems reasonable in their circumstances?

Workbook
Pages 219–220

Read the following test sample. Study the tips in the boxes. Work with a partner to answer the questions.

The New Writing Tablet

Not too many years ago, children in school learned to write carefully with a pen and paper. This type of writing was called *penmanship*. In penmanship classes, students learned a type of writing known as *cursive*. Cursive is writing with a pen where all the letters are pretty and connected to each other. Children learned cursive at a time when very few people used typing skills in their everyday lives. Only people who planned to work in offices learned to type. Everybody else wrote letters, school papers, and other things with a pen and paper.

This changed when computers became available to everyone in the early 1990s. More people began to type. Typing was taught along with cursive in school. Now, with the Internet and cell phones that act like computers, many schools no longer teach cursive or penmanship. This is because people do more typing than they do handwriting. Students as young as four years old have typing classes in school where they learn to find letters on a keyboard. How we write to each other and keep information for others has changed a lot in the past thirty years.

1 Why did students in the past learn penmanship instead of typing?
   A   Very few people used typing in their day-to-day lives.
   B   Learning to type was too difficult for young people to learn.
   C   No one worked in offices where things were typed.
   D   Learning penmanship was needed before one could learn to type.

2 For what activity would you use cursive instead of typing?
   F   Sending an e-mail
   G   Signing a contract or receipt
   H   Writing a very long essay
   J   Writing a resume for a job

UNIT 6 PRACTICE

Read the following test sample. Study the tips in the boxes. Work with a partner to answer the questions.

Traveling Elephants

(1) Elephants travel in groups of adult females and young elephants, or offspring. (2) Younger male elephants will remain with these groups until they are about seven years old. (3) Then they leave and join one or two other male elephants their age. (4) Once a young male elephant becomes an adult, he travels alone until he is ready to mate. (5) When this happens, he goes back to a group of females and their offspring.

(6) Elephant herds eat a lot of grass, though they will eat bark and tree leaves also. (7) Because groups of females and young elephants eat so much, they must keep traveling in search of food. (8) Sometimes a group of elephants finds a crop on a farm. (9) The elephants love the taste of the corn, wheat, and sugar cane. (10) A group of elephants can destroy an entire crop very quickly. (11) This causes a lot of problems for farmers in India who depend on those crops for food and money. (12) Farmers are more important than elephants, and the government has to find a way to stop the elephants without harming them.

1　What does the word *offspring* in sentence 1 refer to?
  A　Young elephants
  B　Male elephants
  C　Elephant herds
  D　Older elephants

2　Which sentence is an opinion?
  F　Sentence 1
  G　Sentence 6
  H　Sentence 11
  J　Sentence 12

Taking Tests
You will often take tests to show what you know. Study the tips below to help you improve your test-taking skills.

Tip
Opinions can sound like facts, especially if they are included in a series of facts. Remember, a fact is something that can be proven, or is true. An opinion is what someone believes or thinks. It's not necessarily true.

Tip
If a question asks whether a sentence is an opinion, watch out for sentences that tell you what someone else thinks.

Workbook
Pages 223–224

Taking Tests

You will often take tests to show what you know. Study the tips below to help you improve your test-taking skills.

Tip

Words like *first* or *next* or *finally* can help you understand the order that the steps take.

Tip

Don't choose an answer just because it "looks" like the correct answer. Make sure it answers the question.

Workbook
Pages 225–226

UNIT 7 PRACTICE

Read the following test sample. Study the tips in the boxes. Work with a partner to answer the questions.

Growing Plant Cuttings

Most people know how to grow a plant from a seed. However, there is another way to grow a plant. You can also grow a plant from a piece of another plant, called a cutting. This cutting can be grown, and a plant that is the same in every way as the first plant will grow. In order to grow a plant from a cutting, you have to follow certain directions.

First, you have to water the original plant very well the day before you take your cutting. Water loss is the biggest danger to the new plant. Next, cut either a leaf or a shoot from the first plant. As soon as the root or leaf is cut, it will begin to die. This is why it is important to put it into a rooting mix, which is water and certain minerals, right away. Once the cutting has sprouted roots, plant it in soil and care for it like any other plant.

1 Why do you have to water the original plant the day before you take the cutting?
  A To force the cutting to grow roots
  B To make sure the original plant is healthy
  C To prevent the cutting from losing water
  D To help the cutting's new roots to form

2 What is the last thing you must do to grow a plant from a cutting?
  F Put the cutting into a rooting mix.
  G Give the roots plenty of light.
  H Give the cutting a lot of water.
  J Plant the cutting in soil.

UNIT 8 PRACTICE

Read the following test sample. Study the tips in the boxes. Work with a partner to answer the questions.

The Eagle and the Raccoon

One day, a smart Raccoon came to the bottom of a hill and saw an Eagle and her eggs. The Raccoon knew how good Eagle eggs tasted, but he could not climb the side of the mountain because it was too smooth and slippery. He ran into the forest and began to gather small sticks, leaves, straw, and dirt. He took these items and began to build a pile beneath the Eagle's nest.

"What are you doing down there?" the Eagle called out.

"I am building a soft place for your eggs to land if they fall," said the Raccoon. "I heard that there is a windstorm coming and was worried about them."

The Eagle became very upset. A windstorm would blow her nest to the ground, and she could lose all of her eggs. She thought it was nice of the Raccoon to think of such things. "How do I know it is soft enough?" the Eagle called to the Raccoon.

"You are right," the Raccoon said, concerned. "Perhaps we should test it. Throw down an egg. If the pile I have built is not soft enough, the egg will bounce before it breaks. I will be here to catch it when it bounces."

The Eagle took her largest egg. She held her claw over the pile the Raccoon had built, closed her eyes, and dropped her egg. Instead of letting the egg fall onto the pile, the Raccoon caught it and ran off into the forest with his dinner. The Eagle realized she had been so afraid of the windstorm that she had forgotten to be afraid of the Raccoon. It is important to see every danger, big and small.

1 What is the purpose of this kind of story?
   A   To explain why eagles do not like raccoons
   B   To teach how eagles built their nests
   C   To teach an important lesson about life
   D   To tell a funny story about animals

2 How was the Raccoon able to trick the Eagle?
   F   He used her fear against her.
   G   He was good at catching eggs.
   H   He could build a better nest.
   J   He tried to make her afraid of him.

Taking Tests
You will often take tests to show what you know. Study the tips below to help you improve your test-taking skills.

Tip
When a question asks you about the purpose of a passage, think about the genre. Knowing the genre will help you identify the purpose.

Tip
Sometimes wrong answers look right because they mention things that happened in the passage. Always focus on the information the question asks for.

Workbook
Pages 227–228

Phonics Handbook

► CONSONANT SOUNDS AND THEIR SPELLINGS

Some letters are called consonants. The **con** part of the word **consonant** means "with." The **sonant** part means "sound." Consonants are letters that stand for speech sounds. Consonant speech sounds go with vowel sounds and other consonant sounds when we speak.

A consonant spelling goes with vowel spellings and other consonant spellings when we write.

Pages 308–315 of this handbook show you twenty-five consonant sounds and how they are spelled. A symbol for each sound is shown in slashes like this //.

Spellings of each consonant sound are shown in color in the samples.

Key words show you words that have this consonant sound. The key words show examples of the sound's spelling at the beginning, middle, or end of the words.

This is the sound symbol.

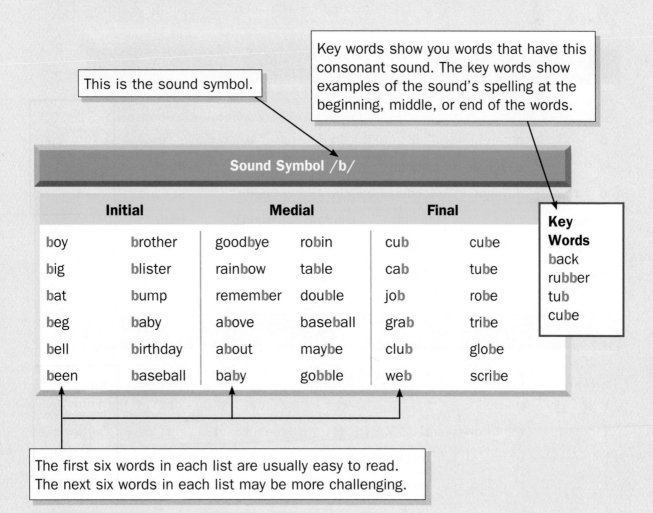

Sound Symbol /b/

Initial		Medial		Final	
boy	brother	goodbye	robin	cub	cube
big	blister	rainbow	table	cab	tube
bat	bump	remember	double	job	robe
beg	baby	above	baseball	grab	tribe
bell	birthday	about	maybe	club	globe
been	baseball	baby	gobble	web	scribe

Key Words
back
rubber
tub
cube

The first six words in each list are usually easy to read.
The next six words in each list may be more challenging.

➤ CONSONANT SOUNDS AND THEIR SPELLINGS

Sound Symbol /p/

Initial		Medial		Final	
pad	plenty	copy	shopping	tip	hiccup
pet	pancake	sample	repeat	stop	gallop
pick	pickle	hoping	report	clap	hope
pill	pineapple	kept	pineapple	jump	ape
pants	pumpkin	slept	pumpkin	keep	ripe
pretty		open	supper	sleep	shape

Key Words
pack
happy
cape

Sound Symbol /d/

Initial		Medial		Final	
dog	different	reading	addition	bad	said
dig	daughter	children	study	kid	hand
do, dew	daylight	wooden	idea	bed	second
down	does	building	window	mud	trade
deep	direction	middle	today	hold	side
drop	December	medal	riding	third	include

Key Words
day
student
read

Sound Symbol /t/

Initial		Medial		Final	
to, too, two	television	city	attack	but, butt	right, write
tan	tomorrow	interview	kitten	aunt, ant	night
tell	traffic	interesting	butter	lost	cute
told	terrible	beautiful	matter	dirt	brought
take	tornado	adjective	pretty	boot	fought
time	Tuesday	entertain	bitter	melt	Internet

Key Words
tie
batter
ant

Sound Symbol /g/

Initial		Medial		Final	
gas	gold	ago	bigger	big	egg
get	good	begin	giggle	bag	flag
girl	group	began	logging	rug	smog
give	grow	together	logo	rag	smug
gone	ground	figure	regret	beg	catalog
game	government	forgotten	struggle	frog	travelogue

Key Words
go
forget
leg

Sound Symbol /k/

Initial		Medial		Final	
cut	kitten	became	recall	black	disk
cap	cola	because	unclear	kick	thank
come	comment	raincoat	ecology	like	music
kept	cream	backward	echo	walk	fantastic
kite	camel	picnic	except	talk	break
color	chorus		excite	sink	mistake

Key Words
cat
key
chorus
become
ticket
lake
back
arc

Sound Symbol /v/

Initial		Medial		Final	
very	valley	never	shove	have	drive
visit	view	ever	shiver	cave	drove
violin	value	over	invest	give	move
voice	vital	even	review	live	twelve
vowel	villain	eleven	prove	five	believe
visa	victory	cover	move	of	relieve

Key Words
van
river
love

309

➤ CONSONANT SOUNDS AND THEIR SPELLINGS

Sound Symbol /f/

Initial		Medial		Final	
for	funny	after	beautiful	if	life
find	found	before	cupful	off	half
first	face	often	snowflake	wolf	laugh
fire	family	careful	afraid	half	graph
feet	friends	different	telephone	myself	enough
fish	February	outfit	coughing	cliff	rough

Key Words
fan
photo
offer
golf
tough

Sound Symbol /ð/

Initial		Medial		Final	
this	their	father	northern	smooth	
that	they	mother	leather	breathe	
there	these	brother	farther	writhe	
them	then	other	together	scythe	
those	than	either	gather	tithe	
though		feather	soothing		

Key Words
the
whether
weather
bathe

Sound Symbol /θ/

Initial		Medial		Final	
throw	thousand	anything	author	with	cloth
threw	thunder	nothing	birthday	tooth	math
thank	thirty	athlete	mathematics	teeth	south
think	thirteen	bathrobe	without	fifth	north
thing	thick	bathtub	earthquake	earth	both
thumb	Thursday	toothbrush	northeast	truth	worth

Key Words
three
something
bath

Sound Symbol /z/

Initial		Medial		Final		Key Words
zip	zap	lazy	citizen	jazz	as	zoo
zero	zeal	puzzle	organized	quiz	is	easy
zoom	zest	dozen	magazine	freeze	flies	runs
zebra	zinc	frozen	rising	prize	was	buzz
zipper	zoology	breezy	choosing	size	says	rise
zone		music		please	wise	

Sound Symbol /s/

Initial		Medial		Final		Key Words
sat	science	also	pencil	books	address	sun
sell, cell	cent	person	decide	units	across	city
soon	cereal	answer	percent	products	ice	best
said	citizen	inside	dancing	marks	advice	less
so, sew	certain	lesson	bicycle	plus	place	fence
sea, see	circus	herself		less	force	

Sound Symbol /ʒ/

Medial		Final	Key Words
treasure	division	beige	vision
pleasure	revision	rouge	beige
leisure			
casual			
Caucasian			
azure			

➤ CONSONANT SOUNDS AND THEIR SPELLINGS

Sound Symbol /ʃ/

Initial		Medial		Final	
she	show	washing	machine	wish	leash
ship	shower	bushes	station	fish	finish
short	shell	brushed	vacation	rush	punish
shape	shame	cushion	addition	wash	publish
shoes	chef	fraction	subtraction	ash	establish
shine	chic	description	magician	push	abolish

Key Words
shop
fishing
nation
musician
dish

Sound Symbol /h/

Initial				Medial	
he	here	house	hospital	ahead	rehearse
his	have	horse	heard	behind	inherit
her	has	high	happened	overhead	inhuman
how	half	hand	hundred	behave	unheard
home	hill	head	hair	household	withhold
happy	help	hard	hole	uphill	downhill

Key Words
hot
unhappy

Sound Symbol /tʃ/

Initial		Medial		Final	
chip	chapter	lunchroom	pitcher	pinch	itch
chin	champion	branches	catcher	rich	ditch
chop	chew	unchanged	structure	bunch	pitch
cheek	chalk	inches	century	coach	watch
cheap	cheer	teacher	lecture	peach	fetch
child	children		actually	reach	March

Key Words
check
lunches
ketchup
picture
such
match

Sound Symbol /dʒ/

Initial		Medial		Final	
jam	gym, Jim	magic	algebra	cage	huge
jar	genes, jeans	tragic	biology	wage	large
jacket	genius	region	ecology	range	fudge
general	June	register		change	badge
geography	July	majority		strange	hinge
generous	January	legislate		bridge	singe

Key Words
giant
joy
biology
legend
judge

Sound Symbol /m/

Initial		Medial		Final	
my	much	family	remove	am	system
many	miles	example	important	him, hymn	come
more	music	number	immediately	harm	name
man	morning	became	summer	farm	some
must	May	remain	government	swim	limb
means	Monday	sometimes	camera	time	comb

Key Words
mother
animal
seem
home
lamb

Sound Symbol /n/

Initial		Medial		Final	
no, know	number	under	inches	in	children
net	notice	second	front	on	done
new, knew	note	once	scientist	one	person
near	nothing	wonder	manner	run	shown, shone
never	next	stand	inner	down	machine
not, knot	noun	ground		upon	plane, plain

Key Words
nest
know
mind
cannot
fun
cone

313

► CONSONANT SOUNDS AND THEIR SPELLINGS

Sound Symbol /ŋ/

	Medial		Final	
	fangs	language	song	strong
	tongs	tangles	wrong	floating
	jungle	single	long	going
	hanger	youngster	lung	running
	singer	kingdom	spring	watering
	lengthen	longed	thing	sitting

Key Words
stronger
sing

Sound Symbol /l/

Initial		Medial		Final	
lip	large	alive	reply	real, reel	small
look	learn	only	world	seal	tell
like	light	belong	palace	wheel	vowel
live	land	family	follow	girl	hole
list	lunch	really	wealthy	heal, heel	single
long	little	smaller	schoolroom	people	regular

Key Words
last
slowly
pull
bottle
until

Sound Symbol /r/

Initial		Medial		Final	
red	rudder	girls	overcome	our	other
ran	review	worked	largest	are	after
read, reed	ready	three	different	year	before
room	religion	earth	triangle	here, hear	there, their
road	right, write	learn	Thursday	for, four	near
reef	wrong	hungry	Friday	water	square

Key Words
run
very
far
care

Sound Symbol /w/

Initial		Medial	
we	were	forward	awake
will	word	backward	rework
was	world	upward	between
water	want	halfway	northwest
way, weigh	woman	sandwich	catwalk
walk	Wednesday	unwilling	highway

Key Words
win
away

Sound Symbol /hw/

Initial		Medial	
when	wheel	everywhere	awhile
where	whip	meanwhile	buckwheat
which	while	cartwheel	overwhelm
why	whale	somewhat	bobwhite
whether	whine	somewhere	
wheat	whistle	anywhere	

Key Words
white
somewhere

Sound Symbol /y/

Initial		Medial	
yes	you	papaya	lawyer
year	your	backyard	vineyard
yen	young	barnyard	beyond
yellow	yak	courtyard	
yet	yoga	canyon	
yard	yesterday	unyielding	

Key Words
you
yoyo

► VOWEL SOUNDS AND THEIR SPELLINGS

Vowel sounds are speech sounds. A vowel sound in a word usually lasts longer than a consonant sound.

Vowels are also letters. Vowel letters are **a, e, i, o, u,** and sometimes **y.** Vowel letters sometimes go together in pairs such as **ai, ea, oi,** and **ay.**

This handbook shows you sixteen speech sounds that are spelled with one or two vowel letters. The word **bat** is an example of a word that has one vowel letter and vowel sound. The word **banana** is an example of a word with three vowel letters and vowel sounds. The word **antidisestablishmentarianism** has eleven vowel letters and sounds. It is one of the longest words in English.

Key words show you examples of words with the vowel sound. The key words show you ways that the vowel sound is spelled. The vowel sound is in color.

This is the symbol that stands for the vowel sound.

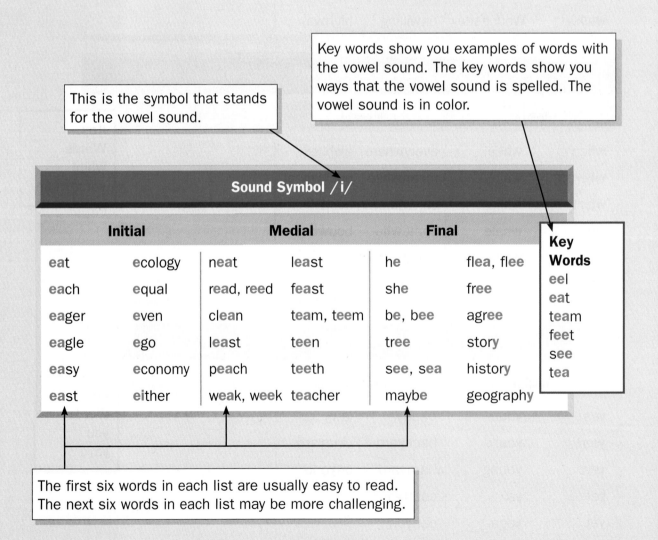

Sound Symbol /i/

Initial		Medial		Final		Key Words
eat	ecology	neat	least	he	flea, flee	eel
each	equal	read, reed	feast	she	free	eat
eager	even	clean	team, teem	be, bee	agree	team
eagle	ego	least	teen	tree	story	feet
easy	economy	peach	teeth	see, sea	history	see
east	either	weak, week	teacher	maybe	geography	tea

The first six words in each list are usually easy to read. The next six words in each list may be more challenging.

316

Sound Symbol / ɪ /

Initial		Medial	
in	insect	did	giving
if	igloo	with	whip
is	instant	his	silver
inch	itself	this	hidden
into	inform	little	finger
illness	interrupt	city	gym

Sound Symbol /eɪ/

Initial		Medial		Final	
ate, eight	aged	gave	baseball	hey	weigh
apron	acre	state	playoff	they	neigh
agent	ail, ale	main, mane	daylight	obey	sleigh
able	ache	quake	volcano	stay	gangway
aim	eighteen	straight, strait	neighbor	today	birthday
aide	April	equation	rain, reign	bluejay	Saturday

Sound Symbol / ɛ /

Initial		Medial		
egg	explain	ten	next	bread
ever	enjoy	send	spelling	head
extra	engine	when	helpful	dead
edge	enter	then	melon	said
elephant	exit	get	themselves	says
		let	together	

➤ VOWEL SOUNDS AND THEIR SPELLINGS

Sound Symbol /æ/

Initial		Medial		Key Words
at	addition	that	than	and
as	adjective	have	happen	had
act	answer	can	began	
add	actor	fact	planted	
ask	animal	black	vacuum	
ant	axle	hand		

Sound Symbol /ɑ/

Initial		Medial		Key Words
on	observation	not, knot	clock	odd
ox	obvious	box	bottom	top
olive	oddity	hot	product	
opera	operation	stop	copy	
object	opportunity	job	comrade	
octopus	October	crop	concentration	

Sound Symbol /ɔ/

Initial		Medial		Key Words
all	awning	salt	walk	awesome
also	author	false	chalk	caught
although	auto	call	crawl	mall
always	audio	ball, bawl	caution	talk
already	auditorium	mall, maul	because	cough
altogether	August	stall	bought	

318

Sound Symbol /oʊ/

Initial		Medial		Final		Key Words
oh, owe	only	poem	coat	go	echo	**old**
open	own	program	road	hello	volcano	**pole**
over	oats	total	loaded	also	show	**boat**
ocean	oak	broken	floating	zero	row	**no**
obey	oath	home	known	radio	tomorrow	**snow**
okay, OK		alone	bowling	piano	yellow	

Sound Symbol /ʊ/

Medial		Key Words
look	push	**book**
took	pull	**foot**
book	pulley	**put**
good	cookie	
wood	understood	
hoof	neighborhood	

Sound Symbol /u/

Initial		Medial		Final		Key Words
ooze		cool	troop, troupe	do, dew, due	grew	**ooze**
oodles		food	tooth	to, too, two	zoo	**pool**
oops		balloon	truce	blue	who	**spruce**
		boot	loose	flew, flu, flue	issue	**soup**
		smooth	soon	crew	tissue	**stew**
		group	Tuesday	new, knew	you, yew	**true**

319

► VOWEL SOUNDS AND THEIR SPELLINGS

Sound Symbol /aɪ/

Initial		Medial		Final	
I, eye	iron	time	life	high, hi	fly
ice	icon	like	while	sigh	sty
icy	iota	find	sight, site, cite	reply	tie
aisle, isle	ion	light	title	by, buy	beautify
item	ivy	right	flying	my	magnify
iris	ivory	night	trying	lie, lye	purify

Key Words
idea
pilot
smile
cry
pie

Sound Symbol /aʊ/

Initial		Medial		Final	
ouch	outcry	about	towel	how	vow
our	outlook	down	mountain	cow	snowplow
outdoors	ounce	sound	vowel	somehow	
ourselves	outfield	around	proud	bow	
outline	owl	ground	loud	eyebrow	
outside	oust	howl	mouth	sow	

Key Words
out
owl
pound
hound
allow

Sound Symbol /ɔɪ/

Initial		Medial		Final	
oyster		point	appointment	boy	employ
oink		join	enjoyment	joy	cowboy
oily		soil	soybean	coy	alloy
oilcloth		voice	voyage	destroy	corduroy
ointment		coin	loyal	annoy	decoy
oilwell		royal	employee	enjoy	Troy

Key Words
oil
noise
royal
toy

Sound Symbol /ʌ/

	Initial		Medial		Key Words
us	upset	but	submarine		up
under	unseen	much	number		cut
ugly	unpack	jump	son, sun		something
uncle	unnecessary	summer	someone		trouble
upper	umpire	funny	double		front
utter	understand	front	frontier		

Sound Symbol /ɚ/

	Initial		Medial		Final	Key Words
earn, urn	earth	govern	squirrel	fir	sure	earth
early	urban	liberty	turn	stir	future	bird
earnings	urgent	western	burned	her	creature	hurry
earthworm	earnest	butterfly	church	player	terror	humor
urge	earthquake	circus	hurdle	answer	rumor, roomer	teacher
irk		dirt	worry	November		feature

Sound Symbol /ə/

	Initial		Medial		Final	Key Words
ago	opinion	level	second	idea	iguana	about
again	occur	different	focus	antenna	lava	banana
away	until	animal	family	comma	fava	
aside	upon	together	fasten	bandanna	retina	
above	unless	often	guacamole	guava	sauna	
official	upholstery	children		mantilla	saga	

Grammar Handbook

➤ THE PARTS OF SPEECH

In English, there are eight **parts of speech**: nouns, pronouns, adjectives, verbs, adverbs, prepositions, conjunctions, and interjections.

Nouns

Nouns name people, places, and things. There are two kinds of nouns: **common nouns** and **proper nouns**.

A **common noun** is a general person, place, or thing.

>   person   thing   place
> The **student** brings a **notebook** to **class**.

A **proper noun** is a specific person, place, or thing. Proper nouns start with a capital letter.

>   person   place   thing
> **Margaret** goes to **California** every **June**.

A noun that is made up of two words is called a **compound noun**. A compound noun can be one word or two words. Some compound nouns have hyphens.

> One word: **newspaper**, **bathroom**
> Two words: **vice president**, **pet shop**
> Hyphens: **sister-in-law**, **grown-up**

Articles identify nouns. *A, an,* and *the* are articles.

A and *an* are called **indefinite articles**. Use the article *a* or *an* to talk about one general person, place, or thing.

Use *an* before a word that begins with a vowel sound. Use *a* before a word that begins with a consonant sound.

> I have **an** idea.
> May I borrow **a** pen?

The is called a **definite article**. Use *the* to talk about one or more specific people, places, or things.

> **The** box in your room contains **the** books.

Pronouns

Pronouns are words that take the place of nouns or proper nouns. In this example, the pronoun *she* replaces, or refers to, the proper noun *Anita.*

proper noun   pronoun
Anita is not home. **She** is babysitting.

Pronouns can be subjects or objects. They can be singular or plural.

	Subject Pronouns	Object Pronouns
Singular	I, you, he, she, it	me, you, him, her, it
Plural	we, you, they	us, you, them

A **subject pronoun** replaces a noun or proper noun that is the subject of a sentence. A **subject** is who or what a sentence is about. In these sentences, *He* replaces *Dan.*

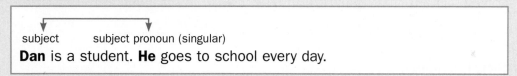

subject   subject pronoun (singular)
Dan is a student. **He** goes to school every day.

In these sentences, *We* replaces *Jaime* and *I.*

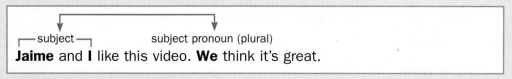

subject   subject pronoun (plural)
Jaime and **I** like this video. **We** think it's great.

An **object pronoun** replaces a noun or proper noun that is the object of a verb. A verb tells the action in a sentence. An **object** receives the action of a verb.

In these sentences, *him* replaces *Ed,* which is the object of the verb *gave.*

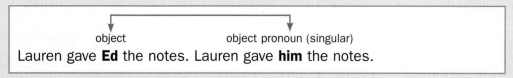

object   object pronoun (singular)
Lauren gave **Ed** the notes. Lauren gave **him** the notes.

An object pronoun can also replace a noun or proper noun that is the **object of a preposition**. Prepositions are words such as *for, to,* and *with*. In these sentences, *them* replaces *José and Yolanda,* which is the object of the preposition *with.*

object of a preposition	object pronoun (plural)

I went to the mall with **José and Yolanda**. I went to the mall with **them**.

Pronouns can also be possessive. A **possessive pronoun** replaces a noun or proper noun. It shows who owns something.

	Possessive Pronouns
Singular	mine, yours, his, hers, its
Plural	ours, yours, theirs

In these sentences, *hers* replaces the words *Alicia's coat*. It shows that Alicia owns the coat.

It is **Alicia's coat**. It is **hers**.

When an auxiliary verb (such as the verb *be*) follows a subject pronoun, it is usually contracted, especially in spoken English. In contractions, an apostrophe (') replaces the deleted letter.

Full Form	Contractions
I **am**	I**'m**
He She **is** It	He**'s** She**'s** It**'s**
You We **are** They	You**'re** We**'re** They**'re**

The **reciprocal pronouns** *each other* and *one another* are used in situations in which an action is carried out by two (or more) people at the same time. Using a reciprocal pronoun makes a sentence less complex. For example, instead of saying, "Lester gave Monica a gift, and Monica gave Lester a gift," you could use a reciprocal pronoun and say, "Lester and Monica gave **each other** gifts." Use the reciprocal pronoun, *one another* when referring to three or more people. Note that reciprocal pronouns can take the possessive form.

Danny and David met **each other** when they were in eighth grade.
When we were babies, my sisters and I looked similar to **one another**.
Scientists believe that lions can recognize **one another's** roars.

Adjectives

Adjectives describe nouns. An adjective usually comes before the noun it describes.

---

tall grass   **big** truck   **two** kittens

An adjective can come *after* the noun it describes. This happens in these kinds of sentences.

The book bag is **heavy**. The books are **old**.

Do not add -*s* to adjectives that describe plural nouns.

---

the **red** houses   the **funny** jokes   the **smart** teachers

---

Verbs

Verbs express an action or a state of being.

---

subject verb   subject verb
Jack **walks** to school. The school **is** near his house.

An **action verb** tells what someone or something does or did. You cannot always see the action of an action verb.

Actions You Can See		Actions You Cannot See	
dance	swim	know	sense
play	talk	name	think
sit	write	remember	understand

A **linking verb** shows no action. It links the subject with another word that describes the subject.

	Linking Verbs
Forms of *be*	am, is, are, was, were
Verbs related to the five senses	look, smell, sound, taste, feel
Verbs that reflect a state of being	appear, become, grow, remain, seem, turn

In this sentence, the adjective *tired* tells something about the subject, *dog*. *Seems* is the linking verb.

Our dog **seems** tired.

In this sentence, the noun *friend* tells something about the subject, *brother*. *Is* is the linking verb.

Your brother **is** my friend.

A **helping verb** comes before the main verb. It adds to the main verb's meaning. Helping verbs can be forms of the verb *be, do,* or *have.*

	Helping Verbs
Forms of *be*	am, is, are, was, were
Forms of *do*	do, does, did
Forms of *have*	have, has, had
Other helping verbs	can, must, could, have (to), should, may, will, would

In this sentence, *am* is the helping verb; *walking* is the action verb.

helping action
  verb   verb
I **am walking** to my English class.

In questions, the subject comes between a helping verb and a main verb.

> subject
> **Did** Liang **give** you the CD?

Mood in verbs relates to the attitude of the speaker or writer. The **indicative** mood expresses factual statements (either an assertion, a denial, or a question). Most of the sentences on this page are in the indicative mood. The **imperative** mood expresses commands, instructions, or requests. The understood subject of an imperative sentence is *you*. The **subjunctive** mood expresses something that is doubtful or not factual. This includes sentences that express things such as wishes, commands, emotion, possibility, necessity, or something that is contrary to fact.

Indicative mood	I **am reading** a book right now.
Imperative mood	**Read** Chapter 12 for Monday.
Subjunctive mood	She didn't understand the book. If she **were** older, she would have understood it better.

Adverbs

Adverbs describe the action of verbs. They tell *how* an action happens. Adverbs answer the questions *Where? When? How?* and *How much?* or *How often?*

Many adverbs end in *-ly.*

> easily   slowly   carefully

Some adverbs do not end in *-ly.*

> seldom   fast   very

In this sentence, the adverb *everywhere* modifies the verb *looked.* It answers the question *Where?*

> verb   adverb
> Nicole looked **everywhere** for her ring.

In this sentence, the adverb *quickly* modifies the verb *walked*. It answers the question *How?*

> verb   adverb
> They walked home **quickly**.

Adverbs also modify adjectives. They answer the question *How much?* or *How little?*

In this sentence, the adjective *dangerous* modifies the noun *road*. The adverb *very* modifies the adjective *dangerous*.

> adverb   adjective   noun
> This is a **very** dangerous road.

Adverbs can also modify other adverbs. In this sentence, the adverb *fast* modifies the verb *runs*. The adverb *quite* modifies the adverb *fast*.

> verb adverb adverb
> Joe runs **quite** fast.

Prepositions
Prepositions can show time, place, and direction.

Time	Place	Direction
after	above	across
before	below	down
during	in	into
since	near	to
until	under	up

In this sentence, the preposition *above* shows where the bird flew. It shows place.

> preposition
> A bird flew **above** my head.

In this sentence, the preposition *across* shows direction.

> preposition
> The children walked **across** the street.

A **prepositional phrase** starts with a preposition and ends with a noun or pronoun.

In this sentence, the preposition is *near* and the noun is *school.*

> prepositional phrase
> The library is **near the new school**.

Conjunctions

A **conjunction** joins words, groups of words, and whole sentences.

Conjunctions						
and	but	for	nor	or	so	yet

In this sentence, the conjunction *and* joins two proper nouns: *Allison* and *Teresa.*

> noun   noun
> Allison **and** Teresa are in school.

In this sentence, the conjunction *or* joins two prepositional phrases: *to the movies* and *to the mall.*

> prepositional   prepositional
> ┌ phrase ┐ ┌ phrase ┐
> They want to go to the movies **or** to the mall.

In this sentence, the conjunction *and* joins two independent clauses: *Alana baked the cookies,* and *Eric made the lemonade.*

> ┌── independent clause ──┐ ┌── independent clause ──┐
> Alana baked the cookies, **and** Eric made the lemonade.

Interjections

Interjections are words or phrases that express emotion.

Interjections that express strong emotion are followed by an exclamation point.

> **Wow!** Did you see that catch?
> **Hey!** Watch out for the ball!

Interjections that express mild emotion are followed by a comma.

> **Gee,** I'm sorry that your team lost.
> **Oh,** it's OK. We'll do better next time.

A Note About Case

Case refers to a word's grammatical role or function within a sentence. In English, nouns and pronouns have three cases: **nominative, objective,** and **possessive**. The nominative refers to the subject of the sentence; the objective refers to something that is the object of a verb or preposition; and the possessive refers to a noun that possesses or owns another noun. The nominative and objective cases of nouns are identical, but the possessive case takes a different form.

Case	Noun	Pronoun
Nominative	<u>Adam</u> has a new puppy.	<u>He</u> has a new puppy.
Objective	They gave <u>Adam</u> a puppy.	They gave <u>him</u> a puppy.
Possessive	<u>Adam's</u> puppy is cute.	<u>His</u> puppy is cute.

► CLAUSES

Clauses are groups of words with a subject and a verb. Some clauses form complete sentences; they tell a complete thought. Others do not.

This clause is a complete sentence. Clauses that form complete sentences are called **independent clauses**.

> subject   verb
> The dog's **tail wagged**.

This clause is not a complete sentence. Clauses that don't form complete sentences are called **dependent clauses**.

> subject verb
> when the **boy petted** him

Independent clauses can be combined with dependent clauses to form a sentence.

In this sentence, *The dog's tail wagged* is an independent clause. *When the boy petted him* is a dependent clause.

> ┌─independent clause─┐ ┌─dependent clause─┐
> The dog's tail wagged when the boy petted him.

► SENTENCES

Sentences have a subject and a verb, and tell a complete thought. A sentence always begins with a capital letter. It always ends with a period, question mark, or exclamation point.

> subject   action verb
> The **cheetah runs** very fast.
>
> helping verb   subject   action verb
> **Do you play** soccer?
>
> subject   linking verb
> **I am** so late!

Simple, Compound, and Complex Sentences

Some sentences are called simple sentences. Others are called compound sentences. A **simple sentence** has one independent clause. Here is an example.

> ⸻ independent clause ⸻
> The dog barked at the mail carrier.

Compound sentences are made up of two or more simple sentences, or independent clauses. They are joined together by a **conjunction** such as *and* or *but*.

> ⸻ independent clause ⸻   ⸻ independent clause ⸻
> The band has a lead singer, **but** they need a drummer.

Complex sentences have an independent clause and one or more dependent clauses. In a complex sentence, the main idea is in the independent clause.

> ⸻dependent clause⸻   ⸻dependent clause⸻   ⸻independent clause⸻
> Although it's raining, and in spite of the cold, we still plan to go for a run.

Compound-complex sentences have more than one independent clause and at least one dependent clause.

> ⸻dependent clause⸻   ⸻independent clause⸻   ⸻independent clause⸻
> After the movie ended, we all said it was good, but secretly, we didn't like it.

Sentence Types

There are four types of sentences. All four have different purposes: **declarative** sentences are statements, **interrogative** sentences are questions, **imperative** sentences are commands, and **exclamatory** sentences express strong feelings.

Sentence Type	Example	Ending Punctuation
Declarative	We're going to the beach on Saturday.	a period
Interrogative	Will you come with us?	a question mark
Imperative	Put on your life jacket. Now jump into the water!	a period or an exclamation point
Exclamatory	I swam all the way from the boat to the shore!	an exclamation point

▶ MECHANICS

End Marks

End marks come at the end of sentences. There are three kinds of end marks: periods, question marks, and exclamation points.

Use a **period** to end a statement (declarative sentence).

> The spacecraft *Magellan* took pictures of Jupiter**.**

Use a **period** to end a command or request (imperative sentence) that isn't strong enough to need an exclamation point.

> Please change the channel**.**

Use a **question mark** to end a sentence that asks a question (interrogative sentence).

> Where does Mrs. Contreras live**?**

Use an **exclamation point** to end a sentence that expresses strong feeling (exclamatory sentence).

> That was a great party**!**
> Look at that huge house**!**

Use an **exclamation point** to end an imperative sentence that gives a strong command.

> Don't get too close to the pool**!**

Periods are also used after initials and many abbreviations.

Use a **period** after a person's initial or abbreviated title.

Ms. Susan Vargas	Mrs. Fiske	J. D. Salinger
Gov. Lise Crawford	Mr. Vargas	Dr. Sapirstein

Use a **period** after the abbreviation of streets, roads, and so on.

Avenue ⟶ Ave.	Road ⟶ Rd.
Boulevard ⟶ Blvd.	Street ⟶ St.
Highway ⟶ Hwy.	

Use a **period** after the abbreviation of many units of measurement. Abbreviations for metric units do *not* use periods.

inch ⟶ in.	centimeter ⟶ cm
foot ⟶ ft.	meter ⟶ m
pound ⟶ lb.	kilogram ⟶ kg
gallon ⟶ gal.	liter ⟶ l

Commas

Commas separate, or set off, parts of a sentence or phrase.

Use a comma to separate two independent clauses linked by a conjunction. In this sentence, the comma goes before the conjunction *but.*

┌──── independent clause ────┐ ┌ independent clause ┐
We went to the museum**,** **but** it was closed.

Use commas to separate the parts in a series. A series is a group of three or more words, phrases, or very brief clauses.

	Commas in Series
To separate words	Lucio's bike is red, white, and silver.
To separate phrases	Today, he rode over the lawn, down the sidewalk, and up the hill.
To separate clauses	Lucio washed the bike, his dad washed the car, and his mom washed the dog.

Use a comma to set off an introductory word, phrase, or clause.

	Commas with Introductory Words, Phrases, or Clauses
To set off a word	Yes, Stacy likes to go swimming. Alma, do you like to swim?
To set off a phrase	In a month, she may join the swim team again.
To set off a clause	If she joins the swim team, I'll miss her at softball practice.

Use commas to set off an interrupting word, nonrestrictive phrase, or nonrestrictive clause. (Note: A nonrestrictive phrase or clause can be left out of a sentence without changing the sentence's meaning.)

	Commas with Interrupting Words, Phrases, or Clauses
To set off a word	We left, finally, to get some fresh air.
To set off a phrase	Carol's dog, a brown pug, shakes when he gets scared.
To set off a clause	The assignment, I'm sorry to say, was too hard for me.

Use a comma to set off a contrasting expression.

> I like tea, not coffee.
> The exam is this Friday, not next Friday.

Use a comma to set off a speaker's quoted words in a sentence.

> Jeanne asked, "Where is that book I just had?"
> "I just saw it," said Billy, "on the kitchen counter."

In a **direct address**, one speaker talks directly to another. Use commas to set off the name of the person being addressed.

> Thank you, Dee, for helping to put away the dishes.
> Sophia, why are you late again?

Use a comma between the day and the year.

> My cousin was born on September 9, 2001.

If the date appears in the middle of a sentence, use a comma before *and* after the year.

> Daria's mother was born on June 8, 1965, in New Jersey.

Use a comma between a city and a state and between a city and a nation.

> My father grew up in Bakersfield, California.
> We are traveling to Acapulco, Mexico.

If the names appear in the middle of a sentence, use a comma before *and* after the state or nation.

> My friend Carl went to Bombay, India, last year.

Use a comma after the greeting in a friendly letter. Use a comma after the closing in both a friendly letter and formal letter. Do this in e-mail letters, too.

Dear Margaret,   Sincerely,   Yours truly,

Semicolons and Colons

Semicolons can connect two independent clauses. Use them when the clauses are closely related in meaning or structure.

The team won again; it was their ninth victory.
Ana usually studies right after school; Rita prefers to study in the
  evening.

Colons introduce a list of items or important information.

Use a colon after an independent clause to introduce a list of items. (The clause often has the words *as follows, the following, these, those,* or *this.*)

The following animals live in Costa Rica: monkeys, lemurs, toucans, and jaguars.

Use a colon to introduce important information. If the information is in an independent clause, use a capital letter to begin the first word after the colon.

There is one main rule: Do not talk to anyone during the test.
You must remember this: Stay away from the train tracks!

Use a colon to separate hours and minutes when writing the time.

1:30   7:45   11:08

Dashes

Dashes are used to make a break in a sentence. They can be used as a replacement for commas, semicolons, colons, and parentheses. They appear more often in informal writing than formal writing.

Dashes are used to express added emphasis.

There's only one person who can lead our team to victory—Steve.
Once I saw the cute puppy—tiny paws, big eyes, curly tail—I just knew I
  had to own it.

338

Dashes are used to indicate an interruption.

> We were walking in the quiet park when—suddenly—we heard a loud noise over by the lake.

Dashes help to set off an abrupt change of thought.

> Could you please get me a—oh, never mind. I'll get it myself.

Quotation Marks

Quotation marks set off direct quotations, dialogue, and some titles. A **direct quotation** is the exact words that somebody said, wrote, or thought.

Commas and periods *always* go inside quotation marks. If a question mark or exclamation point is part of the quotation, it is also placed *inside* the quotation marks.

> "Can you please get ready**?**" Mom asked.
> My sister shouted, "Look out for that bee**!**"

If a question mark or exclamation point is *not* part of the quotation, it goes *outside* the quotation marks. In these cases there is no punctuation before the end quotation marks.

> Did you say, "I can't do this"**?**

Conversation between two or more people is called **dialogue**. Use quotation marks to set off dialogue words.

> "What a great ride!" Pam said. "Let's go on it again."
> José shook his head and said, "No way. I'm feeling sick."

Writers will sometimes use quotation marks around a word or phrase to change its meaning from literal to ironic or sarcastic. Read this example of quotation marks used to indicate sarcasm:

> Our teacher gave us a "simple" homework assignment to do over the weekend. It's going to take me all weekend to finish it!

From context, we can infer that the writer was told an assignment was going to be simple, but he or she doesn't believe that it will be.

Now read this example of quotation marks used to indicate irony:

> The army fired shots at houses in the "safe haven" of the war zone.

Here the writer seems to be implying that even though an area is called a safe haven, it really isn't a safe place to be.

Be careful when trying to use quotation marks in this way. There is a chance that the reader will misunderstand your intended meaning, and think you are being literal instead of ironic or sarcastic.

Use quotation marks around the titles of short works of writing or other art forms. The following kinds of titles take quotation marks:

Chapters	"The Railroad in the West"
Short stories	"The Perfect Cat"
Articles	"California in the 1920s"
Songs	"This Land Is Your Land"
Single TV episodes	"Charlie's New Idea"
Short poems	"The Bat"

Titles of all other written work and artwork are underlined. These include books, magazines, newspapers, plays, movies, TV series, and paintings.

Apostrophes

Apostrophes can be used with singular and plural nouns to show ownership or possession. To form the possessive, follow these rules:

For singular nouns: Add an apostrophe and an *s.*

> Maria**'s** eyes   hamster**'s** cage   the sun**'s** warmth

For singular nouns that end in *s:* Add an apostrophe and an *s* to these nouns, too.

> her boss**'s** office   Carlos**'s** piano   the grass**'s** length

For plural nouns that do not end in *s*: Add an apostrophe and an *s*.

women**'s** clothes   men**'s** shoes   children**'s** books

For plural nouns that end in *s*: Add an apostrophe.

teachers' lounge   dogs' leashes   kids' playground

Apostrophes are also used in **contractions**. A contraction is a shortened form of two words that have been combined. The apostrophe shows where a letter or letters have been taken away.

I will
I'll be home in one hour.
    do not
We **don't** have any soup.

Capitalization

There are five main reasons to use capital letters:
1. to begin a sentence and in a direct quotation
2. to write the word *I*
3. to write the name of a specific person, place, or thing
4. to write a person's title
5. to write the title of a work (artwork, written work)

Use a capital letter to begin the first word in a sentence.

Cows eat grass. **T**hey also eat hay.

Use a capital letter for the first word of a direct quotation. Use the capital letter even if the quotation is in the middle of a sentence.

Sophie said, "**W**e need more sand for the sand castle."

Use a capital letter for the word *I*.

How will **I** ever learn all these things? **I** guess **I** will learn them little by little.

Use a capital letter for the name of a specific person, place, or thing. Capitalize the important words in names.

Robert **E**. Lee   **M**exico   **T**uesday   **T**ropic of **C**ancer

	Capital Letters in Place Names
Streets	Interstate 95, Center Street, Atwood Avenue
City sections	Greenwich Village, Shaker Heights, East Side
Cities and towns	Rome, Chicago, Fresno
States	California, North Dakota, Maryland
Regions	Pacific Northwest, Great Plains, Eastern Europe
Nations	China, Dominican Republic, Italy
Continents	North America, Africa, Asia
Mountains	Mount Shasta, Andes Mountains, Rocky Mountains
Deserts	Mojave Desert, Sahara Desert, Gobi Desert
Islands	Fiji Islands, Capri, Virgin Islands
Rivers	Amazon River, Nile River, Mississippi River
Lakes	Lake Superior, Great Bear Lake, Lake Tahoe
Bays	San Francisco Bay, Hudson Bay, Galveston Bay
Seas	Mediterranean Sea, Sea of Japan
Oceans	Pacific Ocean, Atlantic Ocean, Indian Ocean

	Capital Letters for Specific Things
Historical periods, events	Renaissance, Battle of Bull Run
Historical texts	Constitution, Bill of Rights
Days and months	Monday, October
Holidays	Thanksgiving, Labor Day
Organizations, schools	Greenpeace, Central High School
Government bodies	Congress, State Department
Political parties	Republican Party, Democratic Party
Ethnic groups	Chinese, Latinos
Languages, nationalities	Spanish, Canadian
Buildings	Empire State Building, City Hall
Monuments	Lincoln Memorial, Washington Monument
Religions	Hinduism, Christianity, Judaism, Islam

Use a capital letter for a person's title if the title comes before the name. In the second sentence below, a capital letter is not needed because the title does not come before a name.

I heard **S**enator Harkin's speech about jobs.
The **s**enator may come to our school.

Use a capital letter for the first and last word and all other important words in titles of books, newspapers, magazines, short stories, plays, movies, songs, paintings, and sculptures.

Lucy wants to read **T**he **L**ord of the **R**ings.
The newspaper my father reads is **T**he **N**ew **Y**ork **T**imes.
Did you like the painting called **W**ork in the **F**ields?
This poem is called "**T**he **B**irch **T**ree."

Reading Resources Handbook

▶ DICTIONARY

You can find the **spelling, pronunciation, part of speech,** and **definitions** of words in the dictionary. Many words in English have more than one meaning. Some words, such as *court,* can be both a noun and a verb. The part of speech is usually abbreviated (*n* for *noun, v* for *verb, adj* for *adjective,* and *adv* for *adverb*). The part of speech comes after the word's pronunciation. Then the meanings, or definitions, are numbered. Sometimes **example sentences** are given in italics.

Here is a sample dictionary **entry** for the word *court.* You learned one meaning of *court* in Unit 3. This entry gives that definition and others:

Pronunciation   **Part of speech**

court 1 /kôrt/ *n* **1** a room or building where judges and lawyers try legal cases: *He appeared in court as a witness.* **2** an area for playing sports such as tennis or basketball: *The girls were on the tennis court.* **3** the official place where a king or queen lives and works: *We received an invitation to the king's court.* ◀——— **Example sentence**

Definitions

court 2 *v* **1** to try to make someone like you: *The senator will court voters before the election.* **2** to do something that makes a problem likely to happen: *Martin is courting disaster if he goes to the movies instead of studying for his exam.* **3** to try to win the romantic love of someone: *Andrew courted Susan with flowers and candy.*

——— **Example sentence**

344

Dictionary pages also have other helpful information.

Guide words are at the top of dictionary pages. They tell you the first or the last entry on the page. Guide words can help you find words in a dictionary.

Words can be divided into **syllables**, or parts.

A **stress mark** (') shows which syllable in a word to stress—to pronounce stronger and louder.

Many dictionaries include **illustrations** to help explain the meanings of some words.

An **idiom** is two or more words that have a special meaning when used together. Dictionaries explain what each idiom means. Note that each idiom including the word *hang* has a different meaning.

---

handle

handle² *verb* (**handling, handled**)
1 to hold or touch something: *Handle the package with care.*
2 to control or deal with someone or something: *I can't handle the children by myself.*

han•dle•bars /ˈhændl‚barz/ *plural noun*
the parts of a bicycle that you hold when you ride it

hand•some /ˈhænsəm/ *adjective*
attractive, usually used about a man compare ▶▶ BEAUTIFUL

hand•writ•ing /ˈhænd‚raɪtɪŋ/ *noun* [U]
the way someone writes with his or her hand: *He has very neat handwriting.*

hand•y /ˈhændi/ *adjective* (**handier, handiest**)
1 useful: *A second car comes in handy sometimes.*
2 near: *Keep the medicine handy in case we need it.*

*He **hung** the clothes out to dry.*

hang /hæŋ/ *verb*
1 (*past* **hung** /hʌŋ/) to fasten something at the top so that the bottom part is free to move: *I hung up my coat in the closet.*
2 (*past* **hanged**) to kill someone by holding him or her above the ground with a rope around his or her neck
3 **hang around** to stay in one place and do nothing, or to wait around for someone: *He was hanging around outside my house.*
4 **hang on** to hold something tightly: *Hang on to your hat, it's very windy.*
5 **hang out** to stay in one place and not do very much: *We usually hang out at Jill's house after school.*
6 **hang up** to finish speaking to someone on the telephone by putting the telephone down

hang•er /ˈhæŋɚ/ *noun*
a curved piece of wire or wood that you hang clothes on

► MAPS

Maps help us learn more about our world. They show the location of places such as countries, states, and cities. Some maps show where mountains, rivers, and lakes are located.

Maps usually have helpful features. For example, a **compass rose** shows which way is north. A **scale** shows how miles or kilometers are represented on the map.

▲ Routes of the Underground Railroad

Street maps help give directions within a city or town. They tell how to go from one place to another. Look at the map of New Orleans. Can you find the Public Library? What streets is it near?

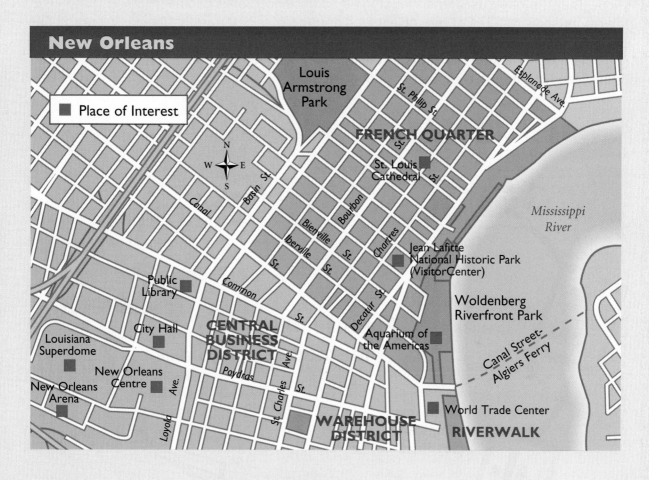

New Orleans

■ Place of Interest

Louis Armstrong Park

St. Philip St.

Esplanade Ave.

FRENCH QUARTER

St. Louis Cathedral

Basin St.

Canal

Bienville St.

Iberville St.

Bourbon St.

Chartres St.

St.

Mississippi River

Jean Lafitte National Historic Park (Visitor Center)

Public Library

Common St.

Decatur St.

Woldenberg Riverfront Park

City Hall

CENTRAL BUSINESS DISTRICT

Aquarium of the Americas

Canal Street-Algiers Ferry

Louisiana Superdome

New Orleans Centre

Poydras

St. Charles Ave.

St.

New Orleans Arena

Loyola Ave.

World Trade Center

WAREHOUSE DISTRICT

RIVERWALK

► DIAGRAMS

Diagrams are drawings or plans used to explain things or show how things work. They are often used in social studies and science books. Some diagrams show pictures of how objects look on the outside or on the inside. Others show the different steps in a process.

This diagram shows the steps of the Scientific Method. It helps you understand the order and importance of each step.

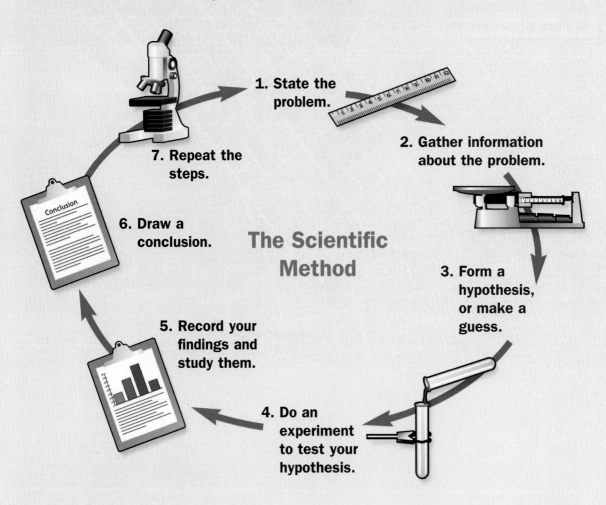

The Scientific Method

1. State the problem.

2. Gather information about the problem.

3. Form a hypothesis, or make a guess.

4. Do an experiment to test your hypothesis.

5. Record your findings and study them.

6. Draw a conclusion.

7. Repeat the steps.

Cross-Section Diagrams

A **cross-section diagram** shows what something looks like on the inside. This diagram shows the stored food and the plant embryo inside a kernel of corn.

Corn Kernel

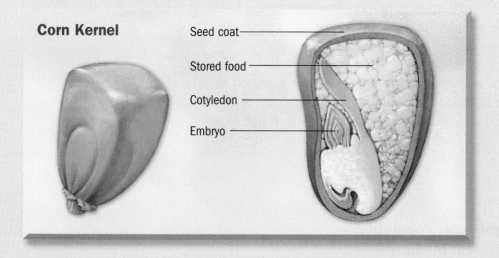

Seed coat

Stored food

Cotyledon

Embryo

Flowcharts

A **flowchart** is a diagram that uses shapes and arrows to show a step-by-step process. The flowchart below shows the steps involved in making spaghetti. Each arrow points to the next step.

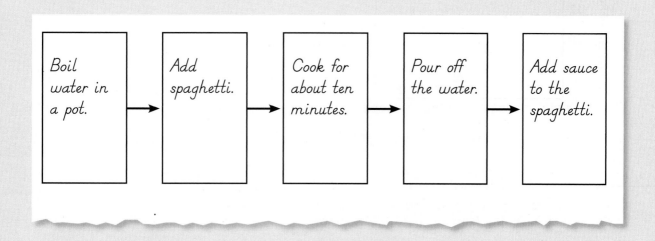

Boil water in a pot. → Add spaghetti. → Cook for about ten minutes. → Pour off the water. → Add sauce to the spaghetti.

► GRAPHS

Graphs organize and explain information. They show how two or more kinds of information are related, or how they are alike. Graphs are often used in math, science, and social studies books. Three common kinds of graphs are **line graphs**, **bar graphs**, and **circle graphs**.

Line Graphs

A **line graph** shows how information changes over a period of time. This line graph explains how, over a period of about 100 years, the Native American population of Central Mexico decreased, or got smaller, by more than 20 million people. Can you find the population in the year 1540? In 1580?

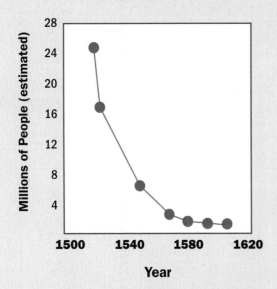

Native American Population of Central Mexico

Bar Graphs

We use **bar graphs** to compare information. For example, this bar graph compares the populations of the thirteen United States in 1790. It shows that, in 1790, Virginia had over ten times as many people as Delaware.

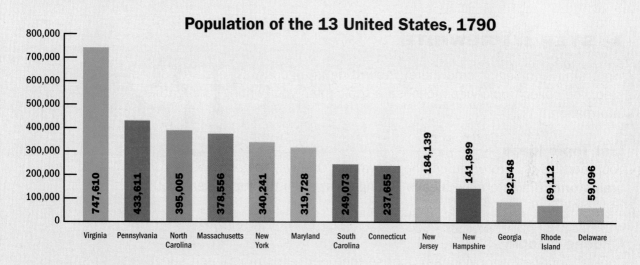

Population of the 13 United States, 1790

State	Population
Virginia	747,610
Pennsylvania	433,611
North Carolina	395,005
Massachusetts	378,556
New York	340,241
Maryland	319,728
South Carolina	249,073
Connecticut	237,655
New Jersey	184,139
New Hampshire	141,899
Georgia	82,548
Rhode Island	69,112
Delaware	59,096

Circle Graphs

A **circle graph** is sometimes called a pie chart because it looks like a pie cut into slices, or pieces. Circle graphs are used to show how different parts of a whole thing compare to each other. In a circle graph, all the "slices" add up to 100 percent. This circle graph shows that only 29 percent of the earth's surface is land. It also shows that the continent of Asia takes up 30 percent of the earth's land.

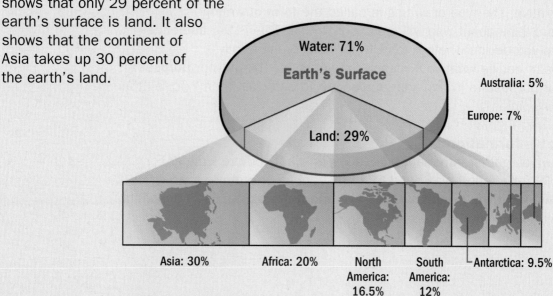

Water: 71%
Earth's Surface
Land: 29%

Australia: 5%
Europe: 7%
Asia: 30%
Africa: 20%
North America: 16.5%
South America: 12%
Antarctica: 9.5%

Writing Process Handbook

Writing allows you to express what you think and to share information. The **Writing Process** is a series of steps that can help you write clearly and effectively.

► STEP 1: PREWRITE

Writers have to begin somewhere. **Prewriting** is a good way to start. In this step, you collect topic ideas, choose a topic, plan your writing, and gather information.

List Topic Ideas
You need ideas before you can begin writing. One way to get ideas is to **brainstorm**. Brainstorming means writing a list of all the topic ideas you can think of.

Choose a Topic
Look at your list of topic ideas. Choose the one that is most interesting. This is your **topic**, the subject you will write about.

Plan Your Writing
Plan your writing by following these steps:
- First, decide on the type of writing that works best with your topic. For example, you may want to write a description, a story, or a personal narrative. The type of writing is called the **form** of writing.
- Then, think about who will read your writing. This is the **audience**. It will help you decide whether to write formally or informally.
- Finally, decide what your reason for writing is. This is your **purpose**. Is your purpose to inform your audience? To entertain them? To tell them your opinion?

Gather Information
The way you gather information depends on what you are writing. For example, for a report, you need to do research. For a movie review, you might list what you liked and didn't like about the movie. For a description, you might write your ideas in a chart.

Here is a chart a student named Rebecca made for her description of her cat. She listed her ideas in the Supporting Details boxes.

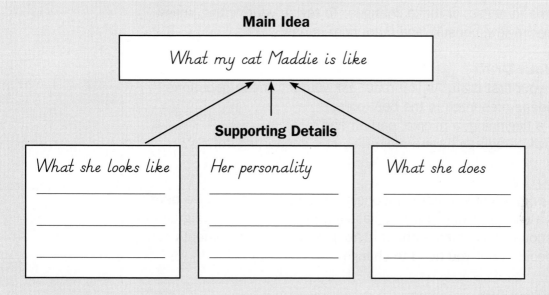

Main Idea

What my cat Maddie is like

Supporting Details

What she looks like	Her personality	What she does

▶ STEP 2: DRAFT

In this step, you start writing. Don't worry too much about spelling and punctuation. Your first draft doesn't have to be perfect. Just put your ideas into sentences.

Here is the first paragraph that Rebecca wrote for her first draft.

Maddie is a pretty cat. Her body is mostly white. There are brown spots on her face and tail. She has big blue eyes and long white whiskers. Maddie has a black spot under her nose. It looks like half a mustache.

► STEP 3: REVISE

Now it's time to revise, or make changes. To revise your writing, follow these steps: review, consult, and mark corrections.

Review Your Draft
Read over your first draft. As you read, ask yourself these questions:
- Are my ideas presented in the best order?
- Is there a beginning, a middle, and an end?
- Does each paragraph have a main idea and supporting details?

Consult Others
When you edit, it helps to get someone's opinion. You can have a **peer review**. In a peer review, you ask a classmate to read your writing and to write questions or comments about it. Your classmate's comments can help you decide what you need to change.

Mark Corrections
Once you know what you want to change, you can mark the corrections on your first draft. Use the **editing marks** in the chart.

Editing Marks		
To:	**Use This Mark:**	**Example:**
add something	$\wedge$	We ate rice, bean^s and corn.
delete something	℮	We ate rice, beans, and corns. ℮
start a new paragraph	¶	¶ We ate rice, beans, and corn.
add a comma	$\wedge$,	We ate rice, beans and corn.
add a period	⊙	We ate rice, beans, and corn ⊙
switch letters or words	∿	We ate rice, baehs, and corn.
change to a capital letter	$\underset{=}{a}$	we ate rice, beans, and corn.
change to a lowercase letter	$\cancel{A}$	WE ate rice, beans, and corn.

Here's how Rebecca revised her first paragraph.

> *really beautiful*
>
> Maddie is a ~~pretty~~ cat. Her body is mostly white, *but* There are
> brown spots on her face and tail. She has big blue eyes and long
> *so*
> white whiskers. Maddie has a black spot under her nose, It looks
> *she has*
> like half a mustache.

▶ STEP 4: EDIT

In this step, you write a new draft that includes the changes you marked on your first draft. Then check your work and make final corrections.

Write Your Second Draft

Make all of the revisions you marked on your first draft. You can also add details you may have thought of since writing your first draft.

Here's Rebecca's first paragraph after she finished editing it.

> My favorite pet is my cat Maddie. Maddie is a really
> beautiful cat. Her body is mostly white, but there are brown
> spots on her face and tail. She has big blue eyes and long white
> whiskers. Maddie has a black spot under her nose, so it looks like
> she has half a mustache.

Check Your Work and Make Final Corrections

Reread your paper. Check for mistakes in spelling and punctuation. Correct any mistakes you find. Your writing is now ready for others to read.

Here is Rebecca's finished paper.

My Cat Maddie

My favorite pet is my cat Maddie. Maddie is a really beautiful cat. Her body is mostly white, but there are brown spots on her face and tail. She has big blue eyes and long white whiskers. Maddie has a black spot under her nose, so it looks like she has half a mustache.

Maddie has a great personality. She is very friendly. She likes to purr a lot, especially when I scratch behind her ears. She often sits on my lap when I'm watching TV or reading a book. Maddie is also very playful. Her favorite toy is a mouse. When I give her the mouse, she hits it and runs around the house. That always makes me laugh.

Sometimes Maddie is too playful. For example, she jumps on the table when my family is eating. Then my Dad yells, "Maddie! Go down!" Then she jumps off the table and runs away. She also likes to jump on the bed and play with my toes when I am sleeping. Then I take her out of the bedroom.

I am always happy to see Maddie when I get home from school. To me, she is the greatest cat in the world.

➤ STEP 5: PUBLISH

Once your paper is revised and proofread, share it with others. Look at these publishing tips.

> **PUBLISHING TIPS**
>
> 1. Photocopy and hand out your work to your classmates.
> 2. Attach it to an e-mail and send it to friends.
> 3. Send it to a school newspaper or magazine for possible publication.

Once you've shared your work with others, you may want to keep it in a **portfolio**, a folder or envelope with your other writing. It's a good idea to organize the work in your portfolio by date.

Each time you write something, add it to your portfolio. Compare recent work with earlier work. See if your writing is improving. See if you have difficulty with some things. If so, focus on these things next time you are writing. That's how writers improve.

Glossary

adjective /aj′ik tiv/
An adjective describes a noun—a person, place, or thing: *I have a blue car*. An adjective can also describe a pronoun: *She is tall*.

adverb /ad′vėrb/
An adverb usually describes the action of a verb. It tells how an action happens: *The boy runs quickly*.

alliteration /ə li tə rā′shən/
Alliteration is a repeat of the first consonant sound in a string of words. For example, *I kindly thank the community for its constant concern for me.*

allusion /ə lü′zhən/
An allusion is making a hint about something or someone: *She was a Scrooge because she never spent money on anyone.*

analogy /ə na′lə jē/
An analogy compares two sets of words that are related in a similar way: *More is to less as loud is to soft.*

antonym /an′tə nim/
An antonym is a word that means the opposite of another word. For example, the antonym for *quick* is *slow*.

archetype /är′ki tīp/
An archetype is an original model or perfect example of a character or situation. A hero is an archetype and an example of a hero is Superman.

article /är′ti kəl/
An article is a word that identifies a noun. Use *a* or *an* to talk about one general person, place, or thing: *I eat a peach or an apple every day*. Use *the* to talk about one or more specific persons, places, or things: *The dog is brown.*

autobiography /ȯ′tə bī og′rə fē/
An autobiography is the story of the writer's own life, told by the writer. It may tell about the person's whole life or only a part of it. Autobiographies are nonfiction.

base form /bās fôrm/
The base form of a verb has no added ending (*-s, -ing, -ed*). *Talk* is the base form of the verb *talk*. (Other forms of *talk* are *talks, talking*, and *talked*.)

biographical narrative
/bī′ə graf′i kəl nar′ə tiv/
A biographical narrative is the true story of a real person's life. Writers often tell the events of a biographical narrative in chronological order, or the order in which they happened.

brainstorming /brān′stôr′ming/
Brainstorming is writing down all the ideas you can think of about a subject or topic as quickly as possible. You can brainstorm alone or with other people.

caption /kap′shən/
A caption is the text written under or next to a photograph, picture, or diagram. A caption explains what the photograph, picture, or diagram shows.

cause and effect /kȯz and ə fekt′/
Why something happens is a cause. What happens is an effect. When you read a text, look for causes and effects. Finding causes and effects as you read can help you better understand a text.

character /kar′ik tər/
A character is a person or an animal in a story.

chronological order (time order) /kron′ə loj′i kəl ôrd′ər/
Chronological order, or time order, is the order in which events happen in a story. To tell story events in chronological order, writers use time phrases such as *in 1976, on May 1,* and *the next year.*

cognate /käg′nāt/
A cognate is a root word in one language that is the same in another language. Spanish and English words share many root words. They usually sound the same and have the same meaning. For example, the English word *important* is *importante* in Spanish.

comparative form of adjectives /kəm par′ə tiv fôrm ov aj′ik tivz/
Use the comparative form of an adjective to compare two people, places, or things. For most one-syllable adjectives, add *-er + than*: *Bigger than* is the comparative form of *big.* For two-syllable adjectives that end in *-y,* change the *y* to *i* and add *-er + than*: *Prettier than* is the comparative form of *pretty.* For most two-syllable adjectives, use *more + adjective + than*: *More famous than* is the comparative form of *famous.*

comparison /kəm′perəsən/
A comparison tells how two or more people, places, or things are alike.

compound sentence /kom′pound sen′təns/
A compound sentence is made up of two or more simple sentences, or independent clauses: *I went to the store, and Joe went to the gym.*

conflict /kän′flikt/
A conflict is a disagreement between people. A conflict is what makes stories interesting.

conjunction /kən jungk′shən/
A conjunction joins words, groups of words, and whole sentences. The words *and, but, so, or, nor, for,* and *yet* are conjunctions.

connotation /kä nə tā′shən/
A connotation is how a word makes you feel. For example, a *blanket* connotes *warmth* and *comfort.*

contraction /kən trak′shən/
A contraction is a word made from two words that have been joined together. An apostrophe shows where a letter or letters have been taken away. For example, the contraction of *I am* is *I'm.* Contractions are common in speaking and informal writing.

contrast /kän′trast/
A contrast tells how two or more people, places, or things are different.

denotation /dē nō tā′shən/
A denotation is the definition of a word. *Confident* and *proud* have the same denotation but have different connotations. *Confident* makes you think of positive feelings, but *proud* can make you think of negative feelings.

description /di skrip′shən/
A description is a form of writing. Writers use adjectives and sensory images to help their readers see, hear, taste, feel, or smell whatever they are describing.

diagram /dī′ə gram/
A diagram is a picture or a plan that gives information in a visual way. Diagrams can help readers understand a text. Science and social studies books often have diagrams. Examples of diagrams include a labeled drawing of parts of a flower and a floor plan of a house.

dialogue /dī′ə log/
A dialogue is a conversation between characters. Dialogue reveals information about characters' personality and situations.

diction /dik′shən/
Diction is a writer's choice of words to express ideas and set a mood.

draft /draft/
A draft is a piece of writing that is not in its finished form.

draw conclusions
/drȯ kən klü′zhənz/
To draw a conclusion means to decide something is true based on information. For example, you see a young person carrying a book bag. You may draw the conclusion that the person is a student.

editorial /e də tor′ē əl/
The kind of writing that states an opinion on something. You can find editorials in newspapers and magazines.

etymology /ət uh mol′uh jee/
Etymology is the study of a word's history.

fable /fā′bəl/
A fable is a brief story, usually with animal characters that speak and act like humans. A fable often teaches a moral, or lesson.

fiction /fik′shən/
Fiction is writing that tells about imaginary characters and events. Short stories and novels are works of fiction.

figurative language
/fi′g(y)ə rə tiv lan′gwij/
Figurative language is when you use one thing to describe something else. For example, the phrase *You are as busy as a bee* is figurative language.

folktale /fōk′tāl/
A folktale is a story that people, or folk, told one another by word of mouth over many generations. In time, people wrote down the stories so that they would not be forgotten.

freewriting /frē′rī ting/
Freewriting is writing down your ideas, thoughts, and feelings as quickly as you can. Freewriting can sometimes help you get ideas for other forms of writing.

genre /zhän′rə/
Genre is writing that is identified by a certain style or form. For example, Agatha Christie writes in the mystery genre. Writing a letter and writing an e-mail are also different genres we use.

imagery /i′mij rē/
Imagery is a description that helps you form pictures in your mind.

imperative /im per′ət iv/
We use the imperative to give directions or orders. The subject of an imperative sentence is usually *you*. The subject is usually not stated: *(You) Open your books to page 5.*

informational text
/in′fər mā′shən əl tekst/
Informational text is nonfiction text. It presents facts and other information about real people, events, places, and situations.

irony /ī′rə nē/

When the reader knows something about a situation in a story that a character in the story does not know, the writer has used irony. Writers use irony to make a story humorous and to teach us about life.

journal /jėr′nəl/

A journal is a book that a person writes in. People write in journals to record their thoughts and feelings about things that happen in their lives. Each separate writing in a journal is called an entry. A journal entry is personal and informal.

legend /lĕj′ənd/

A legend is a story that people tell and retell over many, many years. Legends often change over time.

letter /lĕt′ər/

A letter is a written communication from one person to another. In a personal letter, the writer shares information and ideas with a family member or close friend.

literary nonfiction
/li′tə rer ē nän fik′shən/

Literary nonfiction is a mix of facts and personal examples and descriptions. Biographies and memoirs are examples of literary nonfiction.

main ideas and details
/mān ī dē′əz ənd dē′tālz/

The main ideas are the biggest or most important ideas in a text. Details are facts or examples that support the main ideas.

make inferences /māk in′fər əns əs/

Sometimes writers do not tell you what a story means. Instead, they give you clues. The clues can be things that the characters do and say. You use the clues to make inferences, or guesses, about the story's meaning.

metaphor /me′tə for/

A metaphor directly compares two things without using *like* or *as*: *The flower was perfume in a bottle.*

mood /müd/

Mood is feelings that are created from a piece of writing.

motif /mō tēf′/

A motif is a repeated idea or description that expresses important ideas. Animal motifs are common in folktales. For example, the use of owls usually represents wisdom.

myth /mith/

A myth is a fictional story. Long ago, groups of people created myths to explain natural events. Parents told the myths to their children, and the myths passed from generation to generation. Myths are part of a group's spoken tradition.

narrative /nar′ə tiv/

A narrative is a story. It can be either fiction or nonfiction. Novels and short stories are fictional narratives. Biographies and autobiographies are nonfictional narratives, or true stories. A personal narrative tells about an experience in the writer's life. A biographical narrative tells the true story of a real person's life.

narrator /nar′ā tər/

A narrator is a speaker or character who tells a story. The narrator sometimes takes part in the action. Other times the narrator just speaks about the action.

nonfiction /non fik′shən/

Nonfiction is true information. It tells about real people, places, objects, or events. Biographies, reports, and newspaper articles are examples of nonfiction.

noun /noun/
A noun is the name of a person, place, or thing. Examples of common nouns are *plane*, *building*, and *child*. Examples of proper nouns are *Robert*, *Chicago*, and *Puerto Rico*.

object pronoun /ob′jikt prō′noun/
An object pronoun (*me, you, him, her, it, us, you, them*) replaces a noun that is the object of a sentence: *Bob knows me.*

overstatement /ō′vər stāt′mənt/
An overstatement is expressing more emotion than you would normally expect: *I cried a thousand tears when she waved good-bye.*

paradox /per′ə däks/
A paradox is a statement that doesn't seem to make sense but is true: *America is a rich country with poor people.*

paragraph /par′ə graf/
A paragraph is a group of sentences about one idea in a piece of writing.

personal narrative
/pər′sən əl nar′ə tiv/
A personal narrative is a story about an experience in the writer's life. A writer usually tells a personal narrative in chronological order.

personification /pər sä nə fə kā′shən/
Personification gives human qualities to ideas or objects: *The trees clapped their hands and danced in the wind.*

play /plā/
A play is a story that actors usually perform on a stage in a theater. Although plays are meant to be performed, actors can also read aloud the written version, called a script.

plot /plot/
A plot is what happens in a story. In most stories, the plot has characters and a main problem or conflict. The plot usually begins with information to help the reader understand the story. Then an event introduces the main problem. The problem grows until there is a turning point, or climax, when a character tries to solve the problem. The events after the climax lead to the end of the story.

poem /pō′əm/
A poem is a piece of writing. Poems use patterns of words and sounds to express ideas, experiences, and emotions. Poems are written in lines.

predict /pri dikt′/
To predict means to guess what will happen. When you read, try to look for clues in the story and in the pictures. Think about what will happen next. When you are finished reading, see if your predictions were correct.

preposition /prep′ə zish′ən/
A preposition is a connecting word that shows time, place, or direction. *After*, *above*, *across*, *to*, and *at* are prepositions: *We went to the store.*

prepositional phrase
/prep′ə zish′ə nəl frāz/
A prepositional phrase starts with a preposition and ends with a noun or pronoun: *My family lives in the city.*

previewing /prē′vyüing/
Previewing a text means looking at the pages before you start to read. Previewing includes looking at the headings in dark type as well as the pictures and maps.

pronoun /prō′noun/
A pronoun is a word that takes the place of a noun: *Nadia goes to school. She likes it. She* replaces the proper noun *Nadia*; *it* replaces the noun *school*.

prose /prōz/
Prose is the ordinary language people use in speaking and writing. Most writing that is not poetry, drama, or song is considered prose. Prose occurs in two forms: fiction and nonfiction.

punctuation /pungk′chü ā′shən/
Punctuation is the system of using certain signs or marks, such as periods (.) and commas(,), to divide writing into phrases and sentences so that the meaning is clear. Besides periods and commas, common punctuation marks include exclamation points (!), question marks (?), hyphens (-), semicolons (;), and colons (:).

repetition /re pə ti′shən/
A repetition is a repeat of the same words or phrases.

report /ri pôrt′/
A report is a piece of writing about a topic. You can organize information for a report by writing notes.

revise /rē′vīz/
To revise your writing means to change it in order to make it better.

rhetorical device /ri tor′ikəl di vīs′/
A rhetorical device is a way of writing or speaking that grabs the reader's attention.

root /rüt/
A root is the basic part of a word that tells you the meaning of the word. Separating the word *biology* into two parts can help you understand its definition. *Bio* is the root word that means "life" and *logy* means "the study of." So, *biology* is the study of life.

sarcasm /sär′ka zəm/
Sarcasm is a way of saying one thing but really meaning the opposite: *The babies were crying for hours; it was music to my ears!*

sensory images /sĕn′ sə rē im′ij iz/
Sensory images are words that appeal to one or more of the five senses. Sensory images are like word pictures. They help readers to see, hear, taste, touch, or smell things in a poem or other literary text.

sentence /sen′təns/
A sentence is a group of words with a subject and a verb. A sentence expresses a complete thought.

sequence of events
/sē′kwəns ov i vents′/
A sequence, or order, of events is a series of related actions that has a particular result. In both fiction and nonfiction writing, the sequence of events is often in chronological order.

sequence words /sē′kwəns wėrdz/
Sequence words help make the order of steps or events clear. Some common sequence words are *first, second, next, then, after that*, and *finally*: *First, you should finish your homework. After that, you may go outside.*

setting /set′ing/
The setting of a literary text is the time and place of the action. In most stories, the setting is where the characters interact. Setting can also help create a feeling, or atmosphere.

short story /shôrt stôr′ē/
A short story is a short work of fiction. A short story usually presents a sequence of events, or a plot, and has a clear beginning, middle, and end. One or more characters usually has a problem or conflict. A short story usually presents a message about life.

simile /sim′ə lē/

A simile is a figure of speech that uses the word *like* to compare two different things in an unusual way: *Her hair was like spun gold.*

simple past tense /sim′pəl past tens/

Use the simple past tense to talk about completed actions in the past. For regular verbs, add -ed to the base form: *The girl walked up the hill.* Other verbs have irregular past-tense forms: *The boy ate the apple.*

spatial /spā′shəl/

To use a spatial structure in writing means to describe something in a logical order, such as from left to right, top to bottom, or outside to inside.

speech /spēch/

A speech is a talk given by a speaker to an audience.

song /song/

A song is a piece of music with words.

strategy /strat′ə jē/

A tool or a plan you can use to achieve a goal or learn to do something better.

structure /strək′chər/

Structuring is a way in which a text is put together or organized. Common structures are comparison, contrast, and chronological order (time order).

subject pronoun /sub′jikt prō′noun/

A subject pronoun (*I, you, he, she, it, we, you, they*) replaces a noun that is the subject of a sentence: *Roberto goes to school. He takes the bus.*

subject-verb agreement /sub′jikt vėrb ə grē′mənt/

In the simple present, the subject and verb of a sentence must agree. When the subject is a singular noun or *he, she,* or *it,* add -s or -es to the noun: *A man runs.* When a verb ends in -y, change the *y* to *i* and add -es: *The dog carries his bone.* When the subject is a plural noun or *I, you, we,* or *they,* use the base form of the verb: *The men run.* Do not add -s or -es.

substantiated and unsubstantiated opinion /səb stan′shē āt əd ənd ən səb stan′shē āt əd ə pin′yən/

A substantiated opinion is one that is based on fact, evidence, and/or logical thinking. An unsubstantiated opinion is not based on facts or evidence.

summarize /sum′ə rīz/

To summarize means to write the main ideas of a text in your own words. As you read a text, summarize each section. Be sure to keep your summaries simple. When you are finished reading, reread your summaries. This will help you understand and remember main ideas.

synonym /si′nə nim/

A synonym is a word that means the same as, or almost the same as, another word. For example, the synonym for *quick* is *fast.*

theme /thēm/

A theme is the main idea in a piece of writing.

thesaurus /thi sor′əs/
A thesaurus is a book (or e-book) that groups words that have similar (and opposing) meanings together. For example, if you look up *sad* in a thesaurus, you will find its synonyms, *unhappy, melancholy*. You will also find its antonyms, *happy* and *joyful*.

time phrase /tīm frāz/
Time phrases tell the reader when an event happened: *Yesterday, we went to see a movie. Next week, we will go to see my grandmother.*

timeline /tīm′ līn/
A timeline is a diagram that shows important dates and the order of events in history.

transition /tran si′shən
A transition is a word that indicates a change from one thought to another. However, therefore, and because are transition words.

understatement /ən dər stāt′mənt/
An understatement expresses less emotion than you would normally expect: *Her love was nothing to me. I could have tossed it like a stone into the river.*

verb /vėrb/
A verb expresses action (*swims, drives*) or being (for example, *is*): *Tom swims fast* (action). *Sally is very sick* (being).

viewpoint /vyoo′poīnt/
A viewpoint is a person's opinion or way of thinking about a subject.

visualizing /vizh′ü ə līz′ing/
Visualizing is picturing something in your mind.

writing process /rī′ting pro′ses/
The writing process is a series of steps to help you write. Many writers use the writing process to think of ideas and then to organize, write, and revise their ideas. The steps are: Prewrite, Draft, Edit, Revise, and Publish.

Index

Acknowledgments

Cherry Lane Music Publishing Company, Inc. (ASCAP) and DreamWorks Songs (ASCAP). "Garden Song," words and music by Dave Mallett. Copyright © 1975 Cherry Lane Music Publishing Company, Inc. (ASCAP) and DreamWorks Songs (ASCAP). Worldwide rights for DreamWorks Songs administered by Cherry Lane Music Publishing Company, Inc. International copyright secured. All rights reserved.

HarperCollins Publishers, Inc. "Aaron's Gift," adapted from "Aaron's Gift" from The Witch of Fourth Street and Other Stories, text copyright © 1972 by Myron Levoy. Published by Harper & Row, New York.

Pie Corbett. "Wings" by Pie Corbett. Reprinted by permission of the author.

Paterson Marsh Ltd. "Rain Poem" by Elizabeth Coatsworth. Reprinted by permission of Paterson Marsh Ltd. on behalf of The Estate of Elizabeth Coatsworth.

Dan Scanlan. "Giant Silent Redwood" by Dan Scanlan. Copyright © 1996.

Scholastic Press. "This Big Sky" by Pat Mora, from *This Big Sky* by Pat Mora. Reprinted by permission of Scholastic Press, an imprint of Scholastic Inc.

Credits

199 bottom, B. Borrell Casals/Frank Lane Picture Agency/CORBIS; 200 Dorling Kindersley; 202, Dorling Kindersley; 203, © Cynoclub/Shutterstock; 204, © Shutterstock; 205, © Shutterstock; 206, © Pearson Education/PH College; 207, © EMG Education Management Group; 209, Bluerain/Shutterstock; 210, Photodisc/Getty Images.

UNIT 7: 214-215 background, Shutterstock; 214 bottom left, Phil Schermeister/CORBIS; 214 bottom right, Kyslynskyy/Fotolia; 216 top, © Kavram/Shutterstock; 216 bottom, © Steve Byland/Shutterstock; 217, © Arvind Balaraman/ Shutterstock; 218 top, Dorling Kindersley; 218-219, Getty Images; 218 bottom, Chanelle/ Fotolia; 219 right, Phil Schermeister/CORBIS; 220, © Shutterstock; 221 top, Dorling Kindersley; 221 bottom, Stephen Oliver/Dorling Kindersley; 222, Dorling Kindersley; 225, © Hannah Eckman/ Shutterstock; 231, Sally A. Morgan/Ecoscene/ CORBIS; 233 top, David Nunuk/Science Photo Library/Photo Researchers, Inc.; 233 bottom, Getty Images; 235, © Cathleen A. Clapper/Shutterstock; 239, Kyslynskyy/Fotolia; 242, © PH School.

UNIT 8: 244-245 background, © Victor Shova/ Shutterstock; 244 bottom left, Smithsonian Institution; 244 bottom middle, Kelly Nelson/ Shutterstock; 245 bottom left, Smithsonian Institution; 245 bottom right, Photodisc/Getty Images; 247 left, Underwood & Underwood/CORBIS; 247 top right, Schomburg Center for Research in Black Culture/The New York Public Library; 247 bottom right, United States Postal Service; 248 top, Smithsonian Institution; 248 bottom, Bettmann/ CORBIS; 249 top, CORBIS; 249 bottom, Hulton-Deutsch Collection/CORBIS; 250 top, Smithsonian Institution; 250 middle, Smithsonian Institution; 250 bottom, Dorling Kindersley; 251 top, Courtesy of the Library of Congress; 251 bottom left, United States Postal Service; 195 bottom right, Bettmann/ CORBIS; 253, Library of Congress; 254, © Kelly Nelson/Shutterstock; 255, Dorling Kindersley; 259, Dorling Kindersley; 268, Lawrence Migdale; 269, Getty Images; 270 top, Smithsonian Institution; 270 bottom, Bettmann/CORBIS; 271, Swim Ink/CORBIS; 275, Getty Images; 276, © Lucky Business/Shutterstock; 280, © Pearson Learning Photo Studio; 285, Photodisc/Getty Images; 291, Silver Burdett Ginn; 295, © Monkey Business Images/Shutterstock; 296 top, Getty Images; 296 bottom, The Gorilla Foundation/Ron Cohn.

HANDBOOK: 274 Rebecca Ortman; 275 Will Hart.